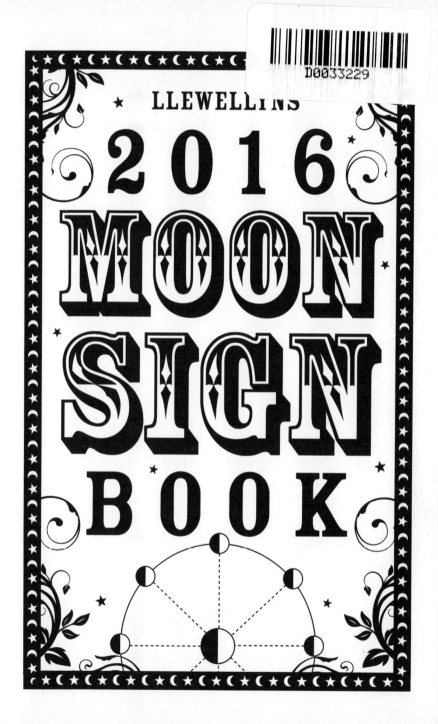

LLEWELLYN'S

2016
MOON
SIGN
BOOK

Llewellyn's 2016 Moon Sign Book®

ISBN 978-0-7387-3404-0

Cover design by Kevin R. Brown
Cover illustrations: Scrolls: iStockphoto.com/4468602/ANGELGILD
  Banner: iStockphoto.com/23088297/DavidGoh
  Moon: iStockphoto.com/12271763/Magnilion
Editing by Jennifer Ackman
Stock photography models used for illustrative purposes only and may not endorse or represent the book's subject.
Copyright 2015 Llewellyn Worldwide Ltd. All rights reserved.
Typography owned by Llewellyn Worldwide Ltd.

Weekly tips by Peg Aloi, Alice DeVille, Mireille Blacke, MA, RD, CD-N, and Penny Kelly.

Any Internet references contained in this work are current at publication time, but the publisher cannot guarantee that a specific location will continue to be maintained.

Astrological data compiled and programmed by Rique Pottenger. Based on the earlier work of Neil F. Michelsen.

You can order Llewellyn annuals and books from *New Worlds*, Llewellyn's catalog. To request a free copy of the catalog, call toll-free 1-877-NEW-WRLD, or visit our website at www.llewellyn.com.

Llewellyn Publications
A Division of Llewellyn Worldwide Ltd.
2143 Wooddale Drive
Woodbury, MN 55125-3989
www.llewellyn.com

Printed in the United States of America

Table of Contents

What's Different About the Moon Sign Book?   5

Weekly Almanac   7

   Gardening by the Moon   61
   A Guide to Planting   69
   Companion Planting Guide   73
   Moon Void-of-Course *by Kim Rogers-Gallagher*   75
   Moon Void-of-Course Tables   76
   The Moon's Rhythm   82
     Moon Aspects   83
     Moon Signs   83
     More About Zodiac Signs   90
   Good Timing *by Sharon Leah*   92
     Personalizing Elections   93
     Llewellyn's Astro Almanac   94
     Astro Almanac   95
   Choose the Best Time for Your Activities   107
   How to Use the Moon Tables
     and Lunar Aspectarian   129
     The Five Basic Steps   130
     Using What You've Learned   133
     A Note About Time and Time Zones   134
   January–December Moon Tables, Lunar Aspectarian,
     Favorable & Unfavorable Days   136
   2016 Retrograde Planets   160
   Egg-Setting Dates   161
   Dates to Hunt and Fish   162
   Dates to Destroy Weeds and Pests   163
   Time Zone Map   164
   Time Zone Conversions   165

Weather, Economic & Lunar Forecasts   **166**

    Forecasting the Weather *by Kris Brandt Riske*   167

    Weather Forecast for 2016 *by Kris Brandt Riske*   171

    Economic Forecast for 2016 *by Christeen Skinner*   214

    New and Full Moon Forecasts for 2016

       by Sally Cragin   230

2016 Moon Sign Book Articles   **245**

    Astrology of Garden Icons *by Robin Ivy Payton*   246

    Lasagna Gardening *by Charlie Rainbow Wolf*   253

    Understanding the Moon Signs of Others

       by David Pond   259

    Hemp: Herb of Many Uses *by Bruce Scofield*   269

    Strawberries *by Mireille Blacke, MA, RD, CD-N*   277

    Spring Bulbs: Why You Need Them!

       by Peg Aloi   284

    Biodynamic Farming *by Michelle Perrin*   291

    The Moon in Midlife *by Amy Herring*   300

About the Authors   310

What's Different About the Moon Sign Book?

Readers have asked why *Llewellyn's Moon Sign Book* says that the Moon is in Taurus when some almanacs indicate that the Moon is in the previous sign of Aries on the same date. It's because there are two different zodiac systems in use today: the tropical and the sidereal. *Llewellyn's Moon Sign Book* is based on the tropical zodiac.

The tropical zodiac takes 0 degrees of Aries to be the Spring Equinox in the Northern Hemisphere. This is the time and date when the Sun is directly overhead at noon along the equator, usually about March 20–21. The rest of the signs are positioned at 30-degree intervals from this point.

The sidereal zodiac, which is based on the location of fixed stars, uses the positions of the fixed stars to determine the starting point of

0 degrees of Aries. In the sidereal system, 0 degrees of Aries always begins at the same point. This does create a problem though, because the positions of the fixed stars, as seen from Earth, have changed since the constellations were named. The term "precession of the equinoxes" is used to describe the change.

Precession of the equinoxes describes an astronomical phenomenon brought about by Earth's wobble as it rotates and orbits the Sun. Earth's axis is inclined toward the Sun at an angle of about 23½ degrees, which creates our seasonal weather changes. Although the change is slight, because one complete circle of Earth's axis takes 25,800 years to complete, we can actually see that the positions of the fixed stars seem to shift. The result is that each year, in the tropical system, the Spring Equinox occurs at a slightly different time.

Does Precession Matter?

There is an accumulative difference of about 23 degrees between the Spring Equinox (0 degrees Aries in the tropical zodiac and 0 degrees Aries in the sidereal zodiac) so that 0 degrees Aries at Spring Equinox in the tropical zodiac actually occurs at about 7 degrees Pisces in the sidereal zodiac system. You can readily see that those who use the other almanacs may be planting seeds (in the garden and in their individual lives) based on the belief that it is occurring in a fruitful sign, such as Taurus, when in fact it would be occurring in Gemini, one of the most barren signs of the zodiac. So, if you wish to plant and plan activities by the Moon, it is helpful to follow *Llewellyn's Moon Sign Book*. Before we go on, there are important things to understand about the Moon, her cycles, and their correlation with everyday living. For more information about gardening by the Moon, see page 61.

Weekly Almanac

Your Guide to Lunar Gardening & Good Timing for Activities

If you have a garden and a library,
you have everything you need.

~Marcus Tullius Cicero

♑ January

December 27–January 2

Anything in life worth having is worth working for.

~Andrew Carnegie

Date	Qtr.	Sign	Activity
Dec 25, 6:12 am– Dec 27, 5:31 am	3rd	Cancer	Plant biennials, perennials, bulbs, and roots. Prune. Irrigate. Fertilize (organic).
Dec 27, 5:31 am– Dec 29, 1:58 pm	3rd	Leo	Cultivate. Destroy weeds and pests. Harvest fruits and root crops for food. Trim to retard growth.
Dec 29, 1:58 pm– Jan 1, 1:41 am	3rd	Virgo	Cultivate, especially for medicinal plants. Destroy weeds and pests. Trim to retard growth.

Small changes add up and can impact health in a big way. Start simply. **Use smaller plates.** Downsizing your dish creates immediate portion control and will help you eat less. **Practice mindful eating.** The brain takes about twenty minutes to register fullness once we start eating. Put your silverware down between bites to slow the pace. **Read nutrition labels thoroughly.** Consider total calories and pay attention to servings per container.

◖
January 2
12:30 am EST

JANUARY

S	M	T	W	T	F	S
					1	2
3	4	5	6	7	8	9
10	11	12	13	14	15	16
17	18	19	20	21	22	23
24	25	26	27	28	29	30
31						

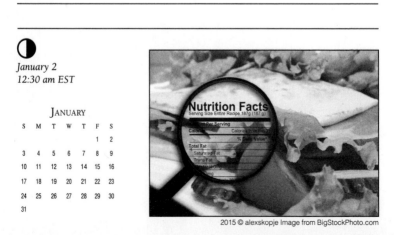

2015 © alexskopje Image from BigStockPhoto.com

January 3–9 ♑

When I get a little money I buy books; and if any is left I buy food and clothes.
    ~DESIDERIUS ERASMUS

Date	Qtr.	Sign	Activity
Jan 3, 2:36 pm– Jan 6, 1:56 am	4th	Scorpio	Plant biennials, perennials, bulbs, and roots. Prune. Irrigate. Fertilize (organic).
Jan 6, 1:56 am– Jan 8, 10:07 am	4th	Sagittarius	Cultivate. Destroy weeds and pests. Harvest fruits and root crops for food. Trim to retard growth.
Jan 8, 10:07 am– Jan 9, 8:31 pm	4th	Capricorn	Plant potatoes and tubers. Trim to retard growth.
Jan 9, 8:31 pm– Jan 10, 3:23 pm	1st	Capricorn	Graft or bud plants. Trim to increase growth.

As winter weeks unfold keep colds, flu, aches, and pains away by drinking a Master Cleansing Drink every morning. Put 2 Tbsp. of lemon juice or apple cider vinegar in a pint jar. Add 1–2 Tbsp. of honey or maple syrup, and ⅛ tsp. of cayenne pepper. Fill the jar with hot water, stir, and drink.

●

January 9
8:31 pm EST

JANUARY

S	M	T	W	T	F	S
					1	2
3	4	5	6	7	8	9
10	11	12	13	14	15	16
17	18	19	20	21	22	23
24	25	26	27	28	29	30
31						

♑ January 10–16

We risk in glory, as we sink in pride: where boasting ends,
there dignity begins. ～EDWARD YOUNG

Date	Qtr.	Sign	Activity
Jan 9, 8:31 pm– Jan 10, 3:23 pm	1st	Capricorn	Graft or bud plants. Trim to increase growth.
Jan 12, 6:53 pm– Jan 14, 9:48 pm	1st	Pisces	Plant grains, leafy annuals. Fertilize (chemical). Graft or bud plants. Irrigate. Trim to increase growth.

Planets in cardinal signs (Aries, Cancer, Libra, and Capricorn) take on a "runaway love scenario" when they cluster in the mutable houses in the chart (third, sixth, ninth, and twelfth). These signs crave exclusive attention in seeking relationships that meet their needs. When such attention is missing, cardinal signs change partners frequently, preferring emotional investments in relationships. Aries and Libra return to the dating game quickly, while Cancer and Capricorn spend time figuring out what went wrong.

_____

_____

_____

◗
January 16
6:26 pm EST

JANUARY

S	M	T	W	T	F	S
					1	2
3	4	5	6	7	8	9
10	11	12	13	14	15	16
17	18	19	20	21	22	23
24	25	26	27	28	29	30
31						

2015 © michaeljung Image from BigStockPhoto.com

January 17–23   ♑

An unreliable person is nobody's friend.   ～IDRIES SHAH

Date	Qtr.	Sign	Activity
Jan 17, 12:48 am– Jan 19, 4:13 am	2nd	Taurus	Plant annuals for hardiness. Trim to increase growth.
Jan 21, 8:28 am– Jan 23, 2:21 pm	2nd	Cancer	Plant grains, leafy annuals. Fertilize (chemical). Graft or bud plants. Irrigate. Trim to increase growth.
Jan 23, 8:46 pm– Jan 25, 10:46 pm	3rd	Leo	Cultivate. Destroy weeds and pests. Harvest fruits and root crops for food. Trim to retard growth.

Capsaicin is the compound in cayenne pepper that provides the spicy burn for which it is known. Capsaicin is sugar- and fat-soluble, but not water-soluble. That is the reason drinking something containing fat (like milk) will soothe your mouth, while water typically will not help. If a chili pepper dish is too hot for your palate, add either something with sugar or fat to reduce the spicy heat.

○

January 23
8:46 pm EST

JANUARY

S	M	T	W	T	F	S
					1	2
3	4	5	6	7	8	9
10	11	12	13	14	15	16
17	18	19	20	21	22	23
24	25	26	27	28	29	30
31						

2015 © Yastremska Image from BigStockPhoto.com

January 24–30

We should not pretend to understand the world only by intellect; we apprehend it just as much by feeling.

~CARL JUNG

Date	Qtr.	Sign	Activity
Jan 23, 8:46 pm– Jan 25, 10:46 pm	3rd	Leo	Cultivate. Destroy weeds and pests. Harvest fruits and root crops for food. Trim to retard growth.
Jan 25, 10:46 pm– Jan 28, 9:59 am	3rd	Virgo	Cultivate, especially medicinal plants. Destroy weeds and pests. Trim to retard growth.
Jan 30, 10:50 pm– Jan 31, 10:28 pm	3rd	Scorpio	Plant biennials, perennials, bulbs, and roots. Prune. Irrigate. Fertilize (organic).

Small amounts of dark chocolate can improve overall heart health, blood pressure, and cholesterol as well as increase blood flow to the brain. But don't wash down your dark chocolate with a glass of milk. This may interfere with the absorption of chocolate's antioxidants and negate its potential benefits. Choose dark chocolate squares or bars with at least 65 percent cacao on the label.

JANUARY

S	M	T	W	T	F	S
					1	2
3	4	5	6	7	8	9
10	11	12	13	14	15	16
17	18	19	20	21	22	23
24	25	26	27	28	29	30
31						

February 〜〜〜

January 31–February 6

When standing over a buried treasure, you need only dig
until you find it.   ~GUY FINLEY

Date	Qtr.	Sign	Activity
Jan 30, 10:50 pm– Jan 31, 10:28 pm	3rd	Scorpio	Plant biennials, perennials, bulbs, and roots. Prune. Irrigate. Fertilize (organic).
Jan 31, 10:28 pm– Feb 2, 10:50 am	4th	Scorpio	Plant biennials, perennials, bulbs, and roots. Prune. Irrigate. Fertilize (organic).
Feb 2, 10:50 am– Feb 4, 7:44 pm	4th	Sagittarius	Cultivate. Destroy weeds and pests. Harvest fruits and root crops for food. Trim to retard growth.
Feb 4, 7:44 pm– Feb 7, 12: am	4th	Capricorn	Plant potatoes and tubers. Trim to retard growth.

There is no better form of meditation than craftwork. It is good for you and productive as well. If you knit, sew, crochet, nurse indoor gardens, do woodworking, scrapbook, or make rugs, lamps, or purses, winter is the time to indulge. Get your supplies and find a quiet corner to work in.

2015 © omgimages Image from BigStockPhoto.com

◐

January 31
10:28 pm EST

FEBRUARY

S	M	T	W	T	F	S
	1	2	3	4	5	6
7	8	9	10	11	12	13
14	15	16	17	18	19	20
21	22	23	24	25	26	27
28	29					

〰 February 7–13

A nation's culture resides in the hearts and the soul of its people.
　　　　　　　　　　　　　　　　　　　　　　~MAHATMA GANDHI

Date	Qtr.	Sign	Activity
Feb 4, 7:44 pm– Feb 7, 12:59 am	4th	Capricorn	Plant potatoes and tubers. Trim to retard growth.
Feb 7, 12:59 am– Feb 8, 9:39 am	4th	Aquarius	Cultivate. Destroy weeds and pests. Harvest fruits and root crops for food. Trim to retard growth.
Feb 9, 3:31 am– Feb 11, 4:55 am	1st	Pisces	Plant grains, leafy annuals. Fertilize (chemical). Graft or bud plants. Irrigate. Trim to increase growth.
Feb 13, 6:36 am– Feb 15, 2:46 am	1st	Taurus	Plant annuals for hardiness. Trim to increase growth.

Think about taking a class in something. Education is a life-long affair, and we begin to age when we stop learning. Many people refuse to change with the times, and this not only dates us, but also limits our contribution to the world and keeps us out of the mainstream of daily living. The myth of retirement is exactly that—a myth. If you want to stay alive, keep yourself educated and engaged in life.

●
February 8
9:39 am EST

FEBRUARY

S	M	T	W	T	F	S
		1	2	3	4	5	6
7	8	9	10	11	12	13
14	15	16	17	18	19	20
21	22	23	24	25	26	27
28	29					

2015 © monkeybusinessimages Image from BigStockPhoto.com

February 14–20 〰️

Be not ashamed to send your valentine; she has your love, but
needs its outward sign.   ~EDGAR A. GUEST

Date	Qtr.	Sign	Activity
Feb 13, 6:36 am– Feb 15, 2:46 am	1st	Taurus	Plant annuals for hardiness. Trim to increase growth.
Feb 15, 2:46 am– Feb 15, 9:35 am	2nd	Taurus	Plant annuals for hardiness. Trim to increase growth.
Feb 17, 2:24 pm– Feb 19, 9:17 pm	2nd	Cancer	Plant grains, leafy annuals. Fertilize (chemical). Graft or bud plants. Irrigate. Trim to increase growth.

February is traditionally known as the month of love. Whether you speak the language of love with flowers, send a tender greeting to your loved one, or share a romantic meal, you can make February 14 memorable. Scope out the romantic vibrations for Valentine's Day. The love planets, Venus and Mars, are in Capricorn and Scorpio for this year's celebration, reflecting the harmonious elements of earth and water. What true romantic could ignore their allure?

2015 © sarsmis Image from BigStockPhoto.com

◗

February 15
2:46 am EST

FEBRUARY

S	M	T	W	T	F	S
	1	2	3	4	5	6
7	8	9	10	11	12	13
14	15	16	17	18	19	20
21	22	23	24	25	26	27
28	29					

♓ February 21–27

A blessing on the printer's art! Books are mentors of the heart. The burning soul, the burdened mind, in books alone companions find.   ～SARAH JOSEPHA HALE

Date	Qtr.	Sign	Activity
Feb 22, 1:20 pm–Feb 24, 5:41 pm	3rd	Virgo	Cultivate, especially medicinal plants. Destroy weeds and pests. Trim to retard growth.
Feb 27, 6:26 am–Feb 29, 6:56 pm	3rd	Scorpio	Plant biennials, perennials, bulbs, and roots. Prune. Irrigate. Fertilize (organic).

March salutes Pisces, the zodiac's last sign. While these Neptune-ruled celebrants wrap up their indoor winter projects and wait for the spring thaw, they long for new adventures, entertainments, and travel. What goes on behind those dreamy eyes? Perhaps it is the knowledge that in a matter of weeks, spring blossoms will emerge from a place of solitude (reflective of mutable Pisces) to fill the landscape with breathtaking beauty and the promise of new beginnings.

February 22
1:20 pm EST

FEBRUARY

S	M	T	W	T	F	S
	1	2	3	4	5	6
7	8	9	10	11	12	13
14	15	16	17	18	19	20
21	22	23	24	25	26	27
28	29					

March

February 28–March 5

We should all be concerned about the future because we will have to spend the rest of our lives there.

~CHARLES FRANKLIN KETTERING

Date	Qtr.	Sign	Activity
Feb 27, 6:26 am–Feb 29, 6:56 pm	3rd	Scorpio	Plant biennials, perennials, bulbs, and roots. Prune. Irrigate. Fertilize (organic).
Feb 29, 6:56 pm–Mar 1, 6:11 pm	3rd	Sagittarius	Cultivate. Destroy weeds and pests. Harvest fruits and root crops for food. Trim to retard growth.
Mar 1, 6:11 pm–Mar 3, 5:01 am	4th	Sagittarius	Cultivate. Destroy weeds and pests. Harvest fruits and root crops for food. Trim to retard growth.
Mar 3, 5:01 am–Mar 5, 11:22 am	4th	Capricorn	Plant potatoes and tubers. Trim to retard growth.
Mar 5, 11:22 am–Mar 7, 2:08 pm	4th	Aquarius	Cultivate. Destroy weeds and pests. Harvest fruits and root crops for food. Trim to retard growth.

Preparing fish or garlic dishes and wondering how to get the smell off your hands? Try rubbing a wedge of lemon over them and then rinse with water. White vinegar may also work. And lastly, stainless steel! Rub your hands over any stainless steel surface and rinse with water.

2015 © Olgany Image from BigStockPhoto.com

March 1
6:11 pm EST

MARCH

S	M	T	W	T	F	S
		1	2	3	4	5
6	7	8	9	10	11	12
13	14	15	16	17	18	19
20	21	22	23	24	25	26
27	28	29	30	31		

March 6–12

Ninety-nine people can approve of you, but if the one
hundredth scowls, your day is ruined.   ~GUY FINLEY

Date	Qtr.	Sign	Activity
Mar 5, 11:22 am– Mar 7, 2:08 pm	4th	Aquarius	Cultivate. Destroy weeds and pests. Harvest fruits and root crops for food. Trim to retard growth.
Mar 7, 2:08 pm– Mar 8, 8:54 pm	4th	Pisces	Plant biennials, perennials, bulbs, and roots. Prune. Irrigate. Fertilize (organic).
Mar 8, 8:54 pm– Mar 9, 2:40 pm	1st	Pisces	Plant grains, leafy annuals. Fertilize (chemical). Graft or bud plants. Irrigate. Trim to increase growth.
Mar 11, 2:44 pm– Mar 13, 4:03 pm	1st	Taurus	Plant annuals for hardiness. Trim to increase growth.

Be ready for unexpected freezes in your garden. Keep an old sheet handy to cover plants in case there's a late frost. Run a cord with a lightbulb out to your garden and put it under the sheet to keep plants warm. Put stakes in the ground—one at each corner and one or two in the middle—and drape the sheet over the stakes. Make sure the sheet goes all the way to the ground so heat doesn't escape.

●
March 8
8:54 pm EST

MARCH

S	M	T	W	T	F	S
		1	2	3	4	5
6	7	8	9	10	11	12
13	14	15	16	17	18	19
20	21	22	23	24	25	26
27	28	29	30	31		

March 13–19 ✄

Nothing in the world can take the place of persistence ... The slogan "press on" has solved, and always will solve, the problems of the human race.   ～CALVIN COOLIDGE

Date	Qtr.	Sign	Activity
Mar 11, 2:44 pm– Mar 13, 4:03 pm	1st	Taurus	Plant annuals for hardiness. Trim to increase growth.
Mar 15, 7:57 pm– Mar 18, 2:54 am	2nd	Cancer	Plant grains, leafy annuals. Fertilize (chemical). Graft or bud plants. Irrigate. Trim to increase growth.

When an onion is cut, a sulfur-containing compound called allicin is produced. Our eyes water as our tear ducts attempt to wash it away. Typically, a simple splash of cool water on the eyes will stop the burning and tears. To reduce eye irritation, cut onions under running water or submerged in a basin of water. Consider refrigerating the onion before cutting to slow the enzymatic reaction rate and also reduce irritation.

*Daylight Saving Time begins
March 13, 2:00 am*

◑

March 15, 1:03 pm EDT

MARCH

S	M	T	W	T	F	S
		1	2	3	4	5
6	7	8	9	10	11	12
13	14	15	16	17	18	19
20	21	22	23	24	25	26
27	28	29	30	31		

♈ **March 20–26**

Perhaps all you need to do to be more fully lit from within is to be around people who see your light. ∼Victoria Moran

Date	Qtr.	Sign	Activity
Mar 23, 12:23 am– Mar 23, 7:01 am	2nd	Libra	Plant annuals for fragrance and beauty. Trim to increase growth.
Mar 25, 1:09 pm– Mar 28, 1:46 am	3rd	Scorpio	Plant biennials, perennials, bulbs, and roots. Prune. Irrigate. Fertilize (organic).

Selling your home in the busy spring market? Did you know that strategically placed roots, herbs, and spices attract potential buyers? Burn cinnamon bark to raise the home's vibration and ignite interest; strew crushed bay leaves near entrances to attract buyers and protect your investment; sprinkle flax seed around the negotiating table to ensure a fair selling price; and put basil in your wallet to attract prosperity and the cash you need to close.

_____

_____

_____

_____

○
March 23
8:01 am EDT

March

S	M	T	W	T	F	S
		1	2	3	4	5
6	7	8	9	10	11	12
13	14	15	16	17	18	19
20	21	22	23	24	25	26
27	28	29	30	31		

April ♈

March 27–April 2

Be kind, for everyone you meet is fighting a hard battle.

~SOCRATES

Date	Qtr.	Sign	Activity
Mar 25, 1:09 pm– Mar 28, 1:46 am	3rd	Scorpio	Plant biennials, perennials, bulbs, and roots. Prune. Irrigate. Fertilize (organic).
Mar 28, 1:46 pm– Mar 30, 12:45 pm	3rd	Sagittarius	Cultivate. Destroy weeds and pests. Harvest fruits and root crops for food. Trim to retard growth.
Mar 30, 12:45 pm– Mar 31, 10:17 am	3rd	Capricorn	Plant potatoes and tubers. Trim to retard growth.
Mar 31, 10:17 am– Apr 1, 8:37 pm	4th	Capricorn	Plant potatoes and tubers. Trim to retard growth.
Apr 1, 8:37 pm– Apr 4, 12:45 am	4th	Aquarius	Cultivate. Destroy weeds and pests. Harvest fruits and root crops for food. Trim to retard growth.

Consider dropping soda, both regular and diet, from your menu for overall health and weight loss. When you guzzle soda, you're choosing to not eat or drink something nutritious in its place. Also, soda drinkers take in more daily calories, partially because sugar increases cravings for more sugar. Replace soda with water and healthier fluid options such as water flavored with lemon, unsweetened tea, or seltzer water.

2015 © Yastremska Image from BigStockPhoto.com

◐

March 31
11:17 am EDT

APRIL

S	M	T	W	T	F	S
					1	2
3	4	5	6	7	8	9
10	11	12	13	14	15	16
17	18	19	20	21	22	23
24	25	26	27	28	29	30

♈ April 3–9

The knowledge of the world is only to be acquired in the world, and not in a closet.   ~Philip Dormer Stanhop

Date	Qtr.	Sign	Activity
Apr 1, 8:37 pm– Apr 4, 12:45 am	4th	Aquarius	Cultivate. Destroy weeds and pests. Harvest fruits and root crops for food. Trim to retard growth.
Apr 4, 12:45 am– Apr 6, 1:46 am	4th	Pisces	Plant biennials, perennials, bulbs, and roots. Prune. Irrigate. Fertilize (organic).
Apr 6, 1:46 am– Apr 7, 6:24 am	4th	Aries	Cultivate. Destroy weeds and pests. Harvest fruits and root crops for food. Trim to retard growth.
Apr 8, 1:10 am– Apr 10, 12:59 am	1st	Taurus	Plant annuals for hardiness. Trim to increase growth.

That "gunk" on the bottom of commercial berry juice bottles is beneficial; bits of the fruit skin are likely to be swirling on the bottom and contribute to the sediment. Consider the blueberry: its skin is its primary source of beneficial antioxidants. You would be losing a significant amount of your juice's nutritional value (and money spent) by not drinking the "gunk." Just be sure to shake the bottle before serving.

●

April 7
7:24 am EDT

April

S	M	T	W	T	F	S
					1	2
3	4	5	6	7	8	9
10	11	12	13	14	15	16
17	18	19	20	21	22	23
24	25	26	27	28	29	30

April 10–16 ♈

Man is only truly great when he acts from the passions.

~BENJAMIN DISRAELI

Date	Qtr.	Sign	Activity
Apr 8, 1:10 am– Apr 10, 12:59 am	1st	Taurus	Plant annuals for hardiness. Trim to increase growth.
Apr 12, 3:07 am– Apr 13, 10:59 pm	1st	Cancer	Plant grains, leafy annuals. Fertilize (chemical). Graft or bud plants. Irrigate. Trim to increase growth.
Apr 13, 10:59 pm– Apr 14, 8:53 am	2nd	Cancer	Plant grains, leafy annuals. Fertilize (chemical). Graft or bud plants. Irrigate. Trim to increase growth.

April gives birth to the splendor of blossoming shrubs and trees. Buds burst forth, promising a shady, green canopy. Neighborhoods come alive with the heady aroma of hyacinths. The visual beauty of colorful tulips fills the landscape with alluring eye candy. Inspiration and energy flow in glowing vibes that usher in the spring. As Ralph Waldo Emerson's poem so aptly declares, the earth truly laughs in flowers.

◐

April 13
11:59 pm EDT

APRIL

S	M	T	W	T	F	S
					1	2
3	4	5	6	7	8	9
10	11	12	13	14	15	16
17	18	19	20	21	22	23
24	25	26	27	28	29	30

2015 © mayabuns Image from BigStockPhoto.com

♈ April 17–23

*Isn't it fine when the day is done, and the petty battles are lost
or won?*
                                                    ~Edgar A. Guest

Date	Qtr.	Sign	Activity
Apr 19, 6:24 am– Apr 21, 7:17 pm	2nd	Libra	Plant annuals for fragrance and beauty. Trim to increase growth.
Apr 21, 7:17 pm– Apr 22, 12:24 pm	2nd	Scorpio	Plant grains, leafy annuals. Fertilize (chemical). Graft or bud plants. Irrigate. Trim to increase growth.
Apr 22, 12:24 am– Apr 24, 7:46 am	3rd	Scorpio	Plant biennials, perennials, bulbs, and roots. Prune. Irrigate. Fertilize (organic).

Giving gifts can be more meaningful when you make an effort to carefully observe people and pay attention to what they like and need. Start organizing early by getting a small notebook and making notes in it all year about the likes, dislikes, characteristics, and true needs of the people you love and want to give gifts to. Add ideas as they come to you. When it's time to shop you won't waste money on meaningless stuff.

_____

_____

_____

_____

O
April 22
1:24 am EDT

April

S	M	T	W	T	F	S
					1	2
3	4	5	6	7	8	9
10	11	12	13	14	15	16
17	18	19	20	21	22	23
24	25	26	27	28	29	30

April 24–30

The richest person is the one with the least desires.
~DEBRA MOFFITT

Date	Qtr.	Sign	Activity
Apr 22, 12:24 am–Apr 24, 7:46 am	3rd	Scorpio	Plant biennials, perennials, bulbs, and roots. Prune. Irrigate. Fertilize (organic).
Apr 24, 7:46 am–Apr 26, 6:54 pm	3rd	Sagittarius	Cultivate. Destroy weeds and pests. Harvest fruits and root crops for food. Trim to retard growth.
Apr 26, 6:54 pm–Apr 29, 3:47 am	3rd	Capricorn	Plant potatoes and tubers. Trim to retard growth.
Apr 29, 3:47 am–Apr 29, 10:29 pm	2nd	Aquarius	Cultivate. Destroy weeds and pests. Harvest fruits and root crops for food. Trim to retard growth.
Apr 29, 10:29 pm–May 1, 9:33 am	4th	Aquarius	Cultivate. Destroy weeds and pests. Harvest fruits and root crops for food. Trim to retard growth.

Water plants in the morning to avoid powdery mildew and other fungal diseases that can be spread by high humidity.

April 29
11:29 pm EDT

APRIL

S	M	T	W	T	F	S
					1	2
3	4	5	6	7	8	9
10	11	12	13	14	15	16
17	18	19	20	21	22	23
24	25	26	27	28	29	30

May
May 1–7

There are moments when everything goes well; don't be frightened, it won't last.   ~JULES RENARD

Date	Qtr.	Sign	Activity
Apr 29, 10:29 pm– May 1, 9:33 am	4th	Aquarius	Cultivate. Destroy weeds and pests. Harvest fruits and root crops for food. Trim to retard growth.
May 1, 9:33 am– May 3, 12:04 pm	4th	Pisces	Plant biennials, perennials, bulbs, and roots. Prune. Irrigate. Fertilize (organic).
May 3, 12:04 pm– May 5, 12:10 pm	4th	Aries	Cultivate. Destroy weeds and pests. Harvest fruits and root crops for food. Trim to retard growth.
May 5, 12:10 pm– May 6, 2:30 pm	4th	Taurus	Plant potatoes and tubers. Trim to retard growth.
May 6, 2:30 pm– May 7, 11:35 am	1st	Taurus	Plant annuals for hardiness. Trim to increase growth.

To get the most nutrients from your strawberries, eat them raw. Assure ripeness by avoiding those with green or white tips. Strawberries absorb high levels of pesticides when grown conventionally. According to the Environmental Working Group, strawberries are the second-highest pesticide-laden and most consistently contaminated fruit or vegetable. Translation: splurge for organic strawberries!

May 6
3:30 pm EDT

MAY

S	M	T	W	T	F	S
1	2	3	4	5	6	7
8	9	10	11	12	13	14
15	16	17	18	19	20	21
22	23	24	25	26	27	28
29	30	31				

May 8–14 ♉

To most people nothing is more troublesome than the effort
of thinking. ~JAMES BRYCE

Date	Qtr.	Sign	Activity
May 9, 12:24 pm– May 11, 4:32 pm	1st	Cancer	Plant grains, leafy annuals. Fertilize (chemical). Graft or bud plants. Irrigate. Trim to increase growth.

Why would your environment need healing? Simply because of the dynamics that occur in everyday life. Moods shift, concerns crop up, relationships change, trauma occurs, and your body and the energy around it responds. It is easy to understand how conflict or chaos pollute your environment. One cure is aromatherapy, the perfect modality to help you balance your body and your life. Explore the benefits of using essential oils to harmonize your space.

◐
May 13
1:02 pm EDT

MAY

S	M	T	W	T	F	S
					1	2
3	4	5	6	7	8	9
10	11	12	13	14	15	16
17	18	19	20	21	22	23
24	25	26	27	28	29	30
31						

May 15–21

A good film is when the price of dinner, the theatre, admission and the babysitter were worth it.   ~ALFRED HITCHCOCK

Date	Qtr.	Sign	Activity
May 16, 12:33 pm– May 19, 1:29 am	2nd	Libra	Plant annuals for fragrance and beauty. Trim to increase growth.
May 19, 1:29 am– May 21, 1:48 pm	2nd	Scorpio	Plant grains, leafy annuals. Fertilize (chemical). Graft or bud plants. Irrigate. Trim to increase growth.
May 21, 4:14 pm– May 24, 12:34 am	3rd	Sagittarius	Cultivate. Destroy weeds and pests. Harvest fruits and root crops for food. Trim to retard growth.

Geminis earn respect for their high energy level, sociability, and fondness for mental stimulation. Known for their communication skills, they are excellent speakers, writers, and teachers. Far too often they juggle multiple complex projects and scatter their forces, resulting in exhaustion and little down time. White chestnut and hornbeam, two Bach flower remedies, help to calm the mind, clear away unwanted clutter, and combat mental fatigue caused by life's trials.

○
May 21
5:14 pm EDT

MAY

S	M	T	W	T	F	S
1	2	3	4	5	6	7
8	9	10	11	12	13	14
15	16	17	18	19	20	21
22	23	24	25	26	27	28
29	30	31				

2015 © marcinmaslowski Image from BigStockPhoto.com

May 22–28 ♊

Never explain yourself to anyone out of fear they may misjudge you.
                                                    ~GUY FINLEY

Date	Qtr.	Sign	Activity
May 21, 4:14 pm– May 24, 12:34 am	3rd	Sagittarius	Cultivate. Destroy weeds and pests. Harvest fruits and root crops for food. Trim to retard growth.
May 24, 12:34 am– May 26, 9:27 am	3rd	Capricorn	Plant potatoes and tubers. Trim to retard growth.
May 26, 9:27 am– May 28, 4:06 pm	3rd	Aquarius	Cultivate. Destroy weeds and pests. Harvest fruits and root crops for food. Trim to retard growth.
May 28, 4:06 pm– May 29, 7:12 am	3rd	Pisces	Plant biennials, perennials, bulbs, and roots. Prune. Irrigate. Fertilize (organic).

Baking soda is a miracle for cleaning many surfaces, but did you know you can wash your hair with it, too? Just wet your hair and scalp and rub baking soda into your scalp with your fingertips, adding water to make a thin paste. Then add diluted apple cider vinegar (yes, it will foam!) and rinse thoroughly. This restores the pH balance to hair and scalp, leaving hair soft and shiny—and it costs only pennies per use!

MAY

S	M	T	W	T	F	S
1	2	3	4	5	6	7
8	9	10	11	12	13	14
15	16	17	18	19	20	21
22	23	24	25	26	27	28
29	30	31				

♊ June

May 29–June 4

You never hear the robins brag about the sweetness of their song.
~Edgar A. Guest

Date	Qtr.	Sign	Activity
May 28, 4:06 pm– May 29, 7:12 am	3rd	Pisces	Plant biennials, perennials, bulbs, and roots. Prune. Irrigate. Fertilize (organic).
May 29, 7:12 am– May 30, 8:09 pm	4th	Pisces	Plant biennials, perennials, bulbs, and roots. Prune. Irrigate. Fertilize (organic).
May 30, 8:09 pm– Jun 1, 9:46 pm	4th	Aries	Cultivate. Destroy weeds and pests. Harvest fruits and root crops for food. Trim to retard growth.
Jun 1, 9:46 pm– Jun 3, 10:01 pm	4th	Taurus	Plant potatoes and tubers. Trim to retard growth.
Jun 3, 10:01 pm– Jun 4, 10:00 pm	4th	Gemini	Cultivate. Destroy weeds and pests. Harvest fruits and root crops for food. Trim to retard growth.

Previous recommended daily allowances of sodium have recently been lowered to 1,500 mg (less than 1 teaspoon!) per day for children and adults. Try salt-free seasonings such as herbs, spices, garlic, vinegar, and black pepper instead. Add fresh lemon juice to fish and vegetables. Combine herbs and spices to make your own salt-free seasonings.

◖ May 29
8:12 am EDT

● June 4
11:00 pm EDT

June

S	M	T	W	T	F	S
			1	2	3	4
5	6	7	8	9	10	11
12	13	14	15	16	17	18
19	20	21	22	23	24	25
26	27	28	29	30		

2015 © Hannamariah Image from BigStockPhoto.com

June 5–11 ♊

The two most important days in your life are the day you
were born, and the day you find out why.

~MARK TWAIN

Date	Qtr.	Sign	Activity
Jun 5, 10:41 pm–Jun 8, 1:47 am	1st	Cancer	Plant grains, leafy annuals. Fertilize (chemical). Graft or bud plants. Irrigate. Trim to increase growth.

Aromatherapy works wonders to clear sacred places like your body, your home, your workplace, your car, and where you play. Most varieties work best when combined with massage oil or inhaled to calm the senses. Venus-ruled Taurus enjoy the healing qualities of bergamot, an uplifting emotional balancer; multipurpose geranium to eliminate fluid retention or to encourage self-expression and communication; and ylang-ylang for lowering blood pressure or for attracting love and peace.

2015 © alexraths Image from BigStockPhoto.com

			JUNE			
S	M	T	W	T	F	S
			1	2	3	4
5	6	7	8	9	10	11
12	13	14	15	16	17	18
19	20	21	22	23	24	25
26	27	28	29	30		

♊ June 12–18

Experience is the name everyone gives to their mistakes.

~WILLARD DUNCAN VANDIVER

Date	Qtr.	Sign	Activity
Jun 12, 7:33 pm– Jun 15, 8:18 am	2nd	Libra	Plant annuals for fragrance and beauty. Trim to increase growth.
Jun 15, 8:18 am– Jun 17, 8:34 pm	2nd	Scorpio	Plant grains, leafy annuals. Fertilize (chemical). Graft or bud plants. Irrigate. Trim to increase growth.

Strawberries are popularly found in cakes, pies, strawberry shortcake, fruit and green salads, as toppings, preserves, or simply eaten raw. For a healthy desert alternative, serve strawberries over ice cream or frozen yogurt with some heart-healthy walnuts, sliced almonds, or macadamia nuts. Or get creative and design a strawberry fruit pizza, or soak strawberries in balsamic vinegar and black pepper to jazz up salads, ice cream, or low-calorie angel food cake.

_____

_____

_____

_____

◑
June 12
4:10 am EDT

JUNE

S	M	T	W	T	F	S
			1	2	3	4
5	6	7	8	9	10	11
12	13	14	15	16	17	18
19	20	21	22	23	24	25
26	27	28	29	30		

June 19–25 ♊

Give what you have. To someone, it may be better than you
dare to think.   ～HENRY WADSWORTH LONGFELLOW

Date	Qtr.	Sign	Activity
Jun 20, 6:02 am– Jun 20, 6:55 am	3rd	Sagittarius	Cultivate. Destroy weeds and pests. Harvest fruits and root crops for food. Trim to retard growth.
Jun 20, 6:55 am– Jun 22, 3:08 pm	3rd	Capricorn	Plant potatoes and tubers. Trim to retard growth.
Jun 22, 3:08 pm– Jun 24, 9:30 pm	3rd	Aquarius	Cultivate. Destroy weeds and pests. Harvest fruits and root crops for food. Trim to retard growth.
Jun 24, 9:30 pm– Jun 27, 2:08 am	3rd	Pisces	Plant biennials, perennials, bulbs, and roots. Prune. Irrigate. Fertilize (organic).

Serious cooks keep shakers filled with tasty seasoning mixes handy for adding flavor to favorite dishes. Grocery stores, gourmet food shops, retail outlets, and county fairs sell pricey commercial mixes for your convenience. Why not make your own? Try this savory mix that works well for meat, poultry, fish, and vegetables: ¼ cup salt, ⅛ cup black pepper, ⅛ cup garlic powder, and ⅛ cup onion powder. Mix and store away from heat.

2015 © Lidante Image from BigStockPhoto.com

○
June 20
7:02 am EDT

JUNE

S	M	T	W	T	F	S
			1	2	3	4
5	6	7	8	9	10	11
12	13	14	15	16	17	18
19	20	21	22	23	24	25
26	27	28	29	30		

♋ July

June 26–July 2

You don't stop laughing because you grow old. You grow old because you stop laughing. ∼MICHAEL PRITCHARD

Date	Qtr.	Sign	Activity
Jun 24, 9:30 pm– Jun 27, 2:08 am	3rd	Pisces	Plant biennials, perennials, bulbs, and roots. Prune. Irrigate. Fertilize (organic).
Jun 27, 2:08 am– Jun 27, 1:19 pm	3rd	Aries	Cultivate. Destroy weeds and pests. Harvest fruits and root crops for food. Trim to retard growth.
Jun 27, 1:19 pm– Jun 29, 5:03 am	4th	Aries	Cultivate. Destroy weeds and pests. Harvest fruits and root crops for food. Trim to retard growth.
Jun 29, 5:03 am– Jul 1, 6:44 am	4th	Taurus	Plant potatoes and tubers. Trim to retard growth.
Jul 1, 6:44 am– Jul 3, 8:20 am	4th	Gemini	Cultivate. Destroy weeds and pests. Harvest fruits and root crops for food. Trim to retard growth.

Peonies are grand dames in the garden, and befitting their station, they don't like to be moved! Once established, they'll bloom for decades with very little fuss. Give them a nice sunny spot with rich, well-drained soil. Trim back the foliage once it gets mildewy or brown in the fall, and add a small top dressing of manure before frost sets in.

◑

June 27
2:19 pm EDT

JULY

S	M	T	W	T	F	S
					1	2
3	4	5	6	7	8	9
10	11	12	13	14	15	16
17	18	19	20	21	22	23
24	25	26	27	28	29	30
31						

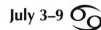

July 3–9 ♋

If opportunity doesn't knock,

ᴸTON Bᴇʀʟᴇ

Date	Qtr.	Sign	
Jul 1, 6:44 am– Jul 3, 8:20 am	4th	Gemini	Cultivate. L ⸍uits and root crops for food. Trim to retard growⁿ.
Jul 3, 8:20 am– Jul 4, 6:01 am	4th	Cancer	Plant biennials, perennials, bulbs, and roots. Prune. Irrigate. Fertilize (organic).
Jul 4, 6:01 am– Jul 5, 11:28 am	1st	Cancer	Plant grains, leafy annuals. Fertilize (chemical). Graft or bud plants. Irrigate. Trim to increase growth.

Whether at the grocery store or farmer's market, pay attention to color and smell. If you can't smell a fruit or vegetable, it isn't ripe. Different nutrients differ in color. Vitamin A and beta-carotene are bright yellow, proanthocyanidins—fabulous antioxidants—are purple, and red nutrients often have lots of Vitamin B12. Orange is the color for Vitamin B, whereas Vitamin C is colorless. A vegetable or fruit that is not rich in color and smell is going to be short on nutrition.

July 4
7:01 am EDT

Jᴜʟʏ

S	M	T	W	T	F	S
					1	2
3	4	5	6	7	8	9
10	11	12	13	14	15	16
17	18	19	20	21	22	23
24	25	26	27	28	29	30
31						

July 10–16

An expert is one who knows more and more about
less and less.   ~NICHOLAS MURRAY BUTLER

Date	Qtr.	Sign	Activity
Jul 10, 3:33 am– Jul 11, 7:52 pm	1st	Libra	Plant annuals for fragrance and beauty. Trim to increase growth.
Jul 11, 7:52 pm– Jul 12, 3:52 pm	2nd	Libra	Plant annuals for fragrance and beauty. Trim to increase growth.
Jul 12, 3:52 pm– Jul 15, 4:14 am	2nd	Scorpio	Plant grains, leafy annuals. Fertilize (chemical). Graft or bud plants. Irrigate. Trim to increase growth.

Essential oils make excellent air fresheners without the artificial scents and chemicals found in commercial products. The antibacterial properties can also help cut down on germs. Fill a spray bottle with water and a few drops of alcohol (vodka works fine) to help disperse it; then add a few drops of your favorite oil, about 15 drops for every 8 ounces of water. Try lavender, lime, lemon, eucalyptus, pine, cypress, cedar, or rosemary. Or make your own blend.

◑
July 11
8:52 pm EDT

JULY

S	M	T	W	T	F	S
					1	2
3	4	5	6	7	8	9
10	11	12	13	14	15	16
17	18	19	20	21	22	23
24	25	26	27	28	29	30
31						

July 17–23 ♋

A well-written life is almost as rare as a well-spent one.

~THOMAS CARLYLE

Date	Qtr.	Sign	Activity
Jul 17, 2:33 pm– Jul 19, 5:57 pm	2nd	Capricorn	Graft or bud plants. Trim to increase growth.
Jul 19, 5:57 pm– Jul 19, 10:10 pm	3rd	Capricorn	Plant potatoes and tubers. Trim to retard growth.
Jul 19, 10:10 pm– Jul 22, 3:35 am	3rd	Aquarius	Cultivate. Destroy weeds and pests. Harvest fruits and root crops for food. Trim to retard growth.
Jul 22, 3:35 am– Jul 24, 7:33 am	3rd	Pisces	Plant biennials, perennials, bulbs, and roots. Prune. Irrigate. Fertilize (organic).

Every home needs a reference library. It should contain books that you can refer to if you lose electricity or the Internet goes down. Think about the kind of information you frequently need or turn to professionals for. Medicine? A physical emergency? Electricity? Plumbing? Food? Go to the bookstore and pick out a few books that you can understand in case of emergency. Read the table of contents and scan through them before buying anything.

○
July 19
6:57 pm EDT

JULY

S	M	T	W	T	F	S
					1	2
3	4	5	6	7	8	9
10	11	12	13	14	15	16
17	18	19	20	21	22	23
24	25	26	27	28	29	30
31						

♌ July 24–30

Everything you've ever wanted is on the other side of fear.

~George Addair

Date	Qtr.	Sign	Activity
Jul 22, 3:35 am– Jul 24, 7:33 am	3rd	Pisces	Plant biennials, perennials, bulbs, and roots. Prune. Irrigate. Fertilize (organic).
Jul 24, 7:33 am– Jul 26, 10:37 am	3rd	Aries	Cultivate. Destroy weeds and pests. Harvest fruits and root crops for food. Trim to retard growth.
Jul 26, 10:37 am– Jul 26, 6:00 pm	3rd	Taurus	Plant potatoes and tubers. Trim to retard growth.
Jul 26, 6:00 pm– Jul 28, 1:17 pm	4th	Taurus	Plant potatoes and tubers. Trim to retard growth.
Jul 28, 1:17 pm– Jul 30, 4:09 pm	4th	Gemini	Cultivate. Destroy weeds and pests. Harvest fruits and root crops for food. Trim to retard growth.
Jul 30, 4:09 pm– Aug 1, 8:12 pm	4th	Cancer	Plant biennials, perennials, bulbs, and roots. Prune. Irrigate. Fertilize (organic).

Amelia Earhart Day honors one of the most famous aviation pioneers in history on July 24 each year, the anniversary of her 1897 birthday. Amelia and her navigator, Fred Noonan, went missing in the Pacific Ocean on July 2, 1937, braving difficult weather conditions while attempting to fly around the world. Their plane was never found, and the public remains fascinated with her life and journey.

◑

July 26
7:00 pm EDT

July

S	M	T	W	T	F	S
					1	2
3	4	5	6	7	8	9
10	11	12	13	14	15	16
17	18	19	20	21	22	23
24	25	26	27	28	29	30
31						

August ♌

July 31–August 6

Opera is where a guy gets stabbed in the back, and instead of
dying, he sings.
           ~Robert Benchley

Date	Qtr.	Sign	Activity
Jul 30, 4:09 pm– Aug 1, 8:12 pm	4th	Cancer	Plant biennials, perennials, bulbs, and roots. Prune. Irrigate. Fertilize (organic).
Aug 1, 8:12 pm– Aug 2, 3:45 pm	4th	Leo	Cultivate. Destroy weeds and pests. Harvest fruits and root crops for food. Trim to retard growth.
Aug 6, 11:57 am– Aug 8, 11:51 pm	1st	Libra	Plant annuals for fragrance and beauty. Trim to increase growth.

Leo rules the natural fifth house in the zodiac. This house relates to your social life, romance, people you date, lovers, children, sports fans, and creative or entrepreneurial partners. Planets in this part of your chart describe how you carry out your social life and shed light on significant relationships. You are likely to meet partners who have similar interests, hobbies, attend the same parties, or prefer similar recreation or vacation choices.

●
August 2
4:45 pm EDT

August

S	M	T	W	T	F	S
	1	2	3	4	5	6
7	8	9	10	11	12	13
14	15	16	17	18	19	20
21	22	23	24	25	26	27
28	29	30	31			

August 7–13

No matter what people tell you, words and ideas can change the world.
                                    ~ROBIN WILLIAMS

Date	Qtr.	Sign	Activity
Aug 6, 11:57 pm–Aug 8, 11:51 pm	1st	Libra	Plant annuals for fragrance and beauty. Trim to increase growth.
Aug 8, 11:51 pm–Aug 10, 1:21 pm	1st	Scorpio	Plant grains, leafy annuals. Fertilize (chemical). Graft or bud plants. Irrigate. Trim to increase growth.
Aug 10, 1:21 pm–Aug 11, 12:24 pm	2nd	Scorpio	Plant grains, leafy annuals. Fertilize (chemical). Graft or bud plants. Irrigate. Trim to increase growth.
Aug 13, 11:11 pm–Aug 16, 6:52 am	2nd	Capricorn	Graft or bud plants. Trim to increase growth.

Love the summer but not the heat and humidity? Stay cool by increasing your fluid intake. Water is the number-one hydrator, so drink lots of it even if you aren't thirsty. Flavor the water with slices of lemon, lime, or orange. Wear light and loose-fitting clothing so your body can breathe. During the "dog days" of August, chill out in air-conditioned spaces and keep your body and mind cool and in healthy working order.

August 10
2:21 pm EDT

AUGUST

S	M	T	W	T	F	S
		1	2	3	4	5	6
7	8	9	10	11	12	13
14	15	16	17	18	19	20
21	22	23	24	25	26	27
28	29	30	31			

August 14–20 ♌

Human history becomes more and more a race between
education and catastrophe.　　　　　　　~H.G. WELLS

Date	Qtr.	Sign	Activity
Aug 13, 11:11 pm– Aug 16, 6:52 am	2nd	Capricorn	Graft or bud plants. Trim to increase growth.
Aug 18, 4:27 am– Aug 18, 11:34 am	3rd	Aquarius	Cultivate. Destroy weeds and pests. Harvest fruits and root crops for food. Trim to retard growth.
Aug 18, 11:34 am– Aug 20, 2:18 pm	3rd	Pisces	Plant biennials, perennials, bulbs, and roots. Prune. Irrigate. Fertilize (organic).
Aug 20, 2:18 pm– Aug 22, 4:19 pm	3rd	Aries	Cultivate. Destroy weeds and pests. Harvest fruits and root crops for food. Trim to retard growth.

Don't just clip those rose hips into a lawn bag! Make tea from them. Rose hips contain very high levels of Vitamins A and C, and they taste delicious when used for tea. Just pour boiling water over them and steep for five minutes, add a bit of honey, and enjoy. Rose hips make a very thirst-quenching iced tea as well.

2015 © teresaterra Image from BigStockPhoto.com

○
August 18
5:27 am EDT

AUGUST

S	M	T	W	T	F	S
		1	2	3	4	5	6
7	8	9	10	11	12	13
14	15	16	17	18	19	20
21	22	23	24	25	26	27
28	29	30	31			

♌ August 21–27

It's a sign of maturity to take control of your own happiness
and be happy, no matter what.   ~RICHARD WEBSTER

Date	Qtr.	Sign	Activity
Aug 20, 2:18 pm– Aug 22, 4:19 pm	3rd	Aries	Cultivate. Destroy weeds and pests. Harvest fruits and root crops for food. Trim to retard growth.
Aug 22, 4:19 pm– Aug 24, 6:40 pm	3rd	Taurus	Plant potatoes and tubers. Trim to retard growth.
Aug 24, 6:40 pm– Aug 24, 10:41 pm	3rd	Gemini	Cultivate. Destroy weeds and pests. Harvest fruits and root crops for food. Trim to retard growth.
Aug 24, 10:41 pm– Aug 26, 10:06 pm	4th	Gemini	Cultivate. Destroy weeds and pests. Harvest fruits and root crops for food. Trim to retard growth.
Aug 26, 10:06 pm– Aug 29, 3:11 am	4th	Cancer	Plant biennials, perennials, bulbs, and roots. Prune. Irrigate. Fertilize (organic).

Ever make a pot of white bean soup and add too many bitter greens? Arugula is more bitter than kale and can make the soup taste astringent and unpleasant. To remedy this, add some very finely grated carrot. The carrot's sweetness will counteract the bitterness of the greens and add some extra Vitamin A and beta-carotene.

◖
August 24
11:41 pm EDT

AUGUST

S	M	T	W	T	F	S
	1	2	3	4	5	6
7	8	9	10	11	12	13
14	15	16	17	18	19	20
21	22	23	24	25	26	27
28	29	30	31			

September ♍
August 28–September 3

The best way out is always through. ～Robert Frost

Date	Qtr.	Sign	Activity
Aug 26, 10:06 pm– Aug 29, 3:11 am	4th	Cancer	Plant biennials, perennials, bulbs, and roots. Prune. Irrigate. Fertilize (organic).
Aug 29, 3:11 am– Aug 31, 10:22 am	4th	Leo	Cultivate. Destroy weeds and pests. Harvest fruits and root crops for food. Trim to retard growth.
Aug 31, 10:22 am– Sep 1, 4:03 am	4th	Virgo	Cultivate, especially medicinal plants. Destroy weeds and pests. Trim to retard growth.
Sep 2, 7:55 pm– Sep 5, 7:38 am	1st	Libra	Plant annuals for fragrance and beauty. Trim to increase growth.

Clean bird feeders in the fall to get them ready for use in the colder months. The birds have done a great job of feasting on garden pests and serenading you all summer. Now is the time to encourage them to stick around another year.

●

September 1
5:03 am EDT

September

S	M	T	W	T	F	S
				1	2	3
4	5	6	7	8	9	10
11	12	13	14	15	16	17
18	19	20	21	22	23	24
25	26	27	28	29	30	

♍ September 4–10

There are women who are not beautiful but only look
that way.

~KARL KRAUS

Date	Qtr.	Sign	Activity
Sep 2, 7:55 pm– Sep 5, 7:38 am	1st	Libra	Plant annuals for fragrance and beauty. Trim to increase growth.
Sep 5, 7:38 am– Sep 7, 8:20 pm	1st	Scorpio	Plant grains, leafy annuals. Fertilize (chemical). Graft or bud plants. Irrigate. Trim to increase growth.
Sep 10, 7:55 am– Sep 12, 4:28 pm	2nd	Capricorn	Graft or bud plants. Trim to increase growth.

When the trees are leafless and the snow is on the ground, a variety of plants and shrubs add greenery and visual interest to the landscape. In many growing zones, hardy camellias display their roselike blooms in the middle of January, winterberry sheds its leaves in the fall and displays bright red berries during the winter, and nandinas flaunt attractive leaves that change colors with the season. Plant wisely in the fall to enjoy the winter bounty.

◐
September 9
7:49 am EDT

SEPTEMBER

S	M	T	W	T	F	S
				1	2	3
4	5	6	7	8	9	10
11	12	13	14	15	16	17
18	19	20	21	22	23	24
25	26	27	28	29	30	

September 11–17 ♍

No one ever keeps a secret so well as a child.

~Victor Hugo

Date	Qtr.	Sign	Activity
Sep 10, 7:55 am– Sep 12, 4:28 pm	2nd	Capricorn	Graft or bud plants. Trim to increase growth.
Sep 14, 9:23 pm– Sep 16, 2:05 pm	2nd	Pisces	Plant grains, leafy annuals. Fertilize (chemical). Graft or bud plants. Irrigate. Trim to increase growth.
Sep 16, 2:05 pm– Sep 16, 11:22 pm	3rd	Pisces	Plant biennials, perennials, bulbs, and roots. Prune. Irrigate. Fertilize (organic).
Sep 16, 11:22 pm– Sep 18, 11:58 pm	3rd	Aries	Cultivate. Destroy weeds and pests. Harvest fruits and root crops for food. Trim to retard growth.

Autumn is wonderful for creating a three- or four-day vacation at home. Choose an exotic recipe and make yourself a dinner you've never had before, read a book that you've been wanting to enjoy, take long, luxurious baths, sleep in, go out for brunch, or visit a local antique store that you've never been in before. It will feel just like you went on a vacation!

2015 © George D. Image from BigStockPhoto.com

○
September 16
3:05 pm EDT

September

S	M	T	W	T	F	S
				1	2	3
4	5	6	7	8	9	10
11	12	13	14	15	16	17
18	19	20	21	22	23	24
25	26	27	28	29	30	

♍ September 18–24

*Men talk too much of gold and fame, and not enough
about a name.*   ~Edgar A. Guest

Date	Qtr.	Sign	Activity
Sep 16, 11:22 pm– Sep 18, 11:58 pm	3rd	Aries	Cultivate. Destroy weeds and pests. Harvest fruits and root crops for food. Trim to retard growth.
Sep 18, 11:58 pm– Sep 21, 12:53 am	3rd	Taurus	Plant potatoes and tubers. Trim to retard growth.
Sep 21, 12:53 am– Sep 23, 3:33 am	3rd	Gemini	Cultivate. Destroy weeds and pests. Harvest fruits and root crops for food. Trim to retard growth.
Sep 23, 3:33 am– Sep 23, 4:56 am	3rd	Cancer	Plant biennials, perennials, bulbs, and roots. Prune. Irrigate. Fertilize (organic).
Sep 23, 4:56 am– Sep 25, 8:48 am	4th	Cancer	Plant biennials, perennials, bulbs, and roots. Prune. Irrigate. Fertilize (organic).

Okra has traditionally been most useful in adding body to and thickening rice-based stews such as gumbo, but the okra plant also produces a colorful flower pretty enough to use as garnish or grow in an ornamental garden. With a resemblance to hollyhock blossoms, the flavor of the okra flower partners well with other late summer crops (garlic, peppers, onions, tomatoes), many of which also fit nicely into a rich, earthy gumbo.

◐
September 23
5:56 am EDT

SEPTEMBER

S	M	T	W	T	F	S
				1	2	3
4	5	6	7	8	9	10
11	12	13	14	15	16	17
18	19	20	21	22	23	24
25	26	27	28	29	30	

October ♎

September 25–October 1

*Life can only be understood backwards; but it must be
lived forwards.*   ~SOREN KIERKEGAARD

Date	Qtr.	Sign	Activity
Sep 23, 4:56 am– Sep 25, 8:48 am	4th	Cancer	Plant biennials, perennials, bulbs, and roots. Prune. Irrigate. Fertilize (organic).
Sep 25, 8:48 am– Sep 27, 4:43 pm	4th	Leo	Cultivate. Destroy weeds and pests. Harvest fruits and root crops for food. Trim to retard growth.
Sep 27, 4:43 pm– Sep 30, 2:52 am	4th	Virgo	Cultivate, especially medicinal plants. Destroy weeds and pests. Trim to retard growth.
Sep 30, 7:11 pm– Oct 2, 2:43 pm	1st	Libra	Plant annuals fragrance and beauty. Trim to increase growth.

Candles have a romantic connotation that helps to harmonize environments. A candle's soft glow adds character and beauty to any space. Lighting a candle is one of the most potent forms of clearing space. The color and type of candle you select to brighten a room sets the tone for the mood and quality you want to create: red candles stimulate physical activity, orange is for fun at gatherings, yellow is for study and concentration, and blue promotes serenity.

2015 © Yastremska Image from BigStockPhoto.com

*September 30
8:11 pm EDT*

OCTOBER

S	M	T	W	T	F	S
						1
2	3	4	5	6	7	8
9	10	11	12	13	14	15
16	17	18	19	20	21	22
23	24	25	26	27	28	29
30	31					

♎ October 2–8

Unhappiness does not come at you, it comes from you.

~GUY FINLEY

Date	Qtr.	Sign	Activity
Sep 30, 7:11 pm– Oct 2, 2:43 pm	1st	Libra	Plant annuals for fragrance and beauty. Trim to increase growth.
Oct 2, 2:43 pm– Oct 5, 3:26 am	1st	Scorpio	Plant grains, leafy annuals. Fertilize (chemical). Graft or bud plants. Irrigate. Trim to increase growth.
Oct 7, 3:40 pm– Oct 8, 11:33 pm	1st	Capricorn	Graft or bud plants. Trim to increase growth.
Oct 8, 11:33 pm– Oct 10, 1:33 am	2nd	Capricorn	Graft or bud plants. Trim to increase growth.

The positive expression of Libra strikes a balance between relationships and alone time, evoking a loving, peaceful nature that showcases talents confidently. When Libra dwells on relationships excessively by ignoring personal needs and intuition, the result is delayed decision-making, uncertain plans, and emotional extremes. Helpful Bach remedies for Libra include agrimony, cerato, and scleranthus to foster self-acceptance, aid in finding stable companionship, and foster the ability to follow and trust your own inner guidance.

OCTOBER

S	M	T	W	T	F	S
						1
2	3	4	5	6	7	8
9	10	11	12	13	14	15
16	17	18	19	20	21	22
23	24	25	26	27	28	29
30	31					

2015 © Nosnibor137 Image from BigStockPhoto.com

October 9–15 ♎

You can tell the ideals of a nation by its advertisements.

~Norman Douglas

Date	Qtr.	Sign	Activity
Oct 8, 11:33 pm– Oct 10, 1:33 am	2nd	Capricorn	Graft or bud plants. Trim to increase growth.
Oct 12, 7:43 am– Oct 14, 10:08 am	2nd	Pisces	Plant grains, leafy annuals. Fertilize (chemical). Graft or bud plants. Irrigate. Trim to increase growth.
Oct 15, 11:23 pm– Oct 16, 10:04 am	3rd	Aries	Cultivate. Destroy weeds and pests. Harvest fruits and root crops for food. Trim to retard growth.

Consider finding a really good esthetician to perform a facial on a monthly basis. They will deep clean the skin, do pulsed light treatments to remove age spots, use powerful masks that clean and tone your skin, and provide transdermal formulas and potions that feed your cells. Choose someone who uses organic products and then tend to your body—face, feet, hands, neck, and back—as if it were your temple, because it is!

October 9
12:33 am EDT

October

S	M	T	W	T	F	S
						1
2	3	4	5	6	7	8
9	10	11	12	13	14	15
16	17	18	19	20	21	22
23	24	25	26	27	28	29
30	31					

2015 © Valua Vitaly Image from BigStockPhoto.com

♎ October 16–22

There's nothing cheers a fellow up just like a hearty greeting.

~Edgar A. Guest

Date	Qtr.	Sign	Activity
Oct 15, 11:23 pm– Oct 16, 10:04 am	3rd	Aries	Cultivate. Destroy weeds and pests. Harvest fruits and root crops for food. Trim to retard growth.
Oct 16, 10:04 am– Oct 18, 9:30 am	3rd	Taurus	Plant potatoes and tubers. Trim to retard growth.
Oct 18, 9:30 am– Oct 20, 10:28 am	3rd	Gemini	Cultivate. Destroy weeds and pests. Harvest fruits and root crops for food. Trim to retard growth.
Oct 20, 10:28 am– Oct 22, 2:14 pm	3rd	Cancer	Plant biennials, perennials, bulbs, and roots. Prune. Irrigate. Fertilize (organic).
Oct 22, 2:14 pm– Oct 22, 2:34 pm	4th	Cancer	Plant biennials, perennials, bulbs, and roots. Prune. Irrigate. Fertilize (organic).
Oct 22, 2:34 pm– Oct 24, 10:16 pm	4th	Leo	Cultivate. Destroy weeds and pests. Harvest fruits and root crops for food. Trim to retard growth.

Want to save some money on your energy bill? When you're using your oven, it's possible your stove has one burner that gets warm or hot. Put a pan of water on the burner and use that water to wash dishes when you're done cooking.

○ October 16
12:23 am EDT

◐ October 22
3:14 pm EDT

October

S	M	T	W	T	F	S
						1
2	3	4	5	6	7	8
9	10	11	12	13	14	15
16	17	18	19	20	21	22
23	24	25	26	27	28	29
30	31					

2015 © AdamEdwards Image from BigStockPhoto.com

October 23–29 ♏

Your True Self can no more get "stuck" somewhere than a
beam of sunlight can be held down by a shadow.

~ GUY FINLEY

Date	Qtr.	Sign	Activity
Oct 22, 2:34 pm– Oct 24, 10:16 pm	4th	Leo	Cultivate. Destroy weeds and pests. Harvest fruits and root crops for food. Trim to retard growth.
Oct 24, 10:16 pm– Oct 27, 8:51 am	4th	Virgo	Cultivate, especially medicinal plants. Destroy weeds and pests. Trim to retard growth.
Oct 29, 9:01 pm– Oct 30, 12:38 pm	4th	Scorpio	Plant biennials, perennials, bulbs, and roots. Prune. Irrigate. Fertilize (organic).

The seventh house elaborates on your marriage partner or soul-mate. It refers to any significant other with whom you have an intimate, live-in relationship. A woman with the Sun and Mars in this house almost always marries at least once. The same is true of a man who has the Moon and Venus. A cluster of planets in the seventh house may indicate the presence of multiple partners.

2015 © Phaendin Image from BigStockPhoto.com

			OCTOBER			
S	M	T	W	T	F	S
						1
2	3	4	5	6	7	8
9	10	11	12	13	14	15
16	17	18	19	20	21	22
23	24	25	26	27	28	29
30	31					

♏ November
October 30–November 5

*Opinions cannot survive if one has no chance to fight
for them.*
                                          ~THOMAS MANN

Date	Qtr.	Sign	Activity
Oct 29, 9:01 pm– Oct 30, 12:38 pm	4th	Scorpio	Plant biennials, perennials, bulbs, and roots. Prune. Irrigate. Fertilize (organic).
Oct 30, 12:38 pm– Nov 1, 9:43 am	1st	Scorpio	Plant grains, leafy annuals. Fertilize (chemical). Graft or bud plants. Irrigate. Trim to increase growth.
Nov 3, 10:05 pm– Nov 6, 8:55 am	1st	Capricorn	Graft or bud plants. Trim to increase growth.

Want a simple and delicious cold weather soup but don't want to go buy ingredients? Dice a few strips of bacon into a pot and cook until soft. Add chopped onion and/or garlic and sauté until translucent. Add in some sliced carrots and diced potatoes. (Add butter or olive oil to help coat the vegetables while you sauté them, if needed). Add enough water to cover them and simmer until the veggies are soft. Yummy, rustic, and easy!

●
October 30
1:38 pm EDT

NOVEMBER

S	M	T	W	T	F	S
		1	2	3	4	5
6	7	8	9	10	11	12
13	14	15	16	17	18	19
20	21	22	23	24	25	26
27	28	29	30			

November 6–12 ♏

Don't ever take a fence down until you know the reason why it was put up.
                    ~GILBERT KEITH CHESTERTON

Date	Qtr.	Sign	Activity
Nov 3, 10:05 pm– Nov 6, 8:55 am	1st	Capricorn	Graft or bud plants. Trim to increase growth.
Nov 8, 4:45 pm– Nov 10, 8:45 pm	2nd	Pisces	Plant grains, leafy annuals. Fertilize (chemical). Graft or bud plants. Irrigate. Trim to increase growth.
Nov 12, 9:24 pm– Nov 14, 8:52 am	2nd	Taurus	Plant annuals for hardiness. Trim to increase growth.

Pluto affiliations include the functions of cleansing and purifying, especially releasing the stored debris from the past, such as grief and anger. Stagnation of these emotions often affects bodily secretions and circulation. Aromatherapies that work to release water retention, relieve night sweats, purify the aura, combat menstrual cramps, and treat stings include sage, cedarwood, jasmine, pennyroyal, and sandalwood.

Daylight Saving Time ends November 6, 2:00 am

November 7, 2:51 pm EST

NOVEMBER

S	M	T	W	T	F	S
		1	2	3	4	5
6	7	8	9	10	11	12
13	14	15	16	17	18	19
20	21	22	23	24	25	26
27	28	29	30			

♏ November 13–19

Kindness lives beyond the memory of him who gives.

*~*EDGAR A. GUEST

Date	Qtr.	Sign	Activity
Nov 12, 9:24 pm– Nov 14, 8:52 am	2nd	Taurus	Plant annuals for hardiness. Trim to increase growth.
Nov 14, 8:52 am– Nov 14, 8:23 pm	3rd	Taurus	Plant potatoes and tubers. Trim to retard growth.
Nov 14, 8:23 pm– Nov 16, 7:57 pm	3rd	Gemini	Cultivate. Destroy weeds and pests. Harvest fruits and root crops for food. Trim to retard growth.
Nov 16, 7:57 pm– Nov 18, 10:14 pm	3rd	Cancer	Plant biennials, perennials, bulbs, and roots. Prune. Irrigate. Fertilize (organic).
Nov 18, 10:14 pm– Nov 21, 3:33 am	3rd	Leo	Cultivate. Destroy weeds and pests. Harvest fruits and root crops for food. Trim to retard growth.

Your astrology chart has specific departments that highlight your social and love lives. Houses five through eight comprise the Zone of Relationships or Intimacy. These houses and the planets that fall in them describe the people you meet and the nature and type of activity that occurs. When you learn the birth date of potential partners and discover that their intimate planets fall near some of your own, you can determine the level of compatibility you'll share.

○
November 14
8:52 am EST

NOVEMBER

S	M	T	W	T	F	S
		1	2	3	4	5
6	7	8	9	10	11	12
13	14	15	16	17	18	19
20	21	22	23	24	25	26
27	28	29	30			

2015 © stefanolunardi Image from BigStockPhoto.com

November 20–26

If you treat others as if they're important, they're likely to extend the same courtesy to you. ~RICHARD WEBSTER

Date	Qtr.	Sign	Activity
Nov 18, 10:14 pm– Nov 21, 3:33 am	3rd	Leo	Cultivate. Destroy weeds and pests. Harvest fruits and root crops for food. Trim to retard growth.
Nov 21, 3:33 am– Nov 21, 4:34 am	4th	Leo	Cultivate. Destroy weeds and pests. Harvest fruits and root crops for food. Trim to retard growth.
Nov 21, 4:34 am– Nov 23, 2:42 pm	4th	Virgo	Cultivate, especially medicinal plants. Destroy weeds and pests. Trim to retard growth.
Nov 26, 3:01 am– Nov 28, 3:46 pm	4th	Scorpio	Plant biennials, perennials, bulbs, and roots. Prune. Irrigate. Fertilize (organic).

Soil amendments can be made from simple household waste: wood ash from your woodstove or charcoal grill, used coffee grounds, old tea bags (remove any staples), and nut shells. Don't use anything that is wet or that will rot quickly. Wood ash makes the soil more alkaline, while the coffee makes it more acidic. Coffee grounds also attract worms and smell great.

November 21
3:33 am EST

NOVEMBER

S	M	T	W	T	F	S
		1	2	3	4	5
6	7	8	9	10	11	12
13	14	15	16	17	18	19
20	21	22	23	24	25	26
27	28	29	30			

↗ December

November 27–December 3

People say that life is the thing, but I prefer reading.

~Logan Pearsall Smith

Date	Qtr.	Sign	Activity
Nov 26, 3:01 am– Nov 28, 3:46 pm	4th	Scorpio	Plant biennials, perennials, bulbs, and roots. Prune. Irrigate. Fertilize (organic).
Nov 28, 3:46 pm– Nov 29, 7:18 am	4th	Sagittarius	Cultivate. Destroy weeds and pests. Harvest fruits and root crops for food. Trim to retard growth.
Dec 1, 3:52 am– Dec 3, 2:44 pm	1st	Capricorn	Graft or bud plants. Trim to increase growth.

Expand your consciousness by reading newspapers and listening to radio programs outside your usual circle of information. We are all global citizens now, and it is important to keep at least one finger on the pulse of information coming from other places of the world. When you read or hear something good, spread the news. When you hear something bad, remember, "trouble comes knocking more and more when you spread it door to door."

―――――――――――――――――――――

―――――――――――――――――――――

―――――――――――――――――――――

●
November 29
7:18 am EST

December

S	M	T	W	T	F	S
				1	2	3
4	5	6	7	8	9	10
11	12	13	14	15	16	17
18	19	20	21	22	23	24
25	26	27	28	29	30	31

December 4–10

But underneath this winter face, a world of golden summer sleeps!   ~ANITA McLEAN WASHINGTON

Date	Qtr.	Sign	Activity
Dec 5, 11:31 pm– Dec 7, 4:03 am	1st	Pisces	Plant grains, leafy annuals. Fertilize (chemical). Graft or bud plants. Irrigate. Trim to increase growth.
Dec 7 4:03 am– Dec 8, 5:15 am	2nd	Pisces	Plant grains, leafy annuals. Fertilize (chemical). Graft or bud plants. Irrigate. Trim to increase growth.
Dec 10, 7:41 am– Dec 12, 7:41 am	2nd	Taurus	Plant annuals for hardiness. Trim to increase growth.

Used as an essential oil, lavender has healing properties to calm the body and mind. Breathe in its sweet aroma and feel the relaxation set in as you breathe out tension. Mix with quality massage oil such as grape seed or almond and apply to sore spots, achy shoulders, or joints. Suffering from insomnia? Use your index finger to dot lavender on the temples, then inhale the essence and enjoy your dream space.

December 7
4:03 am EST

DECEMBER

S	M	T	W	T	F	S
				1	2	3
4	5	6	7	8	9	10
11	12	13	14	15	16	17
18	19	20	21	22	23	24
25	26	27	28	29	30	31

2015 © tashka2000 Image from BigStockPhoto.com

December 11–17

What people say behind your back is your standing in the community. ～EDGAR WATSON HOWE

Date	Qtr.	Sign	Activity
Dec 10, 7:41 am–Dec 12, 7:41 am	2nd	Taurus	Plant annuals for hardiness. Trim to increase growth.
Dec 13, 7:06 am–Dec 14, 7:09 am	3rd	Gemini	Cultivate. Destroy weeds and pests. Harvest fruits and root crops for food. Trim to retard growth.
Dec 14, 7:09 am–Dec 16, 8:15 am	3rd	Cancer	Plant biennials, perennials, bulbs, and roots. Prune. Irrigate. Fertilize (organic).
Dec 16, 8:15 am–Dec 18, 12:52 pm	3rd	Leo	Cultivate. Destroy weeds and pests. Harvest fruits and root crops for food. Trim to retard growth.

Spray your favorite garden shovel with a silicone or Teflon lubricant to make shoveling a breeze. A good coating of this spray will make any type of soil slip right off the shovel without a mess.

_____

_____

_____

_____

_____

○
December 13
7:06 pm EST

DECEMBER

S	M	T	W	T	F	S
				1	2	3
4	5	6	7	8	9	10
11	12	13	14	15	16	17
18	19	20	21	22	23	24
25	26	27	28	29	30	31

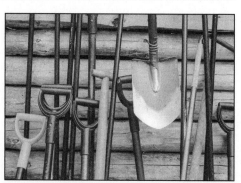

2015 © photoman1551 Image from BigStockPhoto.com

December 18–24

The year is going, let him go; ring out the false, ring in
the true.   ~ALFRED LORD TENNYSON

Date	Qtr.	Sign	Activity
Dec 16, 8:15 am– Dec 18, 12:52 pm	3rd	Leo	Cultivate. Destroy weeds and pests. Harvest fruits and root crops for food. Trim to retard growth.
Dec 18, 12:52 pm– Dec 20, 8:56 pm	3rd	Virgo	Cultivate, especially medicinal plants. Destroy weeds and pests. Trim to retard growth.
Dec 20, 8:56 pm– Dec 20, 9:40 pm	4th	Virgo	Cultivate, especially medicinal plants. Destroy weeds and pests. Trim to retard growth.
Dec 23, 9:32 am– Dec 25, 10:19 pm	4th	Scorpio	Plant biennials, perennials, bulbs, and roots. Prune. Irrigate. Fertilize (organic).

Some commercial hand wash detergents are harsh on fabric and have a strong chemical smell. Use inexpensive shampoo (the kind that costs a dollar a bottle) to hand wash delicates like lingerie or wool sweaters. They'll get just as clean and smell great afterward. You can also add a drop of essential oil to the rinse water—lavender and cedar smell great and will also repel moths from wool.

2015 © kubais Image from BigStockPhoto.com

December 20
8:56 pm EST

DECEMBER

S	M	T	W	T	F	S
				1	2	3
4	5	6	7	8	9	10
11	12	13	14	15	16	17
18	19	20	21	22	23	24
25	26	27	28	29	30	31

♑ December 25–31

Growth is the only evidence of life.

~John Henry Cardinal Newman

Date	Qtr.	Sign	Activity
Dec 23, 9:32 am– Dec 25, 10:19 pm	4th	Scorpio	Plant biennials, perennials, bulbs, and roots. Prune. Irrigate. Fertilize (organic).
Dec 25, 10:19 pm– Dec 28, 10:12 am	4th	Sagittarius	Cultivate. Destroy weeds and pests. Harvest fruits and root crops for food. Trim to retard growth.
Dec 28, 10:12 am– Dec 29, 1:53 am	4th	Capricorn	Plant potatoes and tubers. Trim to retard growth.
Dec 29, 1:53 am– Dec 30, 8:29 pm	1st	Capricorn	Graft or bud plants. Trim to increase growth.

A significant number of personal planets in mutable signs (Gemini, Virgo, Sagittarius, and Pisces) lends a restless quality to feelings and emotions. This group plays the field when not in a committed relationship, but they can be downright fickle even when already involved. Current interests or hobbies bring eligible prospects to the forefront. Moods drive preferences for socializing and meeting new people even though expression by sign varies significantly. The talkative mutable signs are masters when it comes to opening lines.

December 29
1:53 am EST

December

S	M	T	W	T	F	S
				1	2	3
4	5	6	7	8	9	10
11	12	13	14	15	16	17
18	19	20	21	22	23	24
25	26	27	28	29	30	31

2015 © AntonioDiaz Image from BigStockPhoto.com

Gardening by the Moon

Today, people often reject the notion of gardening according to the Moon's phase and sign. The usual nonbeliever is not a scientist but the city dweller who has never had any real contact with nature and little experience of natural rhythms.

Camille Flammarion, the French astronomer, testifies to the success of Moon planting, though:

"Cucumbers increase at Full Moon, as well as radishes, turnips, leeks, lilies, horseradish, and saffron; onions, on the contrary, are much larger and better nourished during the decline and old age of the Moon than at its increase, during its youth and fullness, which is the reason the Egyptians abstained from onions, on account of their antipathy to the Moon. Herbs gathered while the Moon increases are of great efficiency. If the vines are trimmed at night when the Moon is in the sign of the Lion, Sagittarius, the Scorpion, or the Bull, it will save them from field rats, moles, snails, flies, and other animals."

Dr. Clark Timmins is one of the few modern scientists to have conducted tests in Moon planting. Following is a summary of his experiments:

Beets: When sown with the Moon in Scorpio, the germination rate was 71 percent; when sown in Sagittarius, the germination rate was 58 percent.

Scotch marigold: When sown with the Moon in Cancer, the germination rate was 90 percent; when sown in Leo, the rate was 32 percent.

Carrots: When sown with the Moon in Scorpio, the germination rate was 64 percent; when sown in Sagittarius, the germination rate was 47 percent.

Tomatoes: When sown with the Moon in Cancer, the germination rate was 90 percent; but when sown with the Moon in Leo, the germination rate was 58 percent.

Two things should be emphasized. First, remember that this is only a summary of the results of the experiments; the experiments themselves were conducted in a scientific manner to eliminate any variation in soil, temperature, moisture, and so on, so that only the Moon sign is varied. Second, note that these astonishing results were obtained without regard to the phase of the Moon—the other factor we use in Moon planting, and which presumably would have increased the differential in germination rates.

Dr. Timmins also tried transplanting Cancer- and Leo-planted tomato seedlings while the Cancer Moon was waxing. The result was 100 percent survival. When transplanting was done with the waning Sagittarius Moon, there was 0 percent survival. Dr. Timmins's tests show that the Cancer-planted tomatoes had blossoms twelve days earlier than those planted under Leo; the Cancer-planted tomatoes had an average height of twenty inches at that time compared to fifteen inches for the Leo-planted; the first ripe tomatoes were gathered from the Cancer plantings eleven days ahead of the Leo plantings; and a count of the hanging fruit and its size and weight shows an advantage to the Cancer plants over the Leo plants of 45 percent.

Dr. Timmins also observed that there have been similar tests that did not indicate results favorable to the Moon planting theory. As a scientist, he asked why one set of experiments indicated a positive verification of Moon planting, and others did not. He checked these other tests and found that the experimenters had not followed the geocentric system for determining the Moon sign positions, but the heliocentric. When the times used in these other tests were converted to the geocentric system, the dates chosen often were found to be in barren, rather than fertile, signs. Without going into a technical explanation, it is sufficient to point out that geocentric and heliocentric positions often vary by as much as four days. This is a large enough differential to place the Moon in Cancer, for example, in the heliocentric system, and at the same time in Leo by the geocentric system.

Most almanacs and calendars show the Moon's signs heliocentrically—and thus incorrectly for Moon planting—while the *Moon Sign Book* is calculated correctly for planting purposes, using the geocentric system. Some readers are confused because the *Moon Sign Book* talks about first, second, third, and fourth quarters, while other almanacs refer to these same divisions as New Moon, first quarter, Full Moon, and fourth quarter. Thus the almanacs say first quarter when the *Moon Sign Book* says second quarter.

There is nothing complicated about using astrology in agriculture and horticulture in order to increase both pleasure and profit, but there is one very important rule that is often neglected—use common sense! Of course this is one rule that should be remembered in every activity we undertake, but in the case of gardening and farming by the Moon, if it is not possible to use the best dates for planting or harvesting, we must select the next best and just try to do the best we can.

This brings up the matter of the other factors to consider in your gardening work. The dates we give as best for a certain activity apply to the entire country (with slight time correction), but in your section of the country you may be buried under three feet of snow on a date we say is good to plant your flowers. So we have factors of weather, season, temperature, and moisture variations, soil conditions, your own available time and opportunity, and so forth. Some astrologers like to think it is all a matter of science, but gardening is also an art. In art, you develop an instinctive identification with your work and influence it with your feelings and wishes.

The *Moon Sign Book* gives you the place of the Moon for every day of the year so that you can select the best times once you have become familiar with the rules and practices of lunar agriculture. We give you specific, easy-to-follow directions so that you can get right down to work.

We give you the best dates for planting, and also for various related activities, including cultivation, fertilizing, harvesting, irrigation, and getting rid of weeds and pests. But we cannot tell you exactly when it's good to plant. Many of these rules were learned by observation and experience; as the body of experience grew, we could see various patterns emerging that allowed us to make judgments about new things. That's what you should do, too. After you have worked with lunar agriculture for a while and have gained a working knowledge, you will probably begin to try new things—and we hope you will share your experiments and findings with us. That's how the science grows.

Here's an example of what we mean. Years ago Llewellyn George suggested that we try to combine our bits of knowledge about what to expect in planting under each of the Moon signs in order to benefit from several lunar factors in one plant. From this came our rule for developing "thoroughbred seed." To develop thoroughbred seed, save the seed for three successive years from plants grown by the correct Moon sign and phase. You can plant in the first quarter phase and in the sign of Cancer for fruitfulness; the second year, plant seeds from the first year plants in Libra for beauty; and in the third year, plant the seeds from the second year plants in Taurus to produce hardiness. In a similar manner you can combine the fruitfulness of Cancer, the good root growth of Pisces, and the sturdiness and good vine growth of Scorpio. And don't forget the characteristics of Capricorn: hardy like Taurus, but drier and perhaps more resistant to drought and disease.

Unlike common almanacs, we consider both the Moon's phase and the Moon's sign in making our calculations for the proper timing of our work. It is perhaps a little easier to understand this if we remind you that we are all living in the center of a vast electromagnetic field that is Earth and its environment in space. Everything that occurs within this electromagnetic field has an effect on everything else within the field. The Moon and the Sun are the most important of the factors affecting the life of Earth, and it is their relative positions to Earth that we project for each day of the year.

Many people claim that not only do they achieve larger crops gardening by the Moon, but that their fruits and vegetables are much tastier. A number of organic gardeners have also become lunar gardeners using the natural rhythm of life forces that we experience through the relative movements of the Sun and Moon. We provide a few basic rules and then give you day-by-day guidance for your gardening work. You will be able to choose the best dates to meet your own needs and opportunities.

Planting by the Moon's Phases

During the increasing or waxing light—from New Moon to Full Moon—plant annuals that produce their yield above the ground. An annual is a plant that completes its entire life cycle within one growing season and has to be seeded each year. During the decreasing or waning light—from Full Moon to New Moon—plant biennials, perennials, and bulb and root plants. Biennials include crops that are planted one season to winter over and produce crops the next, such as winter wheat. Perennials and bulb and root plants include all plants that grow from the same root each year.

A simpler, less-accurate rule is to plant crops that produce above the ground during the waxing Moon, and to plant crops that produce below the ground during the waning Moon. Thus the old adage, "Plant potatoes during the dark of the Moon." Llewellyn George's system divided the lunar month into quarters. The first two from New Moon to Full Moon are the first and second quarters, and the last two from Full Moon to New Moon the third and fourth quarters. Using these divisions, we can increase our accuracy in timing our efforts to coincide with natural forces.

First Quarter

Plant annuals producing their yield above the ground, which are generally of the leafy kind that produce their seed outside the fruit. Some examples are asparagus, broccoli, brussels sprouts, cabbage, cauliflower, celery, cress, endive, kohlrabi, lettuce, parsley, and spinach. Cucumbers are an exception, as they do best in the first quarter rather than the second, even though the seeds are inside the fruit. Also plant cereals and grains.

Second Quarter

Plant annuals producing their yield above the ground, which are generally of the viney kind that produce their seed inside the fruit. Some examples include beans, eggplant, melons, peas, peppers, pumpkins, squash, tomatoes, etc. These are not hard-and-fast divisions. If you can't plant during the first quarter, plant during the second, and vice versa. There are many plants that seem to do equally well planted in either quarter, such as watermelon, hay, and cereals and grains.

Third Quarter

Plant biennials, perennials, bulbs, root plants, trees, shrubs, berries, grapes, strawberries, beets, carrots, onions, parsnips, rutabagas, potatoes, radishes, peanuts, rhubarb, turnips, winter wheat, etc.

Fourth Quarter

This is the best time to cultivate, turn sod, pull weeds, and destroy pests of all kinds, especially when the Moon is in Aries, Leo, Virgo, Gemini, Aquarius, and Sagittarius.

The Moon in the Signs

Moon in Aries

Barren, dry, fiery, and masculine. Use for destroying noxious weeds.

Moon in Taurus

Productive, moist, earthy, and feminine. Use for planting many crops when hardiness is important, particularly root crops. Also used for lettuce, cabbage, and similar leafy vegetables.

Moon in Gemini

Barren and dry, airy and masculine. Use for destroying noxious growths, weeds, and pests, and for cultivation.

Moon in Cancer

Fruitful, moist, feminine. Use for planting and irrigation.

Moon in Leo

Barren, dry, fiery, masculine. Use for killing weeds or cultivation.

Moon in Virgo

Barren, dry, earthy, and feminine. Use for cultivation and destroying weeds and pests.

Moon in Libra

Semi-fruitful, moist, and airy. Use for planting crops that need good pulp growth. A very good sign for flowers and vines. Also used for seeding hay, corn fodder, and the like.

Moon in Scorpio

Very fruitful and moist, watery and feminine. Nearly as productive as Cancer; use for the same purposes. Especially good for vine growth and sturdiness.

Moon in Sagittarius

Barren and dry, fiery and masculine. Use for planting onions, seeding hay, and for cultivation.

Moon in Capricorn

Productive and dry, earthy and feminine. Use for planting potatoes and other tubers.

Moon in Aquarius

Barren, dry, airy, and masculine. Use for cultivation and destroying noxious growths and pests.

Moon in Pisces

Very fruitful, moist, watery, and feminine. Especially good for root growth.

A Guide to Planting

Plant	Quarter	Sign
Annuals	1st or 2nd	
Apple tree	2nd or 3rd	Cancer, Pisces, Virgo
Artichoke	1st	Cancer, Pisces
Asparagus	1st	Cancer, Scorpio, Pisces
Aster	1st or 2nd	Virgo, Libra
Barley	1st or 2nd	Cancer, Pisces, Libra, Capricorn, Virgo
Beans (bush & pole)	2nd	Cancer, Taurus, Pisces, Libra
Beans (kidney, white, & navy)	1st or 2nd	Cancer, Pisces
Beech tree	2nd or 3rd	Virgo, Taurus
Beets	3rd	Cancer, Capricorn, Pisces, Libra
Biennials	3rd or 4th	
Broccoli	1st	Cancer, Scorpio, Pisces, Libra
Brussels sprouts	1st	Cancer, Scorpio, Pisces, Libra
Buckwheat	1st or 2nd	Capricorn
Bulbs	3rd	Cancer, Scorpio, Pisces
Bulbs for seed	2nd or 3rd	
Cabbage	1st	Cancer, Scorpio, Pisces, Taurus, Libra
Canes (raspberry, blackberry, & gooseberry)	2nd	Cancer, Scorpio, Pisces
Cantaloupe	1st or 2nd	Cancer, Scorpio, Pisces, Taurus, Libra
Carrots	3rd	Cancer, Scorpio, Pisces, Taurus, Libra
Cauliflower	1st	Cancer, Scorpio, Pisces, Libra
Celeriac	3rd	Cancer, Scorpio, Pisces
Celery	1st	Cancer, Scorpio, Pisces
Cereals	1st or 2nd	Cancer, Scorpio, Pisces, Libra
Chard	1st or 2nd	Cancer, Scorpio, Pisces
Chicory	2nd or 3rd	Cancer, Scorpio, Pisces
Chrysanthemum	1st or 2nd	Virgo
Clover	1st or 2nd	Cancer, Scorpio, Pisces

Plant	Quarter	Sign
Coreopsis	2nd or 3rd	Libra
Corn	1st	Cancer, Scorpio, Pisces
Corn for fodder	1st or 2nd	Libra
Cosmos	2nd or 3rd	Libra
Cress	1st	Cancer, Scorpio, Pisces
Crocus	1st or 2nd	Virgo
Cucumber	1st	Cancer, Scorpio, Pisces
Daffodil	1st or 2nd	Libra, Virgo
Dahlia	1st or 2nd	Libra, Virgo
Deciduous trees	2nd or 3rd	Cancer, Scorpio, Pisces, Virgo, Libra
Eggplant	2nd	Cancer, Scorpio, Pisces, Libra
Endive	1st	Cancer, Scorpio, Pisces, Libra
Flowers	1st	Cancer, Scorpio, Pisces, Libra, Taurus, Virgo
Garlic	3rd	Libra, Taurus, Pisces
Gladiola	1st or 2nd	Libra, Virgo
Gourds	1st or 2nd	Cancer, Scorpio, Pisces, Libra
Grapes	2nd or 3rd	Cancer, Scorpio, Pisces, Virgo
Hay	1st or 2nd	Cancer, Scorpio, Pisces, Libra, Taurus
Herbs	1st or 2nd	Cancer, Scorpio, Pisces
Honeysuckle	1st or 2nd	Scorpio, Virgo
Hops	1st or 2nd	Scorpio, Libra
Horseradish	1st or 2nd	Cancer, Scorpio, Pisces
Houseplants	1st	Cancer, Scorpio, Pisces, Libra
Hyacinth	3rd	Cancer, Scorpio, Pisces
Iris	1st or 2nd	Cancer, Virgo
Kohlrabi	1st or 2nd	Cancer, Scorpio, Pisces, Libra
Leek	2nd or 3rd	Sagittarius
Lettuce	1st	Cancer, Scorpio, Pisces, Libra, Taurus
Lily	1st or 2nd	Cancer, Scorpio, Pisces
Maple tree	2nd or 3rd	Taurus, Virgo, Cancer, Pisces
Melon	2nd	Cancer, Scorpio, Pisces
Moon vine	1st or 2nd	Virgo

Plant	Quarter	Sign
Morning glory	1st or 2nd	Cancer, Scorpio, Pisces, Virgo
Oak tree	2nd or 3rd	Taurus, Virgo, Cancer, Pisces
Oats	1st or 2nd	Cancer, Scorpio, Pisces, Libra
Okra	1st or 2nd	Cancer, Scorpio, Pisces, Libra
Onion seed	2nd	Cancer, Scorpio, Sagittarius
Onion set	3rd or 4th	Cancer, Pisces, Taurus, Libra
Pansies	1st or 2nd	Cancer, Scorpio, Pisces
Parsley	1st	Cancer, Scorpio, Pisces, Libra
Parsnip	3rd	Cancer, Scorpio, Taurus, Capricorn
Peach tree	2nd or 3rd	Cancer, Taurus, Virgo, Libra
Peanuts	3rd	Cancer, Scorpio, Pisces
Pear tree	2nd or 3rd	Cancer, Scorpio, Pisces, Libra
Peas	2nd	Cancer, Scorpio, Pisces, Libra
Peony	1st or 2nd	Virgo
Peppers	2nd	Cancer, Scorpio, Pisces
Perennials	3rd	
Petunia	1st or 2nd	Libra, Virgo
Plum tree	2nd or 3rd	Cancer, Pisces, Taurus, Virgo
Poppies	1st or 2nd	Virgo
Portulaca	1st or 2nd	Virgo
Potatoes	3rd	Cancer, Scorpio, Libra, Taurus, Capricorn
Privet	1st or 2nd	Taurus, Libra
Pumpkin	2nd	Cancer, Scorpio, Pisces, Libra
Quince	1st or 2nd	Capricorn
Radishes	3rd	Cancer, Scorpio, Pisces, Libra, Capricorn
Rhubarb	3rd	Cancer, Pisces
Rice	1st or 2nd	Scorpio
Roses	1st or 2nd	Cancer, Virgo
Rutabaga	3rd	Cancer, Scorpio, Pisces, Taurus
Saffron	1st or 2nd	Cancer, Scorpio, Pisces
Sage	3rd	Cancer, Scorpio, Pisces

Plant	Quarter	Sign
Salsify	1st	Cancer, Scorpio, Pisces
Shallot	2nd	Scorpio
Spinach	1st	Cancer, Scorpio, Pisces
Squash	2nd	Cancer, Scorpio, Pisces, Libra
Strawberries	3rd	Cancer, Scorpio, Pisces
String beans	1st or 2nd	Taurus
Sunflowers	1st or 2nd	Libra, Cancer
Sweet peas	1st or 2nd	Any
Tomatoes	2nd	Cancer, Scorpio, Pisces, Capricorn
Trees, shade	3rd	Taurus, Capricorn
Trees, ornamental	2nd	Libra, Taurus
Trumpet vine	1st or 2nd	Cancer, Scorpio, Pisces
Tubers for seed	3rd	Cancer, Scorpio, Pisces, Libra
Tulips	1st or 2nd	Libra, Virgo
Turnips	3rd	Cancer, Scorpio, Pisces, Taurus, Capricorn, Libra
Valerian	1st or 2nd	Virgo, Gemini
Watermelon	1st or 2nd	Cancer, Scorpio, Pisces, Libra
Wheat	1st or 2nd	Cancer, Scorpio, Pisces, Libra

Companion Planting Guide

Plant	Companions	Hindered by
Asparagus	Tomatoes, parsley, basil	None known
Beans	Tomatoes, carrots, cucumbers, garlic, cabbage, beets, corn	Onions, gladiolas
Beets	Onions, cabbage, lettuce, mint, catnip	Pole beans
Broccoli	Beans, celery, potatoes, onions	Tomatoes
Cabbage	Peppermint, sage, thyme, tomatoes	Strawberries, grapes
Carrots	Peas, lettuce, chives, radishes, leeks, onions, sage	Dill, anise
Citrus trees	Guava, live oak, rubber trees, peppers	None known
Corn	Potatoes, beans, peas, melon, squash, pumpkin, sunflowers, soybeans	Quack grass, wheat, straw, mulch
Cucumbers	Beans, cabbage, radishes, sunflowers, lettuce, broccoli, squash	Aromatic herbs
Eggplant	Green beans, lettuce, kale	None known
Grapes	Peas, beans, blackberries	Cabbage, radishes
Melons	Corn, peas	Potatoes, gourds
Onions, leeks	Beets, chamomile, carrots, lettuce	Peas, beans, sage
Parsnip	Peas	None known
Peas	Radishes, carrots, corn, cucumbers, beans, tomatoes, spinach, turnips	Onion, garlic
Potatoes	Beans, corn, peas, cabbage, hemp, cucumbers, eggplant, catnip	Raspberries, pumpkins, tomatoes, sunflowers
Radishes	Peas, lettuce, nasturtiums, cucumbers	Hyssop
Spinach	Strawberries	None known
Squash/Pumpkin	Nasturtiums, corn, mint, catnip	Potatoes
Tomatoes	Asparagus, parsley, chives, onions, carrots, marigolds, nasturtiums, dill	Black walnut roots, fennel, potatoes
Turnips	Peas, beans, brussels sprouts	Potatoes

Plant	Companions	Uses
Anise	Coriander	Flavor candy, pastry, cheeses, cookies
Basil	Tomatoes	Dislikes rue; repels flies and mosquitoes
Borage	Tomatoes, squash	Use in teas
Buttercup	Clover	Hinders delphinium, peonies, monkshood, columbine
Catnip		Repels flea beetles
Chamomile	Peppermint, wheat, onions, cabbage	Roman chamomile may control damping-off disease; use in herbal sprays
Chervil	Radishes	Good in soups and other dishes
Chives	Carrots	Use in spray to deter black spot on roses
Coriander	Plant anywhere	Hinders seed formation in fennel
Cosmos		Repels corn earworms
Dill	Cabbage	Hinders carrots and tomatoes
Fennel	Plant in borders	Disliked by all garden plants
Horseradish		Repels potato bugs
Horsetail		Makes fungicide spray
Hyssop		Attracts cabbage flies; harmful to radishes
Lavender	Plant anywhere	Use in spray to control insects on cotton, repels clothes moths
Lovage		Lures horn worms away from tomatoes
Marigolds		Pest repellent; use against Mexican bean beetles and nematodes
Mint	Cabbage, tomatoes	Repels ants, flea beetles, cabbage worm butterflies
Morning glory	Corn	Helps melon germination
Nasturtium	Cabbage, cucumbers	Deters aphids, squash bugs, pumpkin beetles
Okra	Eggplant	Attracts leafhopper (lure insects from other plants)
Parsley	Tomatoes, asparagus	Freeze chopped-up leaves to flavor foods
Purslane		Good ground cover
Rosemary		Repels cabbage moths, bean beetles, carrot flies
Savory		Plant with onions for added sweetness
Tansy		Deters Japanese beetles, striped cucumber beetles, squash bugs
Thyme		Repels cabbage worms
Yarrow		Increases essential oils of neighbors

Moon Void-of-Course

By Kim Rogers-Gallagher

The Moon circles the Earth in about twenty-eight days, moving through each zodiac sign in two-and-a-half days. As she passes through the thirty degrees of each sign, she "visits" with the planets in numerical order, forming aspects with them. Because she moves one degree in just two to two and a half hours, her influence on each planet lasts only a few hours. She eventually reaches the planet that's in the highest degree of any sign and forms what will be her final aspect before leaving the sign. From this point until she enters the next sign, she is referred to as void-of-course.

Think of it this way: the Moon is the emotional "tone" of the day, carrying feelings with her particular to the sign she's "wearing" at the moment. After she has contacted each of the planets, she symbolically "rests" before changing her costume, so her instinct is temporarily on hold. It's during this time that many people feel "fuzzy" or "vague." Plans or decisions made now often do not pan out. Without the instinctual "knowing" the Moon provides as she touches each planet, we tend to be unrealistic or exercise poor judgment. The traditional definition of the void Moon is that "nothing will come of this." Actions initiated under a void Moon are often wasted, irrelevant, or incorrect—usually because information is hidden, missing, or has been overlooked.

Although it's not a good time to initiate plans, routine tasks seem to go along just fine. This period is ideal for reflection. On the lighter side, remember there are good uses for the void Moon. It is the period when the universe seems to be most open to loopholes. It's a great time to make plans you don't want to fulfill or schedule things you don't want to do. See the tables on pages 76–81 for a schedule of the Moon's void-of-course times.

Last Aspect   **Moon Enters New Sign**

		January		
1	12:33 am	1	Libra	1:41 am
2	11:23 am	3	Scorpio	2:36 pm
5	12:47 pm	6	Sagittarius	1:56 am
7	9:44 pm	8	Capricorn	10:07 am
10	12:39 pm	10	Aquarius	3:23 pm
11	8:09 pm	12	Pisces	6:53 pm
14	11:31 am	14	Aries	9:48 pm
16	6:26 pm	17	Taurus	12:48 am
19	1:50 am	19	Gemini	4:13 am
21	3:01 am	21	Cancer	8:28 am
23	1:21 am	23	Leo	2:21 pm
24	9:51 pm	25	Virgo	10:46 pm
27	7:11 pm	28	Libra	9:59 am
29	8:34 pm	30	Scorpio	10:50 pm
		February		
1	7:35 pm	2	Sagittarius	10:50 am
4	5:04 am	4	Capricorn	7:44 pm
6	10:54 am	7	Aquarius	12:59 am
8	9:39 am	9	Pisces	3:31 am
10	11:25 pm	11	Aries	4:55 am
13	5:32 am	13	Taurus	6:36 am
15	5:54 am	15	Gemini	9:35 am
17	11:37 am	17	Cancer	2:24 pm
19	9:36 am	19	Leo	9:17 pm
21	8:17 pm	22	Virgo	6:24 am
24	9:22 am	24	Libra	5:41 pm
26	6:18 am	27	Scorpio	6:26 am
29	2:55 pm	29	Sagittarius	6:56 pm

Last Aspect   Moon Enters New Sign

			March		
2	9:55 pm	3		Capricorn	5:01 am
5	11:05 am	5		Aquarius	11:22 am
7	3:46 am	7		Pisces	2:08 pm
8	8:54 pm	9		Aries	2:40 pm
11	1:24 pm	11		Taurus	2:44 pm
13	5:46 am	13		Gemini	5:03 pm
15	1:03 pm	15		Cancer	8:57 pm
18	12:09 pm	18		Leo	3:54 am
19	4:43 pm	20		Virgo	1:39 pm
21	11:55 pm	23		Libra	1:23 am
24	4:55 pm	25		Scorpio	2:09 pm
27	3:25 am	28		Sagittarius	2:46 am
29	9:55 pm	30		Capricorn	1:45 pm
			April		
1	12:39 pm	1		Aquarius	9:37 pm
3	7:16 pm	4		Pisces	1:45 am
5	6:33 am	6		Aries	2:46 am
7	10:56 am	8		Taurus	2:10 am
9	5:49 am	10		Gemini	1:59 am
11	2:57 pm	12		Cancer	4:07 am
13	11:59 pm	14		Leo	9:53 am
16	1:48 pm	16		Virgo	7:23 pm
18	8:29 am	19		Libra	7:24 am
21	2:13 am	21		Scorpio	8:17 pm
23	5:46 pm	24		Sagittarius	8:46 am
26	11:51 am	26		Capricorn	7:54 pm
29	3:07 am	29		Aquarius	4:47 am
30	10:56 pm	5/1		Pisces	10:33 am

Last Aspect   Moon Enters New Sign

May				
3	1:08 am	3	Aries	1:04 pm
5	12:17 am	5	Taurus	1:10 pm
6	10:10 pm	7	Gemini	12:35 pm
9	12:15 am	9	Cancer	1:24 pm
11	3:34 am	11	Leo	5:32 pm
13	1:02 pm	14	Virgo	1:52 am
16	5:20 am	16	Libra	1:33 pm
18	11:23 am	19	Scorpio	2:29 am
21	7:40 am	21	Sagittarius	2:48 pm
23	11:37 am	24	Capricorn	1:34 am
25	9:11 pm	26	Aquarius	10:27 am
28	4:19 pm	28	Pisces	5:06 pm
30	7:10 pm	30	Aries	9:09 pm
June				
1	11:42 am	1	Taurus	10:46 pm
3	7:02 pm	3	Gemini	11:01 pm
5	12:47 pm	5	Cancer	11:41 pm
7	8:18 pm	8	Leo	2:47 am
10	3:14 am	10	Virgo	9:46 am
12	10:47 am	12	Libra	8:33 pm
15	3:00 am	15	Scorpio	9:18 am
17	9:52 am	17	Sagittarius	9:34 pm
20	7:02 am	20	Capricorn	7:55 am
22	4:57 am	22	Aquarius	4:08 pm
24	11:48 am	24	Pisces	10:30 pm
26	3:55 pm	27	Aries	3:08 am
29	3:46 am	29	Taurus	6:03 am
30	8:19 pm	7/1	Gemini	7:44 am

Last Aspect   Moon Enters New Sign

		July		
2	11:43 pm	3	Cancer	9:20 am
5	2:29 am	5	Leo	12:28 pm
7	8:07 am	7	Virgo	6:41 pm
9	11:28 pm	10	Libra	4:32 am
12	11:01 am	12	Scorpio	4:52 pm
14	6:22 pm	15	Sagittarius	5:14 am
17	4:57 am	17	Capricorn	3:33 pm
19	6:57 pm	19	Aquarius	11:10 pm
21	9:56 pm	22	Pisces	4:35 am
24	3:06 am	24	Aries	8:33 am
26	2:19 am	26	Taurus	11:37 am
28	11:13 am	28	Gemini	2:17 pm
30	7:46 am	30	Cancer	5:09 pm
		August		
1	8:44 pm	1	Leo	9:12 pm
3	12:13 am	4	Virgo	3:34 am
5	11:20 pm	6	Libra	12:57 pm
8	1:41 pm	9	Scorpio	12:51 am
11	1:22 am	11	Sagittarius	1:24 pm
13	1:37 pm	14	Capricorn	12:11 am
15	10:45 pm	16	Aquarius	7:52 am
18	5:27 am	18	Pisces	12:34 pm
20	8:21 am	20	Aries	3:18 pm
22	7:48 am	22	Taurus	5:19 pm
24	3:38 pm	24	Gemini	7:40 pm
26	8:30 pm	26	Cancer	11:06 pm
29	2:23 am	29	Leo	4:11 am
31	12:20 am	31	Virgo	11:22 am

Last Aspect   Moon Enters New Sign

		September		
2	6:13 pm	2	Libra	8:55 pm
4	8:30 pm	5	Scorpio	8:38 am
7	8:43 pm	7	Sagittarius	9:20 pm
9	8:51 pm	10	Capricorn	8:55 am
12	6:00 am	12	Aquarius	5:28 pm
14	11:31 am	14	Pisces	10:23 pm
16	3:05 pm	17	Aries	12:22 am
18	4:11 pm	19	Taurus	12:58 am
20	11:32 pm	21	Gemini	1:53 am
23	3:57 am	23	Cancer	4:33 am
24	9:42 pm	25	Leo	9:48 am
27	4:52 am	27	Virgo	5:43 pm
29	6:05 am	30	Libra	3:52 am
		October		
2	1:43 am	2	Scorpio	3:43 pm
4	9:04 pm	5	Sagittarius	4:26 am
7	2:26 am	7	Capricorn	4:40 pm
9	12:51 pm	10	Aquarius	2:33 am
11	7:49 pm	12	Pisces	8:43 am
14	3:13 am	14	Aries	11:08 am
16	12:23 am	16	Taurus	11:04 am
17	10:47 am	18	Gemini	10:30 am
20	7:17 am	20	Cancer	11:28 am
22	3:14 pm	22	Leo	3:34 pm
24	8:21 am	24	Virgo	11:16 pm
26	2:33 pm	27	Libra	9:51 am
29	6:09 am	29	Scorpio	10:01 pm
31	10:44 pm	11/1	Sagittarius	10:43 am

Last Aspect   Moon Enters New Sign

		November		
3	6:35 am	3	Capricorn	11:05 pm
6	4:56 am	6	Aquarius	8:55 am
8	8:54 am	8	Pisces	4:45 pm
10	6:16 pm	10	Aries	8:45 pm
12	7:45 am	12	Taurus	9:24 pm
14	8:52 am	14	Gemini	8:23 pm
16	5:58 am	16	Cancer	7:57 pm
18	5:02 pm	18	Leo	10:14 pm
21	3:33 am	21	Virgo	4:34 am
22	12:41 pm	23	Libra	2:42 pm
25	8:52 am	26	Scorpio	3:01 am
27	4:48 pm	28	Sagittarius	3:46 pm
30	11:08 pm	12/1	Capricorn	3:52 am
		December		
3	5:16 am	3	Aquarius	2:44 pm
5	6:23 am	5	Pisces	11:31 pm
7	9:05 am	8	Aries	5:15 am
9	8:06 pm	10	Taurus	7:41 am
11	11:04 pm	12	Gemini	7:41 am
14	12:58 am	14	Cancer	7:09 am
15	4:37 pm	16	Leo	8:15 am
18	11:55 am	18	Virgo	12:52 pm
20	8:56 pm	20	Libra	9:40 pm
22	2:31 pm	23	Scorpio	9:32 am
25	2:22 am	25	Sagittarius	10:19 pm
27	8:45 pm	28	Capricorn	10:12 am
30	3:07 am	30	Aquarius	8:29 pm

The Moon's Rhythm

The Moon journeys around Earth in an elliptical orbit that takes about 27.33 days, which is known as a sidereal month (period of revolution of one body about another). She can move up to 15 degrees or as few as 11 degrees in a day, with the fastest motion occurring when the Moon is at perigee (closest approach to Earth). The Moon is never retrograde, but when her motion is slow, the effect is similar to a retrograde period.

Astrologers have observed that people born on a day when the Moon is fast will process information differently from those who are born when the Moon is slow in motion. People born when the Moon is fast process information quickly and tend to react quickly, while those born during a slow Moon will be more deliberate.

The time from New Moon to New Moon is called the synodic month (involving a conjunction), and the average time span between this Sun-Moon alignment is 29.53 days. Since 29.53

won't divide into 365 evenly, we can have a month with two Full Moons or two New Moons.

Moon Aspects

The aspects the Moon will make during the times you are considering are also important. A trine or sextile, and sometimes a conjunction, are considered favorable aspects. A trine or sextile between the Sun and Moon is an excellent foundation for success. Whether or not a conjunction is considered favorable depends upon the planet the Moon is making a conjunction to. If it's joining the Sun, Venus, Mercury, Jupiter, or even Saturn, the aspect is favorable. If the Moon joins Pluto or Mars, however, that would not be considered favorable. There may be exceptions, but it would depend on what you are electing to do. For example, a trine to Pluto might hasten the end of a relationship you want to be free of.

It is important to avoid times when the Moon makes an aspect to or is conjoining any retrograde planet, unless, of course, you want the thing started to end in failure.

After the Moon has completed an aspect to a planet, that planetary energy has passed. For example, if the Moon squares Saturn at 10:00 am, you can disregard Saturn's influence on your activity if it will occur after that time. You should always look ahead at aspects the Moon will make on the day in question, though, because if the Moon opposes Mars at 11:30 pm on that day, you can expect events that stretch into the evening to be affected by the Moon-Mars aspect. A testy conversation might lead to an argument, or more.

Moon Signs

Much agricultural work is ruled by earth signs—Virgo, Capricorn, and Taurus. The air signs—Gemini, Aquarius, and Libra—rule flying and intellectual pursuits.

Each planet has one or two signs in which its characteristics are enhanced or "dignified," and the planet is said to "rule" that sign. The Sun rules Leo and the Moon rules Cancer, for example. The ruling planet for each sign is listed below. These should not be considered complete lists. We recommend that you purchase a book of planetary rulerships for more complete information.

Aries Moon

The energy of an Aries Moon is masculine, dry, barren, and fiery. Aries provides great start-up energy, but things started at this time may be the result of impulsive action that lacks research or necessary support. Aries lacks staying power.

Use this assertive, outgoing Moon sign to initiate change, but have a plan in place for someone to pick up the reins when you're impatient to move on to the next thing. Work that requires skillful, but not necessarily patient, use of tools—hammering, cutting down trees, etc.—is appropriate in Aries. Expect things to occur rapidly but to also quickly pass. If you are prone to injury or accidents, exercise caution and good judgment in Aries-related activities.

RULER: Mars

IMPULSE: Action

RULES: Head and face

Taurus Moon

A Taurus Moon's energy is feminine, semi-fruitful, and earthy. The Moon is exalted—very strong—in Taurus. Taurus is known as the farmer's sign because of its associations with farmland and precipitation that is the typical day-long "soaker" variety. Taurus energy is good to incorporate into your plans when patience, practicality, and perseverance are needed. Be aware, though, that you may also experience stubbornness in this sign.

Things started in Taurus tend to be long lasting and to increase in value. This can be very supportive energy in a marriage election. On the downside, the fixed energy of this sign resists change or the letting go of even the most difficult situations. A divorce following a marriage that occurred during a Taurus Moon may be difficult and costly to end. Things begun now tend to become habitual and hard to alter. If you want to make changes in something you started, it would be better to wait for Gemini. This is a good time to get a loan, but expect the people in charge of money to be cautious and slow to make decisions.

RULER: Venus

IMPULSE: Stability

RULES: Neck, throat, and voice

Gemini Moon

A Gemini Moon's energy is masculine, dry, barren, and airy. People are more changeable than usual and may prefer to follow intellectual pursuits and play mental games rather than apply themselves to practical concerns.

This sign is not favored for agricultural matters, but it is an excellent time to prepare for activities, to run errands, and write letters. Plan to use a Gemini Moon to exchange ideas, meet people, go on vacations that include walking or biking, or be in situations that require versatility and quick thinking on your feet.

RULER: Mercury

IMPULSE: Versatility

RULES: Shoulders, hands, arms, lungs, and nervous system

Cancer Moon

A Cancer Moon's energy is feminine, fruitful, moist, and very strong. Use this sign when you want to grow things—flowers, fruits, vegetables, commodities, stocks, or collections—for example. This sensitive sign stimulates rapport between people. Considered the most fertile of the signs, it is often associated with mothering. You can use this moontime to build personal friendships that support mutual growth.

Cancer is associated with emotions and feelings. Prominent Cancer energy promotes growth, but it can also turn people pouty and prone to withdrawing into their shells.

RULER: The Moon

IMPULSE: Tenacity

RULES: Chest area, breasts, and stomach

Leo Moon

A Leo Moon's energy is masculine, hot, dry, fiery, and barren. Use it whenever you need to put on a show, make a presentation, or entertain colleagues or guests. This is a proud yet playful energy that exudes self-confidence and is often associated with romance.

This is an excellent time for fundraisers and ceremonies or to be straightforward, frank, and honest about something. It is advisable not to put yourself in a position of needing public approval or where you might have to cope with underhandedness, as trouble in these areas can bring out the worst Leo traits. There is a tendency in this sign to become arrogant or self-centered.

RULER: The Sun

IMPULSE: I am

RULES: Heart and upper back

Virgo Moon

A Virgo Moon is feminine, dry, barren, earthy energy. It is favorable for anything that needs painstaking attention—especially those things where exactness rather than innovation is preferred.

Use this sign for activities when you must analyze information or when you must determine the value of something. Virgo is the sign of bargain hunting. It's friendly toward agricultural matters with an emphasis on animals and harvesting vegetables. It is an excellent time to care for animals, especially training them and veterinary work.

This sign is most beneficial when decisions have already been made and now need to be carried out. The inclination here is to see details rather than the bigger picture.

There is a tendency in this sign to overdo. Precautions should be taken to avoid becoming too dull from all work and no play. Build a little relaxation and pleasure into your routine from the beginning.

RULER: Mercury

IMPULSE: Discriminating

RULES: Abdomen and intestines

Libra Moon

A Libra Moon's energy is masculine, semi-fruitful, and airy. This energy will benefit any attempt to bring beauty to a place or thing. Libra is considered good energy for starting things of an intellectual nature. Libra is the sign of partnership and unions, which makes it an excellent time to form partnerships of any kind, to make agreements, and to negotiate. Even though this sign is good for initiating things, it is crucial to work with a partner who will provide incentive and encouragement, however. A Libra Moon accentuates teamwork (particularly teams of two) and artistic work (especially work that involves color). Make use of this sign when you are decorating your home or shopping for better-quality clothing.

RULER: Venus

IMPULSE: Balance

RULES: Lower back, kidneys, and buttocks

Scorpio Moon

The Scorpio Moon is feminine, fruitful, cold, and moist. It is useful when intensity (that sometimes borders on obsession) is needed. Scorpio is considered a very psychic sign. Use this Moon sign when you must back up something you strongly believe in, such as union or employer relations. There is strong group loyalty here, but a Scorpio Moon is also a good time to end connections thoroughly. This is also a good time to conduct research.

The desire nature is so strong here that there is a tendency to manipulate situations to get what one wants or to not see one's responsibility in an act.

RULER: Pluto, Mars (traditional)

IMPULSE: Transformation

RULES: Reproductive organs, genitals, groin, and pelvis

Sagittarius Moon

The Moon's energy is masculine, dry, barren, and fiery in Sagittarius, encouraging flights of imagination and confidence in the flow of life. Sagittarius is the most philosophical sign. Candor and honesty are enhanced when the Moon is here. This is an excellent time to "get things off your chest" and to deal with institutions of higher learning, publishing companies, and the law. It's also a good time for sport and adventure.

Sagittarians are the crusaders of this world. This is a good time to tackle things that need improvement, but don't try to be the diplomat while influenced by this energy. Opinions can run strong, and the tendency to proselytize is increased.

RULER: Jupiter

IMPULSE: Expansion

RULES: Thighs and hips

Capricorn Moon

In Capricorn the Moon's energy is feminine, semi-fruitful, and earthy. Because Cancer and Capricorn are polar opposites, the Moon's energy is thought to be weakened here. This energy encourages the need for structure, discipline, and organization. This is a good time to set goals and plan for the future, tend to family business, and to take care of details requiring patience or a businesslike manner. Institutional activities are favored. This sign should be avoided if you're seeking favors, as those in authority can be insensitive under this influence.

RULER: Saturn

IMPULSE: Ambitious

RULES: Bones, skin, and knees

Aquarius Moon

An Aquarius Moon's energy is masculine, barren, dry, and airy. Activities that are unique, individualistic, concerned with humanitarian issues, society as a whole, and making improvements are favored under this Moon. It is this quality of making improvements that has caused this sign to be associated with inventors and new inventions.

An Aquarius Moon promotes the gathering of social groups for friendly exchanges. People tend to react and speak from an intellectual rather than emotional viewpoint when the Moon is in this sign.

RULER: Uranus and Saturn

IMPULSE: Reformer

RULES: Calves and ankles

Pisces Moon

A Pisces Moon is feminine, fruitful, cool, and moist. This is an excellent time to retreat, meditate, sleep, pray, or make that dreamed-of escape into a fantasy vacation. However, things are not always what they seem to be with the Moon in Pisces. Personal boundaries tend to be fuzzy, and you may not be seeing things clearly. People tend to be idealistic under this sign, which can prevent them from seeing reality.

There is a live-and-let-live philosophy attached to this sign, which in the idealistic world may work well enough, but chaos is frequently the result. That's why this sign is also associated with alcohol and drug abuse, drug trafficking, and counterfeiting. On the lighter side, many musicians and artists are ruled by Pisces. It's only when they move too far away from reality that the dark side of substance abuse, suicide, or crime takes away life.

RULER: Jupiter and Neptune

IMPULSE: Empathetic

RULES: Feet

More About Zodiac Signs

Element (Triplicity)

Each of the zodiac signs is classified as belonging to an element; these are the four basic elements:

Fire Signs

Aries, Sagittarius, and Leo are action-oriented, outgoing, energetic, and spontaneous.

Earth Signs

Taurus, Capricorn, and Virgo are stable, conservative, practical, and oriented to the physical and material realm.

Air Signs

Gemini, Aquarius, and Libra are sociable and critical, and they tend to represent intellectual responses rather than feelings.

Water Signs

Cancer, Scorpio, and Pisces are emotional, receptive, intuitive, and can be very sensitive.

Quality (Quadruplicity)

Each zodiac sign is further classified as being cardinal, mutable, or fixed. There are four signs in each quadruplicity, one sign from each element.

Cardinal Signs

Aries, Cancer, Libra, and Capricorn represent beginnings and newly initiated action. They initiate each new season in the cycle of the year.

Fixed Signs

Taurus, Leo, Scorpio, and Aquarius want to maintain the status quo through stubbornness and persistence; they represent that "between" time. For example, Leo is the month when summer really feels like summer.

Mutable Signs

Pisces, Gemini, Virgo, and Sagittarius adapt to change and tolerate situations. They represent the last month of each season, when things are changing in preparation for the coming season.

Nature and Fertility

In addition to a sign's element and quality, each sign is further classified as either fruitful, semi-fruitful, or barren. This classification is the most important for readers who use the gardening information in the *Moon Sign Book* because the timing of most events depends on the fertility of the sign occupied by the Moon. The water signs of Cancer, Scorpio, and Pisces are the most fruitful. The semi-fruitful signs are the earth signs Taurus and Capricorn, and the air sign Libra. The barren signs correspond to fire-signs Aries, Leo, and Sagittarius; air-signs Gemini and Aquarius; and earth-sign Virgo.

Good Timing

By Sharon Leah

Electional astrology is the art of electing times to begin any undertaking. Say, for example, you want to start a business. That business will experience ups and downs, as well as reach its potential, according to the promise held in the universe at the time the business was started—its birth time. The horoscope (birth chart) set for the date, time, and place that a business starts would indicate the outcome—its potential to succeed.

So, you might ask yourself the question: If the horoscope for a business start can show success or failure, why not begin at a time that is more favorable to the venture? Well, you can.

While no time is perfect, there are better times and better days to undertake specific activities. There are thousands of examples that prove electional astrology is not only practical, but that it can make a difference in our lives. There are rules for electing times to begin various activities—even shopping. You'll find detailed instructions about how to make elections beginning on page 107.

Personalizing Elections

The election rules in this almanac are based upon the planetary positions at the time for which the election is made. They do not depend on any type of birth chart. However, a birth chart based upon the time, date, and birthplace of an event has advantages. No election is effective for every person. For example, you may leave home to begin a trip at the same time as a friend, but each of you will have a different experience according to whether or not your birth chart favors the trip.

Not all elections require a birth chart, but the timing of very important events—business starts, marriages, etc.—would benefit from the additional accuracy a birth chart provides. To order a birth chart for yourself or a planned event, visit our Web site at www .llewellyn.com.

Some Things to Consider

You've probably experienced good timing in your life. Maybe you were at the right place at the right time to meet a friend whom you hadn't seen in years. Frequently, when something like that happens, it is the result of following an intuitive impulse—that "gut instinct." Consider for a moment that you were actually responding to planetary energies. Electional astrology is a tool that can help you to align with energies, present and future, that are available to us through planetary placements.

Significators

Decide upon the important significators (planet, sign, and house ruling the matter) for which the election is being made. The Moon is the most important significator in any election, so the Moon should always be fortified (strong by sign and making favorable aspects to other planets). The Moon's aspects to other planets are more important than the sign the Moon is in.

Other important considerations are the significators of the Ascendant and Midheaven—the house ruling the election matter and the ruler of the sign on that house cusp. Finally, any planet or sign that has a general rulership over the matter in question should be taken into consideration.

Nature and Fertility

Determine the general nature of the sign that is appropriate for your election. For example, much agricultural work is ruled by the earth signs of Virgo, Capricorn, and Taurus; while the air signs—Gemini, Aquarius, and Libra—rule intellectual pursuits.

One Final Comment

Use common sense. If you must do something, like plant your garden or take an airplane trip on a day that doesn't have the best aspects, proceed anyway, but try to minimize problems. For example, leave early for the airport to avoid being left behind due to delays in the security lanes. When you have no other choice, do the best that you can under the circumstances at the time.

If you want to personalize your elections, please turn to page 107 for more information. If you want a quick and easy answer, you can refer to Llewellyn's Astro Almanac on the following pages.

Llewellyn's Astro Almanac

The Astro Almanac tables, beginning on the next page, can help you find the dates best suited to particular activities. The dates provided are determined from the Moon's sign, phase, and aspects to other planets. Please note that the Astro Almanac does not take personal factors, such as your Sun and Moon sign, into account. The dates are general, and they will apply for everyone. Some activities will not have ideal dates during a particular month.

Activity	January
Animals (Neuter or spay)	6–10, 13, 14
Animals (Sell or buy)	11, 16, 18, 23
Automobile (Buy)	1, 10, 20, 27
Brewing	4, 31
Build (Start foundation)	11
Business (Conducting for self and others)	4, 14, 19, 29
Business (Start new)	10, 18
Can Fruits and Vegetables	4, 31
Can Preserves	4, 31
Concrete (Pour)	24, 25
Construction (Begin new)	10, 18, 19, 23, 29
Consultants (Begin work with)	1, 5, 6, 10, 14, 18, 23, 27
Contracts (Bid on)	10, 14, 18, 23
Cultivate	no ideal dates
Decorating	10–12, 19–21
Demolition	6, 7, 23, 24
Electronics (Buy)	11, 20
Entertain Guests	1
Floor Covering (Laying new)	1, 2, 24–30
Habits (Break)	8
Hair (Cut to increase growth)	13, 17–20, 23
Hair (Cut to decrease growth)	6–9
Harvest (Grain for storage)	24, 25
Harvest (Root crops)	6, 7, 24, 25
Investments (New)	19, 29
Loan (Ask for)	17–19, 23
Massage (Relaxing)	1, 11
Mow Lawn (Decrease growth)	1–8, 24–31
Mow Lawn (Increase growth)	10–22
Mushrooms (Pick)	22–24
Negotiate (Business for the elderly)	11, 15, 24, 29
Prune for Better Fruit	3–7, 31
Prune to Promote Healing	8, 9
Wean Children	6–12
Wood Floors (Installing)	8, 9
Write Letters or Contracts	7, 10, 11, 24

Activity	February
Animals (Neuter or spay)	2–6, 9, 10
Animals (Sell or buy)	15
Automobile (Buy)	6, 15, 16
Brewing	1, 28, 29
Build (Start foundation)	8
Business (Conducting for self and others)	3, 12, 17, 28
Business (Start new)	14
Can Fruits and Vegetables	1, 28, 29
Can Preserves	1, 28, 29
Concrete (Pour)	7
Construction (Begin new)	3, 6, 12, 14, 17, 19
Consultants (Begin work with)	1, 6, 10, 14, 15, 19, 23, 26, 28
Contracts (Bid on)	10, 14, 15, 19
Cultivate	7
Decorating	8, 15–17
Demolition	2, 3
Electronics (Buy)	8, 15, 16, 26
Entertain Guests	15, 25
Floor Covering (Laying new)	7, 8, 23–26
Habits (Break)	5–7
Hair (Cut to increase growth)	10, 13–16, 19
Hair (Cut to decrease growth)	2–6
Harvest (Grain for storage)	29
Harvest (Root crops)	2–4, 7
Investments (New)	17, 28
Loan (Ask for)	13–15, 19–21
Massage (Relaxing)	15, 25
Mow Lawn (Decrease growth)	1–7, 23–29
Mow Lawn (Increase growth)	9–21
Mushrooms (Pick)	21–23
Negotiate (Business for the elderly)	no ideal dates
Prune for Better Fruit	1–3, 27–29
Prune to Promote Healing	5, 6
Wean Children	3–8
Wood Floors (Installing)	5, 6
Write Letters or Contracts	3, 8, 16, 21

Activity	March
Animals (Neuter or spay)	2–4, 8, 9, 31
Animals (Sell or buy)	12, 17
Automobile (Buy)	15
Brewing	26
Build (Start foundation)	no ideal dates
Business (Conducting for self and others)	4, 13, 18, 28
Business (Start new)	12
Can Fruits and Vegetables	8, 26
Can Preserves	26
Concrete (Pour)	6
Construction (Begin new)	4, 12, 13, 17, 18, 28, 31
Consultants (Begin work with)	2, 4, 7, 12, 17, 21, 26, 29, 31
Contracts (Bid on)	12, 17, 21
Cultivate	1, 5–7, 28–30
Decorating	13–15, 23
Demolition	1, 2, 28, 29
Electronics (Buy)	6, 15
Entertain Guests	16
Floor Covering (Laying new)	5, 6, 24, 25
Habits (Break)	3–6
Hair (Cut to increase growth)	8, 11–14, 18
Hair (Cut to decrease growth)	1–4, 28–31
Harvest (Grain for storage)	1, 28–30
Harvest (Root crops)	1, 2, 5–7, 28–30
Investments (New)	18, 28
Loan (Ask for)	11–13, 18–20
Massage (Relaxing)	7, 16
Mow Lawn (Decrease growth)	1–7, 24–31
Mow Lawn (Increase growth)	9–22
Mushrooms (Pick)	22–24
Negotiate (Business for the elderly)	6, 10, 19, 24
Prune for Better Fruit	1, 2, 25–29
Prune to Promote Healing	3–5, 31
Wean Children	1–7, 29–31
Wood Floors (Installing)	3–5, 31
Write Letters or Contracts	2, 6, 7, 15, 19, 29

Activity	April
Animals (Neuter or spay)	1, 4, 5
Animals (Sell or buy)	9, 13
Automobile (Buy)	11, 18, 28
Brewing	4, 23
Build (Start foundation)	no ideal dates
Business (Conducting for self and others)	2, 11, 16, 27
Business (Start new)	9
Can Fruits and Vegetables	4, 22, 23
Can Preserves	22, 23
Concrete (Pour)	2, 30
Construction (Begin new)	2, 9, 11, 13, 16, 27
Consultants (Begin work with)	3, 8, 9, 13, 17, 18, 22, 27, 28
Contracts (Bid on)	8, 9, 13, 14, 17, 18
Cultivate	2, 3, 6, 24–26, 30
Decorating	10–12, 19–21
Demolition	6, 7, 24, 25
Electronics (Buy)	3, 11, 30
Entertain Guests	15
Floor Covering (Laying new)	1–3, 29, 30
Habits (Break)	1–3, 6, 30
Hair (Cut to increase growth)	8–11, 14
Hair (Cut to decrease growth)	4, 5, 24–28
Harvest (Grain for storage)	24–26, 29
Harvest (Root crops)	1–3, 6, 24–26, 29, 30
Investments (New)	16, 27
Loan (Ask for)	8, 9, 14–16
Massage (Relaxing)	15
Mow Lawn (Decrease growth)	1–6, 23–30
Mow Lawn (Increase growth)	8–20
Mushrooms (Pick)	21–23
Negotiate (Business for the elderly)	15, 20, 30
Prune for Better Fruit	22–25
Prune to Promote Healing	1, 27–29
Wean Children	1–3, 25–30
Wood Floors (Installing)	1, 27–29
Write Letters or Contracts	3, 8, 11, 16, 26

Activity	May
Animals (Neuter or spay)	1–3, 29, 30
Animals (Sell or buy)	10, 15, 20
Automobile (Buy)	9, 15, 25
Brewing	2, 3, 29, 30
Build (Start foundation)	12
Business (Conducting for self and others)	2, 11, 16, 26, 31
Business (Start new)	no ideal dates
Can Fruits and Vegetables	2, 29, 30
Can Preserves	6
Concrete (Pour)	27, 28
Construction (Begin new)	6, 10, 11, 16, 25, 26, 31
Consultants (Begin work with)	3, 6, 10, 15, 20, 25, 29
Contracts (Bid on)	10, 15, 20
Cultivate	4, 5, 21–23, 31
Decorating	7–9, 16–18
Demolition	4, 21–24, 31
Electronics (Buy)	9, 28
Entertain Guests	6, 10
Floor Covering (Laying new)	5, 6, 26–28
Habits (Break)	4, 5, 31
Hair (Cut to increase growth)	7, 8, 11, 21
Hair (Cut to decrease growth)	2, 5, 6, 22–25, 29
Harvest (Grain for storage)	22–24, 26–28
Harvest (Root crops)	4, 5, 22, 23, 26–28, 31
Investments (New)	16, 26
Loan (Ask for)	7, 11–13
Massage (Relaxing)	6, 10, 26
Mow Lawn (Decrease growth)	1–5, 22–31
Mow Lawn (Increase growth)	7–20
Mushrooms (Pick)	20–22
Negotiate (Business for the elderly)	4, 12, 17, 27, 31
Prune for Better Fruit	21–23
Prune to Promote Healing	24–26
Wean Children	22–28
Wood Floors (Installing)	24–26
Write Letters or Contracts	6, 9, 23, 28

Activity	June
Animals (Neuter or spay)	no ideal dates
Animals (Sell or buy)	6, 15, 16
Automobile (Buy)	5
Brewing	25, 26
Build (Start foundation)	9
Business (Conducting for self and others)	9, 14, 25, 29
Business (Start new)	no ideal dates
Can Fruits and Vegetables	25, 26
Can Preserves	2, 3, 30
Concrete (Pour)	2, 3, 23, 24, 30
Construction (Begin new)	2, 6, 9, 14, 21, 29, 30
Consultants (Begin work with)	2, 3, 6, 7, 11, 12, 16, 21, 24, 29, 30
Contracts (Bid on)	6, 7, 11, 12, 16
Cultivate	1, 4, 28
Decorating	4, 5, 12–15
Demolition	27, 287
Electronics (Buy)	5, 12, 24
Entertain Guests	4, 9, 30
Floor Covering (Laying new)	2–4, 22–24, 29, 30
Habits (Break)	1, 28, 29
Hair (Cut to increase growth)	17–19
Hair (Cut to decrease growth)	1–4, 21, 25, 26, 29, 30
Harvest (Grain for storage)	22–24, 27
Harvest (Root crops)	1, 22–24, 27, 28
Investments (New)	14, 25
Loan (Ask for)	8–10
Massage (Relaxing)	9, 15, 30
Mow Lawn (Decrease growth)	1–3, 21–30
Mow Lawn (Increase growth)	5–19
Mushrooms (Pick)	19–21
Negotiate (Business for the elderly)	13, 23, 27
Prune for Better Fruit	no ideal dates
Prune to Promote Healing	20–22
Wean Children	18–24
Wood Floors (Installing)	20–22
Write Letters or Contracts	3, 5, 9, 19, 24

Activity	July
Animals (Neuter or spay)	no ideal dates
Animals (Sell or buy)	4, 15
Automobile (Buy)	2, 9, 30
Brewing	23, 31
Build (Start foundation)	6
Business (Conducting for self and others)	9, 14, 24, 29
Business (Start new)	19
Can Fruits and Vegetables	4, 23, 31
Can Preserves	4, 27, 31
Concrete (Pour)	20, 21, 27
Construction (Begin new)	4, 9, 19, 24, 27, 29
Consultants (Begin work with)	4, 9, 14, 15, 19, 25, 27, 30
Contracts (Bid on)	8, 9, 14, 15, 19
Cultivate	1, 2, 29, 30
Decorating	11, 12
Demolition	24, 25
Electronics (Buy)	2, 21, 30
Entertain Guests	4, 30
Floor Covering (Laying new)	1, 2, 20, 21, 26–29
Habits (Break)	1, 3, 29
Hair (Cut to increase growth)	5, 15–18
Hair (Cut to decrease growth)	1, 2, 23, 26–29
Harvest (Grain for storage)	20, 21, 24, 25
Harvest (Root crops)	1, 2, 20, 21, 24, 25, 28–30
Investments (New)	14, 24
Loan (Ask for)	6, 7
Massage (Relaxing)	4
Mow Lawn (Decrease growth)	1–3, 20–31
Mow Lawn (Increase growth)	5–18
Mushrooms (Pick)	18–20
Negotiate (Business for the elderly)	20
Prune for Better Fruit	no ideal dates
Prune to Promote Healing	19
Wean Children	16–22
Wood Floors (Installing)	19
Write Letters or Contracts	2, 4, 7, 17, 21, 30

Activity	August
Animals (Neuter or spay)	no ideal dates
Animals (Sell or buy)	9, 14, 15
Automobile (Buy)	4, 15, 26
Brewing	1, 19, 20, 27, 28
Build (Start foundation)	no ideal dates
Business (Conducting for self and others)	7, 13, 22, 27
Business (Start new)	15
Can Fruits and Vegetables	1, 19, 20, 27, 28
Can Preserves	1, 23, 24, 27, 28
Concrete (Pour)	23, 24, 30
Construction (Begin new)	1, 7, 13, 15, 22, 24, 27, 28
Consultants (Begin work with)	1, 4, 5, 10, 11, 15, 24, 28, 29
Contracts (Bid on)	4, 5, 10, 11, 15
Cultivate	2, 25, 26, 29–31
Decorating	6–8, 16–18
Demolition	2, 21, 29, 30
Electronics (Buy)	18, 26
Entertain Guests	24, 29
Floor Covering (Laying new)	2, 22–26, 29–31
Habits (Break)	29–31
Hair (Cut to increase growth)	11–15
Hair (Cut to decrease growth)	1, 19, 22–25, 29
Harvest (Grain for storage)	20–22, 24
Harvest (Root crops)	18, 21, 22, 24–26, 29, 30
Investments (New)	13, 22
Loan (Ask for)	3, 4
Massage (Relaxing)	4, 24, 29
Mow Lawn (Decrease growth)	1, 19–31
Mow Lawn (Increase growth)	3–17
Mushrooms (Pick)	17–19
Negotiate (Business for the elderly)	2, 7, 29
Prune for Better Fruit	no ideal dates
Prune to Promote Healing	no ideal dates
Wean Children	12–18
Wood Floors (Installing)	no ideal dates
Write Letters or Contracts	3, 4, 18, 31

Activity	September
Animals (Neuter or spay)	8
Animals (Sell or buy)	7, 8, 12
Automobile (Buy)	2, 12, 22, 29
Brewing	24
Build (Start foundation)	no ideal dates
Business (Conducting for self and others)	6, 11, 20, 25
Business (Start new)	10
Can Fruits and Vegetables	24
Can Preserves	19, 24
Concrete (Pour)	19, 26, 27
Construction (Begin new)	11, 12, 20, 21, 25
Consultants (Begin work with)	2, 7, 12, 20, 21, 24, 25, 29, 30
Contracts (Bid on)	2, 7, 12
Cultivate	25–29
Decorating	3, 4, 12–14, 30
Demolition	17, 18, 25, 26
Electronics (Buy)	14, 22
Entertain Guests	3, 23
Floor Covering (Laying new)	1, 19–22, 25–30
Habits (Break)	25–27
Hair (Cut to increase growth)	8–11, 15, 16
Hair (Cut to decrease growth)	19–22, 25
Harvest (Grain for storage)	17, 21, 22
Harvest (Root crops)	17, 18, 21, 22, 25–27
Investments (New)	11, 20
Loan (Ask for)	no ideal dates
Massage (Relaxing)	3, 14
Mow Lawn (Decrease growth)	17–29
Mow Lawn (Increase growth)	2–15
Mushrooms (Pick)	15–17
Negotiate (Business for the elderly)	3, 13, 17
Prune for Better Fruit	no ideal dates
Prune to Promote Healing	no ideal dates
Wean Children	8–14
Wood Floors (Installing)	no ideal dates
Write Letters or Contracts	2, 14, 27, 29

Activity	October
Animals (Neuter or spay)	5–8
Animals (Sell or buy)	5, 9, 10, 14
Automobile (Buy)	19, 25
Brewing	21, 22
Build (Start foundation)	no ideal dates
Business (Conducting for self and others)	6, 11, 20, 25
Business (Start new)	8
Can Fruits and Vegetables	21, 22, 30
Can Preserves	17, 21, 22, 30
Concrete (Pour)	17, 23, 24
Construction (Begin new)	5, 6, 10, 11, 19, 20, 23, 25
Consultants (Begin work with)	4, 5, 10, 19, 23, 25, 28, 30
Contracts (Bid on)	4, 5, 10, 11
Cultivate	23–26
Decorating	1, 2, 10, 11
Demolition	23
Electronics (Buy)	10, 11, 19
Entertain Guests	23, 28
Floor Covering (Laying new)	16–19, 23–29
Habits (Break)	23, 24
Hair (Cut to increase growth)	5–9, 13
Hair (Cut to decrease growth)	17–19, 22
Harvest (Grain for storage)	18, 19, 22
Harvest (Root crops)	18, 19, 23, 24
Investments (New)	11, 20
Loan (Ask for)	no ideal dates
Massage (Relaxing)	23, 28
Mow Lawn (Decrease growth)	17–29
Mow Lawn (Increase growth)	1–14, 31
Mushrooms (Pick)	15–17
Negotiate (Business for the elderly)	23, 28
Prune for Better Fruit	30
Prune to Promote Healing	no ideal dates
Wean Children	6–11
Wood Floors (Installing)	no ideal dates
Write Letters or Contracts	11, 19, 24, 30

Activity	November
Animals (Neuter or spay)	1–5, 29, 30
Animals (Sell or buy)	2, 7, 8, 12, 30
Automobile (Buy)	5, 16
Brewing	17, 18, 26, 27
Build (Start foundation)	7
Business (Conducting for self and others)	5, 10, 18, 23
Business (Start new)	4
Can Fruits and Vegetables	17, 18, 26, 27
Can Preserves	17, 18, 26, 27
Concrete (Pour)	19, 20
Construction (Begin new)	2, 5, 7, 15, 18, 20, 23, 30
Consultants (Begin work with)	2, 5, 7, 10, 15, 19, 20, 24, 25, 30
Contracts (Bid on)	2, 5, 7, 10, 30
Cultivate	21–23
Decorating	7, 8
Demolition	19, 20, 29
Electronics (Buy)	8, 16, 25
Entertain Guests	no ideal dates
Floor Covering (Laying new)	15, 16, 19–25
Habits (Break)	no ideal dates
Hair (Cut to increase growth)	2–5, 9, 12, 13, 29, 30
Hair (Cut to decrease growth)	15, 18
Harvest (Grain for storage)	15, 16, 18–20
Harvest (Root crops)	14–16, 19, 20
Investments (New)	10, 18
Loan (Ask for)	12, 13
Massage (Relaxing)	8, 12
Mow Lawn (Decrease growth)	15–27
Mow Lawn (Increase growth)	1–5, 7–13, 30
Mushrooms (Pick)	13–15
Negotiate (Business for the elderly)	7, 11
Prune for Better Fruit	26, 27
Prune to Promote Healing	no ideal dates
Wean Children	2–8, 29, 30
Wood Floors (Installing)	no ideal dates
Write Letters or Contracts	3, 16, 20, 30

Activity	December
Animals (Neuter or spay)	1–3, 6, 26–30
Animals (Sell or buy)	8, 12, 13
Automobile (Buy)	13, 19, 28
Brewing	15, 24, 25
Build (Start foundation)	5
Business (Conducting for self and others)	4, 9, 18, 23
Business (Start new)	2, 30
Can Fruits and Vegetables	15, 24, 25
Can Preserves	15, 24, 25
Concrete (Pour)	17
Construction (Begin new)	4, 5, 9, 13, 17, 18, 27
Consultants (Begin work with)	5, 6, 11, 13, 17, 19, 22, 24, 27, 28
Contracts (Bid on)	5, 6, 11, 13
Cultivate	no ideal dates
Decorating	4, 5, 12, 13
Demolition	16, 17, 26, 27
Electronics (Buy)	5, 13
Entertain Guests	12, 22
Floor Covering (Laying new)	16–22
Habits (Break)	no ideal dates
Hair (Cut to increase growth)	1, 2, 6, 7, 10–13, 29
Hair (Cut to decrease growth)	16, 26–28
Harvest (Grain for storage)	16–18
Harvest (Root crops)	16–18, 26, 27
Investments (New)	9, 18
Loan (Ask for)	10–12
Massage (Relaxing)	22
Mow Lawn (Decrease growth)	14–27
Mow Lawn (Increase growth)	1–12, 30
Mushrooms (Pick)	12–14
Negotiate (Business for the elderly)	9, 17, 22
Prune for Better Fruit	23–27
Prune to Promote Healing	28, 29
Wean Children	1–5, 26–30
Wood Floors (Installing)	28, 29
Write Letters or Contracts	5, 13, 17, 27, 28

Choose the Best Time for Your Activities

When rules for elections refer to "favorable" and "unfavorable" aspects to your Sun or other planets, please refer to the Favorable and Unfavorable Days Tables and Lunar Aspectarian for more information. You'll find instructions beginning on page 129 and the tables beginning on page 136.

The material in this section came from several sources including: *The New A to Z Horoscope Maker and Delineator* by Llewellyn George (Llewellyn, 1999), *Moon Sign Book* (Llewellyn, 1945), and *Electional Astrology* by Vivian Robson (Slingshot Publishing, 2000). Robson's book was originally published in 1937.

Advertise (Internet)

The Moon should be conjunct, sextile, or trine Mercury or Uranus and in the sign of Gemini, Capricorn, or Aquarius.

Advertise (Print)

Write ads on a day favorable to your Sun. The Moon should be conjunct, sextile, or trine Mercury or Venus. Avoid hard aspects to Mars and Saturn. Ad campaigns produce the best results when the Moon is well aspected in Gemini (to enhance communication) or Capricorn (to build business).

Animals

Take home new pets when the day is favorable to your Sun, or when the Moon is trine, sextile, or conjunct Mercury, Venus, or Jupiter, or in the sign of Virgo or Pisces. However, avoid days when the Moon is either square or opposing the Sun, Mars, Saturn, Uranus, Neptune, or Pluto. When selecting a pet, have the Moon well aspected by the planet that rules the animal. Cats are ruled by the Sun, dogs by Mercury, birds by Venus, horses by Jupiter, and fish by Neptune. Buy large animals when the Moon is in Sagittarius or Pisces and making favorable aspects to Jupiter or Mercury. Buy animals smaller than sheep when the Moon is in Virgo with favorable aspects to Mercury or Venus.

Animals (Breed)

Animals are easiest to handle when the Moon is in Taurus, Cancer, Libra, or Pisces, but try to avoid the Full Moon. To encourage healthy births, animals should be mated so births occur when the Moon is increasing in Taurus, Cancer, Pisces, or Libra. Those born during a semi-fruitful sign (Taurus and Capricorn) will produce leaner meat. Libra yields beautiful animals for showing and racing.

Animals (Declaw)

Declaw cats for medical purposes in the dark of the Moon. Avoid the week before and after the Full Moon and the sign of Pisces.

Animals (Neuter or spay)

Have livestock and pets neutered or spayed when the Moon is in Sagittarius, Capricorn, or Pisces, after it has passed through Scorpio, the sign that rules reproductive organs. Avoid the week before and after the Full Moon.

Animals (Sell or buy)

In either buying or selling, it is important to keep the Moon and Mercury free from any aspect to Mars. Aspects to Mars will create discord and increase the likelihood of wrangling over price and quality. The Moon should be passing from the first quarter to full and sextile or trine Venus or Jupiter. When buying racehorses, let the Moon be in an air sign. The Moon should be in air signs when you buy birds. If the birds are to be pets, let the Moon be in good aspect to Venus.

Animals (Train)

Train pets when the Moon is in Virgo or trine to Mercury.

Animals (Train dogs to hunt)

Let the Moon be in Aries in conjunction with Mars, which makes them courageous and quick to learn. But let Jupiter also be in aspect to preserve them from danger in hunting.

Automobiles

When buying an automobile, select a time when the Moon is conjunct, sextile, or trine to Mercury, Saturn, or Uranus and in the sign of Gemini or Capricorn. Avoid times when Mercury is in retrograde motion.

Baking Cakes

Your cakes will have a lighter texture if you see that the Moon is in Gemini, Libra, or Aquarius and in good aspect to Venus or Mercury. If you are decorating a cake or confections are being made, have the Moon placed in Libra.

Beauty Treatments (Massage, etc.)

See that the Moon is in Taurus, Cancer, Leo, Libra, or Aquarius and in favorable aspect to Venus. In the case of plastic surgery, aspects to Mars should be avoided, and the Moon should not be in the sign ruling the part to be operated on.

Borrow (Money or goods)

See that the Moon is not placed between 15 degrees Libra and 15 degrees Scorpio. Let the Moon be waning and in Leo, Scorpio (16 to 30 degrees), Sagittarius, or Pisces. Venus should be in good aspect to the Moon, and the Moon should not be square, opposing, or conjunct either Saturn or Mars.

Brewing

Start brewing during the third or fourth quarter, when the Moon is in Cancer, Scorpio, or Pisces.

Build (Start foundation)

Turning the first sod for the foundation marks the beginning of the building. For best results, excavate the site when the Moon is in the first quarter of a fixed sign and making favorable aspects to Saturn.

Business (Start new)

When starting a business, have the Moon be in Taurus, Virgo, or Capricorn and increasing. The Moon should be sextile or trine Jupiter or Saturn, but avoid oppositions or squares. The planet ruling the business should be well aspected, too.

Buy Goods

Buy during the third quarter, when the Moon is in Taurus for quality or in a mutable sign (Gemini, Sagittarius, Virgo, or Pisces) for savings. Good aspects to Venus or the Sun are desirable. If you are buying for yourself, it is good if the day is favorable for your Sun sign. You may also apply rules for buying specific items.

Canning

Can fruits and vegetables when the Moon is in either the third or fourth quarter and in the water sign Cancer or Pisces. Preserves and jellies use the same quarters and the signs Cancer, Pisces, or Taurus.

Clothing

Buy clothing on a day that is favorable for your Sun sign and when Venus or Mercury is well aspected. Avoid aspects to Mars and Saturn. Buy your clothing when the Moon is in Taurus if you want to remain satisfied. Do not buy clothing or jewelry when the Moon is in Scorpio or Aries. See that the Moon is sextile or trine the Sun during the first or second quarters.

Collections

Try to make collections on days when your natal Sun is well aspected. Avoid days when the Moon is opposing or square Mars or Saturn. If possible, the Moon should be in a cardinal sign (Aries, Cancer, Libra, or Capricorn). It is more difficult to collect when the Moon is in Taurus or Scorpio.

Concrete

Pour concrete when the Moon is in the third quarter of the fixed sign Taurus, Leo, or Aquarius.

Construction (Begin new)

The Moon should be sextile or trine Jupiter. According to Hermes, no building should be begun when the Moon is in Scorpio or Pisces. The best time to begin building is when the Moon is in Aquarius.

Consultants (Work with)

The Moon should be conjunct, sextile, or trine Mercury or Jupiter.

Contracts (Bid on)

The Moon should be in Gemini or Capricorn and either the Moon or Mercury should be conjunct, sextile, or trine Jupiter.

Copyrights/Patents

The Moon should be conjunct, trine, or sextile either Mercury or Jupiter.

Coronations and Installations

Let the Moon be in Leo and in favorable aspect to Venus, Jupiter, or Mercury. The Moon should be applying to these planets.

Cultivate

Cultivate when the Moon is in a barren sign and waning, ideally the fourth quarter in Aries, Gemini, Leo, Virgo, or Aquarius. The third quarter in the sign of Sagittarius will also work.

Cut Timber

Timber cut during the waning Moon does not become worm-eaten; it will season well and not warp, decay, or snap during burning. Cut when the Moon is in Taurus, Gemini, Virgo, or Capricorn—especially in August. Avoid the water signs. Look for favorable aspects to Mars.

Decorating or Home Repairs

Have the Moon waxing and in the sign of Libra, Gemini, or Aquarius. Avoid squares or oppositions to either Mars or Saturn. Venus in good aspect to Mars or Saturn is beneficial.

Demolition

Let the waning Moon be in Leo, Sagittarius, or Aries.

Dental and Dentists

Visit the dentist when the Moon is in Virgo, or pick a day marked favorable for your Sun sign. Mars should be marked

2015 © Flynt Image from BigStockPhoto.com

sextile, conjunct, or trine; avoid squares or oppositions to Saturn, Uranus, or Jupiter.

Teeth are best removed when the Moon is in Gemini, Virgo, Sagittarius, or Pisces and during the first or second quarter. Avoid the Full Moon! The day should be favorable for your lunar cycle, and Mars and Saturn should be marked conjunct, trine, or sextile. Fillings should be done in the third or fourth quarters in the sign of Taurus, Leo, Scorpio, or Pisces. The same applies for dentures.

Dressmaking

William Lilly wrote in 1676: "Make no new clothes, or first put them on when the Moon is in Scorpio or afflicted by Mars, for they will be apt to be torn and quickly worn out." Design, repair, and sew clothes in the first and second quarters of Taurus, Leo, or Libra on a day marked favorable for your Sun sign. Venus, Jupiter, and Mercury should be favorably aspected, but avoid hard aspects to Mars or Saturn.

Egg-setting (see p. 161)

Eggs should be set so chicks will hatch during fruitful signs. To set eggs, subtract the number of days given for incubation or gestation from the fruitful dates. Chickens incubate in twenty-one days, turkeys and geese in twenty-eight days.

A freshly laid egg loses quality rapidly if it is not handled properly. Use plenty of clean litter in the nests to reduce the number of dirty or cracked eggs. Gather eggs daily in mild weather and at least two times daily in hot or cold weather. The eggs should be placed in a cooler immediately after gathering and stored at 50 to 55°F. Do not store eggs with foods or products that give off pungent odors since eggs may absorb the odors.

Eggs saved for hatching purposes should not be washed. Only clean and slightly soiled eggs should be saved for hatching. Dirty eggs should not be incubated. Eggs should be stored in a cool place with the large ends up. It is not advisable to store the eggs longer than one week before setting them in an incubator.

Electricity and Gas (Install)

The Moon should be in a fire sign, and there should be no squares, oppositions, or conjunctions with Uranus (ruler of electricity), Neptune (ruler of gas), Saturn, or Mars. Hard aspects to Mars can cause fires.

Electronics (Buying)

Choose a day when the Moon is in an air sign (Gemini, Libra, Aquarius) and well aspected by Mercury and/or Uranus when buying electronics.

Electronics (Repair)

The Moon should be sextile or trine Mars or Uranus and in a fixed sign (Taurus, Leo, Scorpio, Aquarius).

Entertain Friends

Let the Moon be in Leo or Libra and making good aspects to Venus. Avoid squares or oppositions to either Mars or Saturn by the Moon or Venus.

Eyes and Eyeglasses

Have your eyes tested and glasses fitted on a day marked favorable for your Sun sign, and on a day that falls during your favorable lunar cycle. Mars should not be in aspect with the Moon. The same applies for any treatment of the eyes, which should also be started during the Moon's first or second quarter.

Fence Posts

Set posts when the Moon is in the third or fourth quarter of the fixed sign Taurus or Leo.

Fertilize and Compost

Fertilize when the Moon is in a fruitful sign (Cancer, Scorpio, Pisces). Organic fertilizers are best when the Moon is waning. Use chemical fertilizers when the Moon is waxing. Start compost when the Moon is in the fourth quarter in a water sign.

Find Hidden Treasure

Let the Moon be in good aspect to Jupiter or Venus. If you erect a horoscope for this election, place the Moon in the Fourth House.

Find Lost Articles

Search for lost articles during the first quarter and when your Sun sign is marked favorable. Also check to see that the planet ruling the lost item is trine, sextile, or conjunct the Moon. The Moon rules household utensils; Mercury rules letters and books; and Venus rules clothing, jewelry, and money.

2015 © Nosnibor137 Image from BigStockPhoto.com

Fishing

During the summer months, the best time of the day to fish is from sunrise to three hours after and from two hours before sunset until one hour after. Fish do not bite in cooler months until the air is warm, from noon to three pm. Warm, cloudy days are good. The most favorable winds are from the south and southwest. Easterly winds are unfavorable. The best days of the month for fishing are when the Moon changes quarters, especially if the change occurs on a day when the Moon is in a water sign (Cancer, Scorpio, Pisces). The best period in any month is the day after the Full Moon.

Friendship

The need for friendship is greater when the Moon is in Aquarius or when Uranus aspects the Moon. Friendship prospers when Venus or Uranus is trine, sextile, or conjunct the Moon. The

Moon in Gemini facilitates the chance meeting of acquaintances and friends.

Grafting or Budding

Grafting is the process of introducing new varieties of fruit on less desirable trees. For this process you should use the increasing phase of the Moon in fruitful signs such as Cancer, Scorpio, or Pisces. Capricorn may be used, too. Cut your grafts while trees are dormant, from December to March. Keep them in a cool, dark place, not too dry or too damp. Do the grafting before the sap starts to flow and while the Moon is waxing, preferably while it is in Cancer, Scorpio, or Pisces. The type of plant should determine both cutting and planting times.

Habit (Breaking)

To end an undesirable habit, and this applies to ending everything from a bad relationship to smoking, start on a day when the Moon is in the fourth quarter and in the barren sign of Gemini, Leo, or Aquarius. Aries, Virgo, and Capricorn may be suitable as well, depending on the habit you want to be rid of. Make sure that your lunar cycle is favorable. Avoid lunar aspects to Mars or Jupiter. However, favorable aspects to Pluto are helpful.

Haircuts

Cut hair when the Moon is in Gemini, Sagittarius, Pisces, Taurus, or Capricorn, but not in Virgo. Look for favorable aspects to Venus. For faster growth, cut hair when the Moon is increasing in Cancer or Pisces. To make hair grow thicker, cut when the Moon is full in the signs of Taurus, Cancer, or Leo. If you want your hair to grow more slowly, have the Moon be decreasing in Aries, Gemini, or Virgo, and have the Moon square or opposing Saturn.

Permanents, straightening, and hair coloring will take well if the Moon is in Taurus or Leo and trine or sextile Venus. Avoid hair treatments if Mars is marked as square or in opposition, especially if heat is to be used. For permanents, a trine to Jupiter is helpful. The Moon also should be in the first quarter. Check the lunar cycle for a favorable day in relation to your Sun sign.

Harvest Crops

Harvest root crops when the Moon is in a dry sign (Aries, Leo, Sagittarius, Gemini, Aquarius) and waning. Harvest grain for storage just after the Full Moon, avoiding Cancer, Scorpio, or Pisces. Harvest in the third and fourth quarters in dry signs. Dry crops in the third quarter in fire signs.

Health

A diagnosis is more likely to be successful when the Moon is in Aries, Cancer, Libra, or Capricorn and less so when in Gemini, Sagittarius, Pisces, or Virgo. Begin a recuperation program or enter a hospital when the Moon is in a cardinal or fixed sign and the day is favorable to your Sun sign. For surgery, see "Surgical Procedures." Buy medicines when the Moon is in Virgo or Scorpio.

Home (Buy new)

If you desire a permanent home, buy when the New Moon is in a fixed sign—Taurus or Leo, for example. Each sign will affect your decision in a different way. A house bought when the Moon is in Taurus is likely to be more practical and have a country look—right down to the split-rail fence. A house purchased when the Moon is in Leo will more likely be a real showplace.

If you're buying for speculation and a quick turnover, be certain that the Moon is in a cardinal sign (Aries, Cancer, Libra, Capricorn). Avoid buying when the Moon is in a fixed sign (Leo, Scorpio, Aquarius, Taurus).

Home (Make repairs)

In all repairs, avoid squares, oppositions, or conjunctions to the planet ruling the place or thing to be repaired. For example, bathrooms are ruled by Scorpio and Cancer. You would not want to start a project in those rooms when the Moon or Pluto is receiving hard aspects. The front entrance, hall, dining room, and porch are ruled by the Sun. So you would want to avoid times when Saturn or Mars are square, opposing, or conjunct the Sun. Also, let the Moon be waxing.

Home (Sell)

Make a strong effort to list your property for sale when the Sun is marked favorable in your sign and in good aspect to Jupiter. Avoid adverse aspects to as many planets as possible.

Home Furnishings (Buy new)

Saturn days (Saturday) are good for buying, and Jupiter days (Thursday) are good for selling. Items bought on days when Saturn is well aspected tend to wear longer and purchases tend to be more conservative.

Job (Start new)

Jupiter and Venus should be sextile, trine, or conjunct the Moon. A day when your Sun is receiving favorable aspects is preferred.

Legal Matters

Good Moon-Jupiter aspects improve the outcome in legal decisions. To gain damages through a lawsuit, begin the process during the increasing Moon. To avoid paying damages, a court date during the decreasing Moon is desirable. Good Moon-Sun aspects strengthen your chance of success. A well-aspected Moon in Cancer or Leo, making good aspects to the Sun, brings the best results in custody cases. In divorce cases, a favorable Moon-Venus aspect is best.

Loan (Ask for)

A first and second quarter phase favors the lender, the third and fourth quarters favor the borrower. Good aspects of Jupiter and

Venus to the Moon are favorable to both, as is having the Moon in Leo or Taurus.

Machinery, Appliances, or Tools (Buy)

Tools, machinery, and other implements should be bought on days when your lunar cycle is favorable and when Mars and Uranus are trine, sextile, or conjunct the Moon. Any quarter of the Moon is suitable. When buying gas or electrical appliances, the Moon should be in Aquarius.

Make a Will

Let the Moon be in a fixed sign (Taurus, Leo, Scorpio, or Aquarius) to ensure permanence. If the Moon is in a cardinal sign (Aries, Cancer, Libra, or Capricorn), the will could be altered. Let the Moon be waxing—increasing in light—and in good aspect to Saturn, Venus, or Mercury. In case the will is made in an emergency during illness and the Moon is slow in motion, void-of-course, combust, or under the Sun's beams, the testator will die and the will remain unaltered. There is some danger that it will be lost or stolen, however.

Marriage

The best time for marriage to take place is when the Moon is increasing, but not yet full. Good signs for the Moon to be in are Taurus, Cancer, Leo, or Libra.

The Moon in Taurus produces the most steadfast marriages, but if the partners later want to separate, they may have a difficult time. Make sure that the Moon is well aspected, especially to Venus or Jupiter. Avoid aspects to Mars, Uranus, or Pluto and the signs Aries, Gemini, Virgo, Scorpio, or Aquarius.

The values of the signs are as follows:

- Aries is not favored for marriage
- Taurus from 0 to 19 degrees is good, the remaining degrees are less favorable

- Cancer is unfavorable unless you are marrying a widow
- Leo is favored, but it may cause one party to deceive the other as to his or her money or possessions
- Virgo is not favored except when marrying a widow
- Libra is good for engagements but not for marriage
- Scorpio from 0 to 15 degrees is good, but the last 15 degrees are entirely unfortunate. The woman may be fickle, envious, and quarrelsome
- Sagittarius is neutral
- Capricorn, from 0 to 10 degrees, is difficult for marriage; however, the remaining degrees are favorable, especially when marrying a widow
- Aquarius is not favored
- Pisces is favored, although marriage under this sign can incline a woman to chatter a lot

These effects are strongest when the Moon is in the sign. If the Moon and Venus are in a cardinal sign, happiness between the couple may not continue long.

On no account should the Moon apply to Saturn or Mars, even by good aspect.

Medical Treatment for the Eyes

Let the Moon be increasing in light and motion and making favorable aspects to Venus or Jupiter and be unaspected by Mars. Keep the Moon out of Taurus, Capricorn, or Virgo. If an aspect between the Moon and Mars is unavoidable, let it be separating.

Medical Treatment for the Head

If possible, have Mars and Saturn free of hard aspects. Let the Moon be in Aries or Taurus, decreasing in light, in conjunction or aspect with Venus or Jupiter and free of hard aspects. The Sun should not be in any aspect to the Moon.

Medical Treatment for the Nose

Let the Moon be in Cancer, Leo, or Virgo and not aspecting Mars or Saturn and also not in conjunction with a retrograde or weak planet.

Mining

Saturn rules mining. Begin work when Saturn is marked conjunct, trine, or sextile. Mine for gold when the Sun is marked conjunct, trine, or sextile. Mercury rules quicksilver, Venus rules copper, Jupiter rules tin, Saturn rules lead and coal, Uranus rules radioactive elements, Neptune rules oil, the Moon rules water. Mine for these items when the ruling planet is marked conjunct, trine, or sextile.

Move to New Home

If you have a choice, and sometimes you don't, make sure that Mars is not aspecting the Moon. Move on a day favorable to your Sun sign or when the Moon is conjunct, sextile, or trine the Sun.

Mow Lawn

Mow in the first and second quarters (waxing phase) to increase growth and lushness, and in the third and fourth quarters (waning phase) to decrease growth.

Negotiate

When you are choosing a time to negotiate, consider what the meeting is about and what you want to have happen. If it is agreement or compromise between two parties that you desire, have the Moon be in the sign of Libra. When you are making contracts, it is best to have the Moon in the same element. For example, if your concern is communication, then elect a time when the Moon is in an air sign. If, on the other hand, your concern is about possessions, an earth sign would be more appropriate.

Fixed signs are unfavorable, with the exception of Leo; so are cardinal signs, except for Capricorn. If you are negotiating the end of something, use the rules that apply to ending habits.

Occupational Training

When you begin training, see that your lunar cycle is favorable that day and that the planet ruling your occupation is marked conjunct or trine.

Paint

Paint buildings during the waning Libra or Aquarius Moon. If the weather is hot, paint when the Moon is in Taurus. If the weather is cold, paint when the Moon is in Leo. Schedule the painting to start in the fourth quarter as the wood is drier and paint will penetrate wood better. Avoid painting around the New Moon, though, as the wood is likely to be damp, making the paint subject to scalding when hot weather hits it. If the temperature is below 70°F, it is not advisable to paint while the Moon is in Cancer, Scorpio, or Pisces as the paint is apt to creep, check, or run.

Party (Host or attend)

A party timed so the Moon is in Gemini, Leo, Libra, or Sagittarius, with good aspects to Venus and Jupiter, will be fun and well attended. There should be no aspects between the Moon and Mars or Saturn.

Pawn

Do not pawn any article when Jupiter is receiving a square or opposition from Saturn or Mars or when Jupiter is within 17 degrees of the Sun, for you will have little chance to redeem the items.

Pick Mushrooms

Mushrooms, one of the most promising traditional medicines in the world, should be gathered at the Full Moon.

Plant

Root crops, like carrots and potatoes, are best if planted in the sign Taurus or Capricorn. Beans, peas, tomatoes, peppers, and other fruit-bearing plants are best if planted in a sign that supports seed growth. Leaf plants, like lettuce, broccoli, or cauliflower, are best planted when the Moon is in a water sign.

It is recommended that you transplant during a decreasing Moon, when forces are streaming into the lower part of the plant. This helps root growth.

Promotion (Ask for)

Choose a day favorable to your Sun sign. Mercury should be marked conjunct, trine, or sextile. Avoid days when Mars or Saturn is aspected.

Prune

Prune during the third and fourth quarter of a Scorpio Moon to retard growth and to promote better fruit. Prune when the Moon is in cardinal Capricorn to promote healing.

Reconcile with People

If the reconciliation is with a woman, let Venus be strong and well aspected. If elders or superiors are involved, see that Saturn is receiving good aspects; if the reconciliation is between young people or between an older and younger person, see that Mercury is well aspected.

Romance

There is less control of when a romance starts, but romances begun under an increasing Moon are more likely to be permanent or satisfying, while those begun during the decreasing Moon tend to transform the participants. The tone of the relationship can be guessed from the sign the Moon is in. Romances begun with the Moon in Aries may be impulsive. Those begun in Capricorn will

take greater effort to bring to a desirable conclusion, but they may be very rewarding. Good aspects between the Moon and Venus will have a positive influence on the relationship. Avoid unfavorable aspects to Mars, Uranus, and Pluto. A decreasing Moon, particularly the fourth quarter, facilitates ending a relationship and causes the least pain.

Roof a Building

Begin roofing a building during the third or fourth quarter, when the Moon is in Aries or Aquarius. Shingles laid during the New Moon have a tendency to curl at the edges.

Sauerkraut

The best-tasting sauerkraut is made just after the Full Moon in the fruitful signs of Cancer, Scorpio, or Pisces.

Select a Child's Sex

Count from the last day of menstruation to the first day of the next cycle and divide the interval between the two dates in half.

Pregnancy in the first half produces females, but copulation should take place with the Moon in a feminine sign. Pregnancy in the latter half, up to three days before the beginning of menstruation, produces males, but copulation should take place with the Moon in a masculine sign. The three-day period before the next period again produces females.

Sell or Canvass

Begin these activities during a day favorable to your Sun sign. Otherwise, sell on days when Jupiter, Mercury, or Mars is trine, sextile, or conjunct the Moon. Avoid days when Saturn is square or opposing the Moon, for that always hinders business and causes discord. If the Moon is passing from the first quarter to full, it is best to have the Moon swift in motion and in good aspect with Venus and/or Jupiter.

Sign Papers

Sign contracts or agreements when the Moon is increasing in a fruitful sign and on a day when the Moon is making favorable aspects to Mercury. Avoid days when Mars, Saturn, or Neptune are square or opposite the Moon.

Spray and Weed

Spray pests and weeds during the fourth quarter when the Moon is in the barren sign Leo or Aquarius and making favorable aspects to Pluto. Weed during a waning Moon in a barren sign.

Staff (Fire)

Have the Moon in the third or fourth quarter, but not full. The Moon should not be square any planets.

Staff (Hire)

The Moon should be in the first or second quarter, and preferably in the sign of Gemini or Virgo. The Moon should be conjunct, trine, or sextile Mercury or Jupiter.

Stocks (Buy)

The Moon should be in Taurus or Capricorn, and there should be a sextile or trine to Jupiter or Saturn.

Surgical Procedures

Blood flow, like ocean tides, appears to be related to Moon phases. To reduce hemorrhage after a surgery, schedule it within one week before or after a New Moon. Schedule surgery to occur during the increase of the Moon if possible, as wounds heal better and vitality is greater than during the decrease of the Moon. Avoid surgery within one week before or after the Full Moon. Select a date when the Moon is past the sign governing the part of the body involved in the operation. For example, abdominal operations should be done when the Moon is in Sagittarius, Capricorn, or Aquarius. The further removed the Moon sign is from the sign ruling the afflicted part of the body, the better.

For successful operations, avoid times when the Moon is applying to any aspect of Mars. (This tends to promote inflammation and complications.) See the Lunar Aspectarian on odd pages 137–159 to find days with negative Mars aspects and positive Venus and Jupiter aspects. Never operate with the Moon in the same sign as a person's Sun sign or Ascendant. Let the Moon be in a fixed sign and avoid square or opposing aspects. The Moon should not be void-of-course. Cosmetic surgery should be done in the increase of the Moon, when the Moon is not square or in opposition to Mars. Avoid days when the Moon is square or opposing Saturn or the Sun.

Travel (Air)

Start long trips when the Moon is making favorable aspects to the Sun. For enjoyment, aspects to Jupiter are preferable; for visiting, look for favorable aspects to Mercury. To prevent accidents, avoid squares or oppositions to Mars, Saturn, Uranus, or

Pluto. Choose a day when the Moon is in Sagittarius or Gemini and well aspected to Mercury, Jupiter, or Uranus. Avoid adverse aspects of Mars, Saturn, or Uranus.

Visit

On setting out to visit a person, let the Moon be in aspect with any retrograde planet, for this ensures that the person you're visiting will be at home. If you desire to stay a long time in a place, let the Moon be in good aspect to Saturn. If you desire to leave the place quickly, let the Moon be in a cardinal sign.

Wean Children

To wean a child successfully, do so when the Moon is in Sagittarius, Capricorn, Aquarius, or Pisces—signs that do not rule vital human organs. By observing this astrological rule, much trouble for parents and child may be avoided.

Weight (Reduce)

If you want to lose weight, the best time to get started is when the Moon is in the third or fourth quarter and in the barren sign of Virgo. Review the section on How to Use the Moon Tables and Lunar Aspectarian beginning on page 136 to help you select a date that is favorable to begin your weight-loss program.

Wine and Drink Other Than Beer

Start brewing when the Moon is in Pisces or Taurus. Sextiles or trines to Venus are favorable, but avoid aspects to Mars or Saturn.

Write

Write for pleasure or publication when the Moon is in Gemini. Mercury should be making favorable aspects to Uranus and Neptune.

How to Use the Moon Tables and Lunar Aspectarian

Timing activities is one of the most important things you can do to ensure success. In many Eastern countries, timing by the planets is so important that practically no event takes place without first setting up a chart for it. Weddings have occurred in the middle of the night because the influences were best then. You may not want to take it that far, but you can still make use of the influences of the Moon whenever possible. It's easy and it works!

Llewellyn's Moon Sign Book has information to help you plan just about any activity: weddings, fishing, making purchases, cutting your hair, traveling, and more. We provide the guidelines you need to pick the best day out of the several from which you have to choose. The Moon Tables are the *Moon Sign Book's* primary method for choosing dates. Following are instructions, examples, and directions on how to read the Moon Tables. More advanced information on using the tables containing the Lunar Aspectarian and favorable and unfavorable days (found on odd-numbered pages opposite the Moon Tables), Moon void-of-course and retrograde information to choose the dates best for you is also included.

The Five Basic Steps

Step 1: Directions for Choosing Dates

Look up the directions for choosing dates for the activity that you wish to begin, then go to step 2.

Step 2: Check the Moon Tables

You'll find two tables for each month of the year beginning on page 136. The Moon Tables (on the left-hand pages) include the day, date, and sign the Moon is in; the element and nature of the sign; the Moon's phase; and when it changes sign or phase. If there is a time listed after a date, that time is the time when the Moon moves into that zodiac sign. Until then, the Moon is considered to be in the sign for the previous day.

The abbreviation Full signifies Full Moon and New signifies New Moon. The times listed with dates indicate when the Moon changes sign. The times listed after the phase indicate when the Moon changes phase.

Turn to the month you would like to begin your activity. You will be using the Moon's sign and phase information most often when you begin choosing your own dates. Use the Time Zone Map on page 164 and the Time Zone Conversions table on page 165 to convert time to your own time zone.

When you find dates that meet the criteria for the correct Moon phase and sign for your activity, you may have completed the process. For certain simple activities, such as getting a haircut, the phase and sign information is all that is needed. If the directions for your activity include information on certain lunar aspects, however, you should consult the Lunar Aspectarian. An example of this would be if the directions told you not to perform a certain activity when the Moon is square (Q) Jupiter.

Step 3: Check the Lunar Aspectarian

On the pages opposite the Moon Tables you will find tables containing the Lunar Aspectarian and Favorable and Unfavorable Days. The Lunar Aspectarian gives the aspects (or angles) of the Moon to other planets. Some aspects are favorable, while others are not. To use the Lunar Aspectarian, find the planet that the directions list as favorable for your activity, and run down the column to the date desired. For example, you should avoid aspects to Mars if you are planning surgery. So you would look for Mars across the top and then run down that column looking for days where there are no aspects to Mars (as signified by empty boxes). If you want to find a *favorable* aspect (sextile (X) or trine (T)) to Mercury, run your finger down the column under Mercury until you find an X or T. *Adverse* aspects to planets are squares (Q) or oppositions (O). A conjunction (C) is sometimes beneficial, sometimes not, depending on the activity or planets involved.

Step 4: Favorable and Unfavorable Days

The tables listing favorable and unfavorable days are helpful when you want to choose your personal best dates because your Sun sign is taken into consideration. The twelve Sun signs are listed on the right side of the tables. Once you have determined which days meet your criteria for phase, sign, and aspects, you can determine whether or not those days are positive for you by checking the favorable and unfavorable days for your Sun sign.

To find out if a day is positive for you, find your Sun sign and then look down the column. If it is marked F, it is very favorable. The Moon is in the same sign as your Sun on a favorable day. If it is marked f, it is slightly favorable; U is very unfavorable; and u means slightly unfavorable. A day marked very unfavorable (U) indicates that the Moon is in the sign opposing your Sun.

Once you have selected good dates for the activity you are about to begin, you can go straight to "Using What You've Learned," beginning on the next page. To learn how to fine-tune your selections even further, read on.

Step 5: Void-of-Course Moon and Retrogrades

This last step is perhaps the most advanced portion of the procedure. It is generally considered poor timing to make decisions, sign important papers, or start special activities during a Moon void-of-course period or during a Mercury retrograde. Once you have chosen the best date for your activity based on steps one through four, you can check the Void-of-Course tables, beginning on page 76, to find out if any of the dates you have chosen have void periods.

The Moon is said to be void-of-course after it has made its last aspect to a planet within a particular sign, but before it has moved into the next sign. Put simply, the Moon is "resting" during the void-of-course period, so activities initiated at this time generally don't come to fruition. You will notice that there are many void periods during the year, and it is nearly impossible to avoid all of them. Some people choose to ignore these altogether and do not take them into consideration when planning activities.

Next, you can check the Retrograde Planets tables on page 160 to see what planets are retrograde during your chosen date(s).

A planet is said to be retrograde when it appears to move backward in the sky as viewed from Earth. Generally, the farther a planet is away from the Sun, the longer it can stay retrograde. Some planets will retrograde for several months at a time. Avoiding retrogrades is not as important in lunar planning as avoiding the Moon void-of-course, with the exception of the planet Mercury.

Mercury rules thought and communication, so it is advisable not to sign important papers, initiate important business or legal work, or make crucial decisions during these times. As with the Moon void of course, it is difficult to avoid all planetary retrogrades when beginning events, and you may choose to ignore this step of the process. Following are some examples using some or all of the steps outlined above.

Using What You've Learned

Let's say it's a new year and you want to have your hair cut. It's thin and you would like it to look fuller, so you find the directions for hair care and you see that for thicker hair you should cut hair while the Moon is Full and in the sign of Taurus, Cancer, or Leo. You should avoid the Moon in Aries, Gemini, or Virgo. Look at the January Moon Table on page 136. You see that the Full Moon is on January 23 at 8:46 pm. The Moon is in Leo that day after 2:21 pm and remains in Leo until January 25 at 10:46 pm, so January 23–25 meets both the phase and sign criteria.

Let's move on to a more difficult example using the sign and phase of the Moon. You want to buy a permanent home. After checking the instructions for purchasing a house: "Home (Buy new)" on page 118, you see that you should buy a home when the Moon is in Taurus, Cancer, or Leo. You need to get a loan, so you should also look under "Loan (Ask for)" on page 119. Here it says that the third and fourth quarters favor the borrower (you). You are going to buy the house in October, so go to page 154. The Moon is in the third quarter October 16–22 and fourth quarter October 22–30. The Moon is in Taurus from 11:04 am on October 16 until October 18 at 10:30 am; in Cancer from 11:28 am October 20 until October 22 at 3:34 pm; and in Leo from October 22 at 3:34 pm until October 24 at 11:16 pm. The best days for obtaining a loan would be October 16, 17, 18, 20, 21, 22, 23, or 24.

Just match up the best sign and phase (quarter) to come up with the best date. With all activities, be sure to check the favorable and unfavorable days for your Sun sign in the table adjoining the Lunar Aspectarian. If there is a choice between several dates, pick the one most favorable for you. Because buying a home is an important business decision, you may also wish to see if the Moon is void or if Mercury is retrograde during these dates.

Now let's look at an example that uses signs, phases, and aspects. Our example is starting new home construction. We will use the month of May. Look under "Build (Start foundation)" on page 110 and you'll see that the Moon should be in the first quarter of a fixed sign—Leo, Taurus, Aquarius, or Scorpio. You should select a time when the Moon is not making unfavorable aspects to Saturn. (Conjunctions are usually considered unfavorable if they are to Mars, Saturn, or Neptune.) Look in the May Moon Table. You will see that the Moon is in the first quarter May 6–13 and in Leo from 5:32 pm on May 11 until 1:52 am on May 14. Now, look to the May Lunar Aspectarian. We see that there is a favorable trine to Saturn on May 12 and a challenging opposition on May 8. Therefore, May 12 would be the best date to start a foundation.

A Note About Time and Time Zones

All tables in the Moon Sign Book use Eastern Time. You must calculate the difference between your time zone and the Eastern Time Zone. Please refer to the Time Zone Conversions chart on page 165 for help with time conversions. The sign the Moon is in at midnight is the sign shown in the Aspectarian and Favorable and Unfavorable Days tables.

How Does the Time Matter?

Due to the three-hour time difference between the East and West Coasts of the United States, those of you living on the East Coast may be, for example, under the influence of a Virgo

Moon, while those of you living on the West Coast will still have a Leo Moon influence.

We follow a commonly held belief among astrologers: whatever sign the Moon is in at the start of a day—12:00 am Eastern Time—is considered the dominant influence of the day. That sign is indicated in the Moon Tables. If the date you select for an activity shows the Moon changing signs, you can decide how important the sign change may be for your specific election and adjust your election date and time accordingly.

Use Common Sense

Some activities depend on outside factors. Obviously, you can't go out and plant when there is a foot of snow on the ground. You should adjust to the conditions at hand. If the weather was bad during the first quarter, when it was best to plant crops, do it during the second quarter while the Moon is in a fruitful sign. If the Moon is not in a fruitful sign during the first or second quarter, choose a day when it is in a semi-fruitful sign. The best advice is to choose either the sign or phase that is most favorable, when the two don't coincide.

To Summarize

First, look up the activity under the proper heading, then look for the information given in the tables. Choose the best date considering the number of positive factors in effect. If most of the dates are favorable, there is no problem choosing the one that will fit your schedule. However, if there aren't any really good dates, pick the ones with the least number of negative influences. Please keep in mind that the information found here applies in the broadest sense to the events you want to plan or are considering. To be the most effective, when you use electional astrology, you should also consider your own birth chart in relation to a chart drawn for the time or times you have under consideration. The best advice we can offer you is: read the entire introduction to each section.

January Moon Table

Date	Sign	Element	Nature	Phase
1 Fri 1:41 am	Libra	Air	Semi-fruitful	3rd
2 Sat	Libra	Air	Semi-fruitful	4th 12:30 am
3 Sun 2:36 pm	Scorpio	Water	Fruitful	4th
4 Mon	Scorpio	Water	Fruitful	4th
5 Tue	Scorpio	Water	Fruitful	4th
6 Wed 1:56 am	Sagittarius	Fire	Barren	4th
7 Thu	Sagittarius	Fire	Barren	4th
8 Fri 10:07 am	Capricorn	Earth	Semi-fruitful	4th
9 Sat	Capricorn	Earth	Semi-fruitful	New 8:31 pm
10 Sun 3:23 pm	Aquarius	Air	Barren	1st
11 Mon	Aquarius	Air	Barren	1st
12 Tues 6:53 pm	Pisces	Water	Fruitful	1st
13 Wed	Pisces	Water	Fruitful	1st
14 Thu 9:48 pm	Aries	Fire	Barren	1st
15 Fri	Aries	Fire	Barren	1st
16 Sat	Aries	Fire	Barren	2nd 6:26 pm
17 Sun 12:48 am	Taurus	Earth	Semi-fruitful	2nd
18 Mon	Taurus	Earth	Semi-fruitful	2nd
19 Tue 4:13 am	Gemini	Air	Barren	2nd
20 Wed	Gemini	Air	Barren	2nd
21 Thu 8:28 am	Cancer	Water	Fruitful	2nd
22 Fri	Cancer	Water	Fruitful	2nd
23 Sat 2:21 pm	Leo	Fire	Barren	Full 8:46 pm
24 Sun	Leo	Fire	Barren	3rd
25 Mon 10:46 pm	Virgo	Earth	Barren	3rd
26 Tue	Virgo	Earth	Barren	3rd
27 Wed	Virgo	Earth	Barren	3rd
28 Thu 9:59 am	Libra	Air	Semi-fruitful	3rd
29 Fri	Libra	Air	Semi-fruitful	3rd
30 Sat 10:50 pm	Scorpio	Water	Fruitful	3rd
31 Sun	Scorpio	Water	Fruitful	4th 10:28 pm

Bake Bread (handwritten note beside 9 Sat row)

January Aspectarian/Favorable & Unfavorable Days

Date	Sun	Mercury	Venus	Mars	Jupiter	Saturn	Uranus	Neptune	Pluto
1		T	X						
2	Q					X	O		Q
3		Q		C					
4	X							T	X
5					X				
6		X	C					Q	
7					Q	C	T		
8			X						
9	C					Q	X	C	
10		C		Q	T				
11			X			X	X		
12									
13				T		Q		C	X
14	X	X	Q		O				
15						T			
16	Q	Q	T				C		Q
17				O				X	
18		T			T				T
19	T							Q	
20					Q	O	X		
21			O					T	
22		O	T			Q			O
23	O				X				
24			Q			T	T		
25									
26			T	X				O	
27		T				C	Q		T
28		Q							
29	T	Q				X	O		Q
30									
31	Q		X					T	

Date	Aries	Taurus	Gemini	Cancer	Leo	Virgo	Libra	Scorpio	Sagittarius	Capricorn	Aquarius	Pisces
1	U		f	u	f		F		f	u	f	
2	U		f	u	f		F		f	u	f	
3	U		f	u	f		F		f	u	f	
4		U		f	u	f		F		f	u	f
5		U		f	u	f		F		f	u	f
6	f		U		f	u	f		F		f	u
7	f		U		f	u	f		F		f	u
8	u	f		U		f	u	f		F		f
9	u	f		U		f	u	f		F		f
10	u	f		U		f	u	f		F		f
11	f	u	f		U		f	u	f		F	
12	f	u	f		U		f	u	f		F	
13		f	u	f		U		f	u	f		F
14		f	u	f		U		f	u	f		F
15	F		f	u	f		U		f	u	f	
16	F		f	u	f		U		f	u	f	
17		F		f	u	f		U		f	u	f
18		F		f	u	f		U		f	u	f
19	f		F		f	u	f		U		f	u
20	f		F		f	u	f		U		f	u
21	u	f		F		f	u	f		U		f
22	u	f		F		f	u	f		U		f
23	u	f		F		f	u	f		U		f
24	f	u	f		F		f	u	f		U	
25	f	u	f		F		f	u	f		U	
26		f	u	f		F		f	u	f		U
27		f	u	f		F		f	u	f		U
28	U		f	u	f		F		f	u	f	
29	U		f	u	f		F		f	u	f	
30	U		f	u	f		F		f	u	f	
31		U		f	u	f		F		f	u	f

February Moon Table

Date	Sign	Element	Nature	Phase
1 Mon	Scorpio	Water	Fruitful	4th
2 Tue 10:50 am	Sagittarius	Fire	Barren	4th
3 Wed	Sagittarius	Fire	Barren	4th
4 Thu 7:44 pm	Capricorn	Earth	Semi-fruitful	4th
5 Fri	Capricorn	Earth	Semi-fruitful	4th
6 Sat	Capricorn	Earth	Semi-fruitful	4th
7 Sun 12:59 am	Aquarius	Air	Barren	4th
8 Mon	Aquarius	Air	Barren	New 9:39 am
9 Tue 3:31 am	Pisces	Water	Fruitful	1st
10 Wed	Pisces	Water	Fruitful	1st
11 Thu 4:55 am	Aries	Fire	Barren	1st
12 Fri	Aries	Fire	Barren	1st
13 Sat 6:36 am	Taurus	Earth	Semi-fruitful	1st
14 Sun	Taurus	Earth	Semi-fruitful	1st
15 Mon 9:35 am	Gemini	Air	Barren	2nd 2:46 am
16 Tue	Gemini	Air	Barren	2nd
17 Wed 2:24 pm	Cancer	Water	Fruitful	2nd
18 Thu	Cancer	Water	Fruitful	2nd
19 Fri 9:17 pm	Leo	Fire	Barren	2nd
20 Sat	Leo	Fire	Barren	2nd
21 Sun	Leo	Fire	Barren	2nd
22 Mon 6:24 am	Virgo	Earth	Barren	Full 1:20 pm
23 Tue	Virgo	Earth	Barren	3rd
24 Wed 5:41 pm	Libra	Air	Semi-fruitful	3rd
25 Thu	Libra	Air	Semi-fruitful	3rd
26 Fri	Libra	Air	Semi-fruitful	3rd
27 Sat 6:26 am	Scorpio	Water	Fruitful	3rd
28 Sun	Scorpio	Water	Fruitful	3rd
29 Mon 6:56 pm	Sagittarius	Fire	Barren	3rd

February Aspectarian/Favorable & Unfavorable Days

Date	Sun	Mercury	Venus	Mars	Jupiter	Saturn	Uranus	Neptune	Pluto
1		X		C	X				X
2									
3	X					C	T	Q	
4					Q				
5								X	
6		C	C	X	T		Q		C
7									
8	C			Q		X	X		
9								C	
10		X	X	T	I	Q			X
11									
12	X		Q			T	C		Q
13		Q						X	
14				O	T				T
15	Q	T	T						
16					Q	O	X	Q	
17	T								
18							Q	T	O
19				T	X				
20		O	O						
21				Q		T	T		
22	O								
23					C	Q		O	T
24				X					
25			T						
26		T				X	O		Q
27									
28	T		Q		X			T	X
29		Q		C					

Date	Aries	Taurus	Gemini	Cancer	Leo	Virgo	Libra	Scorpio	Sagittarius	Capricorn	Aquarius	Pisces
1		U		f	u	f		F		f	u	f
2	f		U		f	u	f		F		f	u
3	f		U		f	u	f		F		f	u
4	f		U		f	u	f		F		f	u
5	u	f		U		f	u	f		F		f
6	u	f		U		f	u	f		F		f
7	f	u	f		U		f	u	f		F	
8	f	u	f		U		f	u	f		F	
9		f	u	f		U		f	u	f		F
10		f	u	f		U		f	u	f		F
11	F		f	u	f		U		f	u	f	
12	F		f	u	f		U		f	u	f	
13		F		f	u	f		U		f	u	f
14		F		f	u	f		U		f	u	f
15	f		F		f	u	f		U		f	u
16	f		F		f	u	f		U		f	u
17	f		F		f	u	f		U		f	u
18	u	f		F		f	u	f		U		f
19	u	f		F		f	u	f		U		f
20	f	u	f		F		f	u	f		U	
21	f	u	f		F		f	u	f		U	
22		f	u	f		F		f	u	f		U
23		f	u	f		F		f	u	f		U
24		f	u	f		F		f	u	f		U
25	U		f	u	f		F		f	u	f	
26	U		f	u	f		F		f	u	f	
27		U		f	u	f		F		f	u	f
28		U		f	u	f		F		f	u	f
29		U		f	u	f		F		f	u	f

March Moon Table

Date	Sign	Element	Nature	Phase
1 Tue	Sagittarius	Fire	Barren	4th 6:11 pm
2 Wed	Sagittarius	Fire	Barren	4th
3 Thu 5:01 am	Capricorn	Earth	Semi-fruitful	4th
4 Fri	Capricorn	Earth	Semi-fruitful	4th
5 Sat 11:22 am	Aquarius	Air	Barren	4th
6 Sun	Aquarius	Air	Barren	4th
7 Mon 2:08 pm	Pisces	Water	Fruitful	4th
8 Tue	Pisces	Water	Fruitful	New 8:54 pm
9 Wed 2:40 pm	Aries	Fire	Barren	1st
10 Thu	Aries	Fire	Barren	1st
11 Fri 2:44 pm	Taurus	Earth	Semi-fruitful	1st
12 Sat	Taurus	Earth	Semi-fruitful	1st
13 Sun 5:03 pm	Gemini	Air	Barren	1st
14 Mon	Gemini	Air	Barren	1st
15 Tue 8:57 pm	Cancer	Water	Fruitful	2nd 1:03 pm
16 Wed	Cancer	Water	Fruitful	2nd
17 Thu	Cancer	Water	Fruitful	2nd
18 Fri 3:54 am	Leo	Fire	Barren	2nd
19 Sat	Leo	Fire	Barren	2nd
20 Sun 1:39 pm	Virgo	Earth	Barren	2nd
21 Mon	Virgo	Earth	Barren	2nd
22 Tue	Virgo	Earth	Barren	2nd
23 Wed 1:23 am	Libra	Air	Semi-fruitful	Full 8:01 am
24 Thu	Libra	Air	Semi-fruitful	3rd
25 Fri 2:09 pm	Scorpio	Water	Fruitful	3rd
26 Sat	Scorpio	Water	Fruitful	3rd
27 Sun	Scorpio	Water	Fruitful	3rd
28 Mon 2:46 am	Sagittarius	Fire	Barren	3rd
29 Tue	Sagittarius	Fire	Barren	3rd
30 Wed 1:45 pm	Capricorn	Earth	Semi-fruitful	3rd
31 Thu	Capricorn	Earth	Semi-fruitful	4th 11:17 am

No MORE Stressin about School, ET KEEP up E daily routines (ART &a Outside/z Fresh Air, Dishes lp and make things l ♡ more importan (sewing ETC) (Baking bread, ETC (Music, ETC)

March Aspectarian/Favorable & Unfavorable Days

Date	Sun	Mercury	Venus	Mars	Jupiter	Saturn	Uranus	Neptune	Pluto
1	Q							Q	
2		X	X			Q	C	T	
3								X	
4	X				T			Q	C
5			X						
6							X	X	
7		C	C	Q					
8	C					O	Q	C	X
9			T						
10							T	C	Q
11			X						
12		X			T			X	T
13	X		Q	O					
14		Q			Q	I		Q	
15	Q							X	
16			T					T	
17		T			X		Q		O
18	T			T					
19						T	T		
20				Q					
21			O		C	Q		O	T
22									
23	O	O		X					
24						X	O		Q
25									
26					X			T	
27			T						X
28	T			C				Q	
29		T	Q		Q	C	T		
30									
31	Q				T			X	C

Date	Aries	Taurus	Gemini	Cancer	Leo	Virgo	Libra	Scorpio	Sagittarius	Capricorn	Aquarius	Pisces
1	f		U		f	u	f		F		f	u
2	f		U		f	u	f		F		f	u
3	f		U		f	u	f		F		f	u
4	u	f		U		f	u	f		F		f
5	u	f		U		f	u	f		F		f
6	f	u	f		U		f	u	f		F	
7	f	u	f		U		f	u	f		F	
8		f	u	f		U		f	u	f		F
9		f	u	f		U		f	u	f		F
10	F		f	u	f		U		f	u	f	
11	F		f	u	f		U		f	u	f	
12		F		f	u	f		U		f	u	f
13		F		f	u	f		U		f	u	f
14	f		F		f	u	f		U		f	u
15	f		F		f	u	f		U		f	u
16	u	f		F		f	u	f		U		f
17	u	f		F		f	u	f		U		f
18	u	f		F		f	u	f		U		f
19	f	u	f		F		f	u	f		U	
20	f	u	f		F		f	u	f		U	
21		f	u	f		F		f	u	f		U
22		f	u	f		F		f	u	f		U
23	U		f	u	f		F		f	u	f	
24	U		f	u	f		F		f	u	f	
25	U		f	u	f		F		f	u	f	
26		U		f	u	f		F		f	u	f
27		U		f	u	f		F		f	u	f
28	f		U		f	u	f		F		f	u
29	f		U		f	u	f		F		f	u
30	f		U		f	u	f		F		f	u
31	u	f		U		f	u	f		F		f

April Moon Table

Date	Sign	Element	Nature	Phase
1 Fri 9:37 pm	Aquarius	Air	Barren	4th
2 Sat	Aquarius	Air	Barren	4th
3 Sun	Aquarius	Air	Barren	4th
4 Mon 1:45 am	Pisces	Water	Fruitful	4th
5 Tue	Pisces	Water	Fruitful	4th
6 Wed 2:46 am	Aries	Fire	Barren	4th
7 Thu	Aries	Fire	Barren	New 7:24 am
8 Fri 2:10 am	Taurus	Earth	Semi-fruitful	1st
9 Sat	Taurus	Earth	Semi-fruitful	1st
10 Sun 1:59 am	Gemini	Air	Barren	1st
11 Mon	Gemini	Air	Barren	1st
12 Tue 4:07 am	Cancer	Water	Fruitful	1st
13 Wed	Cancer	Water	Fruitful	2nd 11:59 pm
14 Thu 9:53 am	Leo	Fire	Barren	2nd
15 Fri	Leo	Fire	Barren	2nd
16 Sat 7:23 pm	Virgo	Earth	Barren	2nd
17 Sun	Virgo	Earth	Barren	2nd
18 Mon	Virgo	Earth	Barren	2nd
19 Tue 7:24 am	Libra	Air	Semi-fruitful	2nd
20 Wed	Libra	Air	Semi-fruitful	2nd
21 Thu 8:17 pm	Scorpio	Water	Fruitful	2nd
22 Fri	Scorpio	Water	Fruitful	Full 1:24 am
23 Sat	Scorpio	Water	Fruitful	3rd
24 Sun 8:46 am	Sagittarius	Fire	Barren	3rd
25 Mon	Sagittarius	Fire	Barren	3rd
26 Tue 7:54 pm	Capricorn	Earth	Semi-fruitful	3rd
27 Wed	Capricorn	Earth	Semi-fruitful	3rd
28 Thu	Capricorn	Earth	Semi-fruitful	3rd
29 Fri 4:47 am	Aquarius	Air	Barren	4th 11:29 pm
30 Sat	Aquarius	Air	Barren	4th

April Aspectarian/Favorable & Unfavorable Days

Date	Sun	Mercury	Venus	Mars	Jupiter	Saturn	Uranus	Neptune	Pluto
1		Q	X					Q	
2	X			X					
3		X				X	X		
4				Q				C	
5					O	Q			X
6			C	T					
7	C					T	C		Q
8		C						X	
9					T				T
10			X	O				Q	
11	X					Q	O	X	
12			Q					T	
13	Q	X		X			Q		O
14									
15		Q	T	T		T			
16	T							T	
17				Q	C			O	
18		T					Q		T
19									
20			O	X		X			Q
21							O		
22	O				X			T	
23		O							X
24									
25					C	Q	C	Q	
26			T					T	
27	T					T		X	
28		T					Q		C
29	Q		Q	X					
30		Q					X	X	

Date	Aries	Taurus	Gemini	Cancer	Leo	Virgo	Libra	Scorpio	Sagittarius	Capricorn	Aquarius	Pisces
1	u	f	U		f	u	f			F		f
2	f	u	f	U		f	u	f			F	
3	f	u	f	U		f	u	f			F	
4		f	u	f		U		f	u	f		F
5		f	u	f		U		f	u	f		F
6	F		f	u	f		U		f	u	f	
7	F		f	u	f		U		f	u	f	
8		F		f	u	f		U		f	u	f
9		F		f	u	f		U		f	u	f
10	f		F		f	u	f		U		f	u
11	f		F		f	u	f		U		f	u
12	u	f		F		f	u	f		U		f
13	u	f		F		f	u	f		U		f
14	f	u	f		F		f	u	f		U	
15	f	u	f		F		f	u	f		U	
16	f	u	f		F		f	u	f		U	
17		f	u	f		F		f	u	f		U
18		f	u	f		F		f	u	f		U
19	U		f	u	f		F		f	u	f	
20	U		f	u	f		F		f	u	f	
21	U		f	u	f		F		f	u	f	
22		U		f	u	f		F		f	u	f
23		U		f	u	f		F		f	u	f
24	f		U		f	u	f		F		f	u
25	f		U		f	u	f		F		f	u
26	f		U		f	u	f		F		f	u
27	u	f		U		f	u	f		F		f
28	u	f		U		f	u	f		F		f
29	f	u	f		U		f	u	f		F	
30	f	u	f		U		f	u	f		F	

May Moon Table

Date	Sign	Element	Nature	Phase
1 Sun 10:33 am	Pisces	Water	Fruitful	4th
2 Mon	Pisces	Water	Fruitful	4th
3 Tue 1:04 pm	Aries	Fire	Barren	4th
4 Wed	Aries	Fire	Barren	4th
5 Thu 1:10 pm	Taurus	Earth	Semi-fruitful	4th
6 Fri	Taurus	Earth	Semi-fruitful	New 3:30 pm
7 Sat 12:35 pm	Gemini	Air	Barren	1st
8 Sun	Gemini	Air	Barren	1st
9 Mon 1:24 pm	Cancer	Water	Fruitful	1st
10 Tue	Cancer	Water	Fruitful	1st
11 Wed 5:32 pm	Leo	Fire	Barren	1st
12 Thu	Leo	Fire	Barren	1st
13 Fri	Leo	Fire	Barren	2nd 1:02 pm
14 Sat 1:52 am	Virgo	Earth	Barren	2nd
15 Sun	Virgo	Earth	Barren	2nd
16 Mon 1:33 pm	Libra	Air	Semi-fruitful	2nd
17 Tue	Libra	Air	Semi-fruitful	2nd
18 Wed	Libra	Air	Semi-fruitful	2nd
19 Thu 2:29 am	Scorpio	Water	Fruitful	2nd
20 Fri	Scorpio	Water	Fruitful	2nd
21 Sat 2:48 pm	Sagittarius	Fire	Barren	Full 5:14 pm
22 Sun	Sagittarius	Fire	Barren	3rd
23 Mon	Sagittarius	Fire	Barren	3rd
24 Tue 1:34 am	Capricorn	Earth	Semi-fruitful	3rd
25 Wed	Capricorn	Earth	Semi-fruitful	3rd
26 Thu 10:27 am	Aquarius	Air	Barren	3rd
27 Fri	Aquarius	Air	Barren	3rd
28 Sat 5:06 pm	Pisces	Water	Fruitful	3rd
29 Sun	Pisces	Water	Fruitful	4th 8:12 am
30 Mon 9:09 pm	Aries	Fire	Barren	4th
31 Tue	Aries	Fire	Barren	4th

May Aspectarian/Favorable & Unfavorable Days

Date	Sun	Mercury	Venus	Mars	Jupiter	Saturn	Uranus	Neptune	Pluto
1			X	Q					
2	X				O	Q		C	X
3		X							
4				T		T			Q
5							C		
6	C	C	C		T			X	T
7					O				
8					Q	O		Q	
9							X		
10		X	X		X			T	O
11	X						Q		
12			Q	T		T			
13	Q	Q					T		
14				Q					
15		T	T		C	Q		O	T
16	T			X					
17							X		
18							O		Q
19									
20		O			X			T	X
21	O		O	C					
22					Q	C		Q	
23							T		
24									
25		T			T		Q	X	C
26	T		T	X					
27		Q				X			
28				Q		X			
29	Q	X	Q		O	Q		C	X
30				T					
31	X		X			T			

Date	Aries	Taurus	Gemini	Cancer	Leo	Virgo	Libra	Scorpio	Sagittarius	Capricorn	Aquarius	Pisces
1	f	u	f		U		f	u	f		F	
2		f	u	f		U		f	u	f		F
3		f	u	f		U		f	u	f		F
4	F		f	u	f		U		f	u	f	
5	F		f	u	f		U		f	u	f	
6		F		f	u	f		U		f	u	f
7		F		f	u	f		U		f	u	f
8	f		F		f	u	f		U		f	u
9	f		F		f	u	f		U		f	u
10	u	f		F		f	u	f		U		f
11	u	f		F		f	u	f		U		f
12	f	u	f		F		f	u	f		U	
13	f	u	f		F		f	u	f		U	
14		f	u	f		F		f	u	f		U
15		f	u	f		F		f	u	f		U
16		f	u	f		F		f	u	f		U
17	U		f	u	f		F		f	u	f	
18	U		f	u	f		F		f	u	f	
19		U		f	u	f		F		f	u	f
20		U		f	u	f		F		f	u	f
21		U		f	u	f		F		f	u	f
22	f		U		f	u	f		F		f	u
23	f		U		f	u	f		F		f	u
24	u	f		U		f	u	f		F		f
25	u	f		U		f	u	f		F		f
26	u	f		U		f	u	f		F		f
27	f	u	f		U		f	u	f		F	
28	f	u	f		U		f	u	f		F	
29		f	u	f		U		f	u	f		F
30		f	u	f		U		f	u	f		F
31	F		f	u	f		U		f	u	f	

June Moon Table

Date	Sign	Element	Nature	Phase
1 Wed 10:46 pm	Taurus	Earth	Semi-fruitful	4th
2 Thu	Taurus	Earth	Semi-fruitful	4th
3 Fri 11:01 pm	Gemini	Air	Barren	4th
4 Sat	Gemini	Air	Barren	New 11:00 pm
5 Sun 11:41 pm	Cancer	Water	Fruitful	1st
6 Mon	Cancer	Water	Fruitful	1st
7 Tue	Cancer	Water	Fruitful	1st
8 Wed 2:47 am	Leo	Fire	Barren	1st
9 Thu	Leo	Fire	Barren	1st
10 Fri 9:46 am	Virgo	Earth	Barren	1st
11 Sat	Virgo	Earth	Barren	1st
12 Sun 8:33 pm	Libra	Air	Semi-fruitful	2nd 4:10 am
13 Mon	Libra	Air	Semi-fruitful	2nd
14 Tue	Libra	Air	Semi-fruitful	2nd
15 Wed 9:18 am	Scorpio	Water	Fruitful	2nd
16 Thu	Scorpio	Water	Fruitful	2nd
17 Fri 9:34 pm	Sagittarius	Fire	Barren	2nd
18 Sat	Sagittarius	Fire	Barren	2nd
19 Sun	Sagittarius	Fire	Barren	2nd
20 Mon 7:55 am	Capricorn	Earth	Semi-fruitful	Full 7:02 am
21 Tue	Capricorn	Earth	Semi-fruitful	3rd
22 Wed 4:08 pm	Aquarius	Air	Barren	3rd
23 Thu	Aquarius	Air	Barren	3rd
24 Fri 10:30 pm	Pisces	Water	Fruitful	3rd
25 Sat	Pisces	Water	Fruitful	3rd
26 Sun	Pisces	Water	Fruitful	3rd
27 Mon 3:08 am	Aries	Fire	Barren	4th 2:19 pm
28 Tue	Aries	Fire	Barren	4th
29 Wed 6:03 am	Taurus	Earth	Semi-fruitful	4th
30 Thu	Taurus	Earth	Semi-fruitful	4th

Straw-berry Full Moon

June Aspectarian/Favorable & Unfavorable Days

Date	Sun	Mercury	Venus	Mars	Jupiter	Saturn	Uranus	Neptune	Pluto
1							C		Q
2					T			X	
3		C		O					T
4	C		C		Q	O		Q	
5							X		
6					X			T	
7		X		T			Q		O
8									
9	X		X			T	T		
10		Q		Q					
11					C	Q		O	T
12	Q	T	Q	X					
13							X		
14	T							O	Q
15			T						
16					X			T	X
17				C					
18		O				C		Q	
19					Q		T		
20	O		O						
21					T			X	C
22			X				Q		
23						X			
24		T		Q			X		
25	T		T			Q		C	
26		Q		T	O				X
27	Q					T			
28		Q					C		Q
29	X	X							
30				X	O	T		X	T

Date	Aries	Taurus	Gemini	Cancer	Leo	Virgo	Libra	Scorpio	Sagittarius	Capricorn	Aquarius	Pisces
1	F		f	u	f		U		f	u	f	
2		F		f	u	f		U		f	u	f
3		F		f	u	f		U		f	u	f
4	f		F		f	u	f		U		f	u
5	f		F		f	u	f		U		f	u
6	u	f		F		f	u	f		U		f
7	u	f		F		f	u	f		U		f
8	f	u	f		F		f	u	f		U	
9	f	u	f		F		f	u	f		U	
10		f	u	f		F		f	u	f		U
11		f	u	f		F		f	u	f		U
12		f	u	f		F		f	u	f		U
13	U		f	u	f		F		f	u	f	
14	U		f	u	f		F		f	u	f	
15		U		f	u	f		F		f	u	f
16		U		f	u	f		F		f	u	f
17		U		f	u	f		F		f	u	f
18	f		U		f	u	f		F		f	u
19	f		U		f	u	f		F		f	u
20	u	f		U		f	u	f		F		f
21	u	f		U		f	u	f		F		f
22	u	f		U		f	u	f		F		f
23	f	u	f		U		f	u	f		F	
24	f	u	f		U		f	u	f		F	
25		f	u	f		U		f	u	f		F
26		f	u	f		U		f	u	f		F
27	F		f	u	f		U		f	u	f	
28	F		f	u	f		U		f	u	f	
29		F		f	u	f		U		f	u	f
30		F		f	u	f		U		f	u	f

July Moon Table

Date	Sign	Element	Nature	Phase
1 Fri 7:44 am	Gemini	Air	Barren	4th
2 Sat	Gemini	Air	Barren	4th
3 Sun 9:20 am	Cancer	Water	Fruitful	4th
4 Mon	Cancer	Water	Fruitful	New 7:01 am
5 Tue 12:28 pm	Leo	Fire	Barren	1st
6 Wed	Leo	Fire	Barren	1st
7 Thu 6:41 pm	Virgo	Earth	Barren	1st
8 Fri	Virgo	Earth	Barren	1st
9 Sat	Virgo	Earth	Barren	1st
10 Sun 4:32 am	Libra	Air	Semi-fruitful	1st
11 Mon	Libra	Air	Semi-fruitful	2nd 8:52 pm
12 Tue 4:52 pm	Scorpio	Water	Fruitful	2nd
13 Wed	Scorpio	Water	Fruitful	2nd
14 Thu	Scorpio	Water	Fruitful	2nd
15 Fri 5:14 am	Sagittarius	Fire	Barren	2nd
16 Sat	Sagittarius	Fire	Barren	2nd
17 Sun 3:33 pm	Capricorn	Earth	Semi-fruitful	2nd
18 Mon	Capricorn	Earth	Semi-fruitful	2nd
19 Tue 11:10 pm	Aquarius	Air	Barren	Full 6:57 pm
20 Wed	Aquarius	Air	Barren	3rd
21 Thu	Aquarius	Air	Barren	3rd
22 Fri 4:35 am	Pisces	Water	Fruitful	3rd
23 Sat	Pisces	Water	Fruitful	3rd
24 Sun 8:33 am	Aries	Fire	Barren	3rd
25 Mon	Aries	Fire	Barren	3rd
26 Tue 11:37 am	Taurus	Earth	Semi-fruitful	4th 7:00 pm
27 Wed	Taurus	Earth	Semi-fruitful	4th
28 Thu 2:17 pm	Gemini	Air	Barren	4th
29 Fri	Gemini	Air	Barren	4th
30 Sat 5:09 pm	Cancer	Water	Fruitful	4th
31 Sun	Cancer	Water	Fruitful	4th

July Aspectarian/Favorable & Unfavorable Days

Date	Sun	Mercury	Venus	Mars	Jupiter	Saturn	Uranus	Neptune	Pluto
1									
2					Q	O	X	Q	
3									
4	C	C	C		X			T	O
5				T				Q	
6							T		
7				Q				T	
8						Q		O	
9	X	X	X	X	C				T
10									
11	Q						X		Q
12		Q	Q					O	
13								T	
14	T			C	X				X
15		T	T						
16					Q	C		Q	
17								T	
18								X	C
19	O			X	T			Q	
20		O	O			X			
21				Q				X	
22						Q			
23					O			C	X
24	T			T					
25		T	T			T			Q
26	Q							C	
27			Q		T			X	T
28		Q		O					
29	X					O		Q	
30		X	X		Q	X			
31								T	O

Date	Aries	Taurus	Gemini	Cancer	Leo	Virgo	Libra	Scorpio	Sagittarius	Capricorn	Aquarius	Pisces
1		F		f	u	f		U		f	u	f
2	f		F		f	u	f		U		f	u
3	f		F		f	u	f		U		f	u
4	u	f		F		f	u	f		U		f
5	u	f		F		f	u	f		U		f
6	f	u	f		F		f	u	f		U	
7	f	u	f		F		f	u	f		U	
8		f	u	f		F		f	u	f		U
9		f	u	f		F		f	u	f		U
10		f	u	f		F		f	u	f		U
11	U		f	u	f		F		f	u	f	
12	U		f	u	f		F		f	u	f	
13		U		f	u	f		F		f	u	f
14		U		f	u	f		F		f	u	f
15		U		f	u	f		F		f	u	f
16	f		U		f	u	f		F		f	u
17	f		U		f	u	f		F		f	u
18	u	f		U		f	u	f		F		f
19	u	f		U		f	u	f		F		f
20	f	u	f		U		f	u	f		F	
21	f	u	f		U		f	u	f		F	
22	f	u	f		U		f	u	f		F	
23		f	u	f		U		f	u	f		F
24		f	u	f		U		f	u	f		F
25	F		f	u	f		U		f	u	f	
26	F		f	u	f		U		f	u	f	
27		F		f	u	f		U		f	u	f
28		F		f	u	f		U		f	u	f
29	f		F		f	u	f		U		f	u
30	f		F		f	u	f		U		f	u
31	u	f		F		f	u	f		U		f

August Moon Table

Date	Sign	Element	Nature	Phase
1 Mon 9:12 pm	Leo	Fire	Barren	4th
2 Tue	Leo	Fire	Barren	New 4:45 pm
3 Wed	Leo	Fire	Barren	1st
4 Thu 3:34 am	Virgo	Earth	Barren	1st
5 Fri	Virgo	Earth	Barren	1st
6 Sat 12:57 pm	Libra	Air	Semi-fruitful	1st
7 Sun	Libra	Air	Semi-fruitful	1st
8 Mon	Libra	Air	Semi-fruitful	1st
9 Tue 12:51 am	Scorpio	Water	Fruitful	1st
10 Wed	Scorpio	Water	Fruitful	2nd 2:21 pm
11 Thu 1:24 pm	Sagittarius	Fire	Barren	2nd
12 Fri	Sagittarius	Fire	Barren	2nd
13 Sat	Sagittarius	Fire	Barren	2nd
14 Sun 12:11 am	Capricorn	Earth	Semi-fruitful	2nd
15 Mon	Capricorn	Earth	Semi-fruitful	2nd
16 Tue 7:52 am	Aquarius	Air	Barren	2nd
17 Wed	Aquarius	Air	Barren	2nd
18 Thu 12:34 pm	Pisces	Water	Fruitful	Full 5:27 am
19 Fri	Pisces	Water	Fruitful	3rd
20 Sat 3:18 pm	Aries	Fire	Barren	3rd
21 Sun	Aries	Fire	Barren	3rd
22 Mon 5:19 pm	Taurus	Earth	Semi-fruitful	3rd
23 Tue	Taurus	Earth	Semi-fruitful	3rd
24 Wed 7:40 pm	Gemini	Air	Barren	4th 11:41 pm
25 Thu	Gemini	Air	Barren	4th
26 Fri 11:06 pm	Cancer	Water	Fruitful	4th
27 Sat	Cancer	Water	Fruitful	4th
28 Sun	Cancer	Water	Fruitful	4th
29 Mon 4:11 am	Leo	Fire	Barren	4th
30 Tue	Leo	Fire	Barren	4th
31 Wed 11:22 am	Virgo	Earth	Barren	4th

August Aspectarian/Favorable & Unfavorable Days

Date	Sun	Mercury	Venus	Mars	Jupiter	Saturn	Uranus	Neptune	Pluto
1				T	X		Q		
2	C					T			
3							T		
4		C	C	Q		Q			
5					C			O	T
6				X					
7	X					X			Q
8							O		
9			X				T		
10	Q	X							X
11				C	X				
12			Q			C	Q		
13	T	Q			Q		T		
14			T					X	
15		T			T		Q		C
16				X					
17						X			
18	O						X		
19			O	Q		Q		C	X
20		O		O					
21				T		T			Q
22	T						C		
23							X		T
24	Q	T	T		T				
25				O		O	Q		
26		Q	Q		Q		X		
27	X						T		
28				X		Q			O
29		X	X		T				
30				T					
31							T		

Date	Aries	Taurus	Gemini	Cancer	Leo	Virgo	Libra	Scorpio	Sagittarius	Capricorn	Aquarius	Pisces
1	u	f		F		f	u	f		U		f
2	f	u	f		F		f	u	f		U	
3	f	u	f		F		f	u	f		U	
4	f	u	f		F		f	u	f		U	
5		f	u	f		F		f	u	f		U
6		f	u	f		F		f	u	f		U
7	U		f	u	f		F		f	u	f	
8	U		f	u	f		F		f	u	f	
9		U		f	u	f		F		f	u	f
10		U		f	u	f		F		f	u	f
11		U		f	u	f		F		f	u	f
12	f		U		f	u	f		F		f	u
13	f		U		f	u	f		F		f	u
14	u	f		U		f	u	f		F		f
15	u	f		U		f	u	f		F		f
16	u	f		U		f	u	f		F		f
17	f	u	f		U		f	u	f		F	
18	f	u	f		U		f	u	f		F	
19		f	u	f		U		f	u	f		F
20		f	u	f		U		f	u	f		F
21	F		f	u	f		U		f	u	f	
22	F		f	u	f		U		f	u	f	
23		F		f	u	f		U		f	u	f
24		F		f	u	f		U		f	u	f
25	f		F		f	u	f		U		f	u
26	f		F		f	u	f		U		f	u
27	u	f		F		f	u	f		U		f
28	u	f		F		f	u	f		U		f
29	u	f		F		f	u	f		U		f
30	f	u	f		F		f	u	f		U	
31	f	u	f		F		f	u	f		U	

September Moon Table

Date	Sign	Element	Nature	Phase
1 Thu	Virgo	Earth	Barren	New 5:03 am
2 Fri 8:55 pm	Libra	Air	Semi-fruitful	1st
3 Sat	Libra	Air	Semi-fruitful	1st
4 Sun	Libra	Air	Semi-fruitful	1st
5 Mon 8:38 am	Scorpio	Water	Fruitful	1st
6 Tue	Scorpio	Water	Fruitful	1st
7 Wed 9:20 pm	Sagittarius	Fire	Barren	1st
8 Thu	Sagittarius	Fire	Barren	1st
9 Fri	Sagittarius	Fire	Barren	2nd 7:49 am
10 Sat 8:55 am	Capricorn	Earth	Semi-fruitful	2nd
11 Sun	Capricorn	Earth	Semi-fruitful	2nd
12 Mon 5:28 pm	Aquarius	Air	Barren	2nd
13 Tue	Aquarius	Air	Barren	2nd
14 Wed 10:23 pm	Pisces	Water	Fruitful	2nd
15 Thu	Pisces	Water	Fruitful	2nd
16 Fri	Pisces	Water	Fruitful	Full 3:05 pm
17 Sat 12:22 am	Aries	Fire	Barren	3rd
18 Sun	Aries	Fire	Barren	3rd
19 Mon 12:58 am	Taurus	Earth	Semi-fruitful	3rd
20 Tue	Taurus	Earth	Semi-fruitful	3rd
21 Wed 1:53 am	Gemini	Air	Barren	3rd
22 Thu	Gemini	Air	Barren	3rd
23 Fri 4:33 am	Cancer	Water	Fruitful	4th 5:56 am
24 Sat	Cancer	Water	Fruitful	4th
25 Sun 9:48 am	Leo	Fire	Barren	4th
26 Mon	Leo	Fire	Barren	4th
27 Tue 5:43 pm	Virgo	Earth	Barren	4th
28 Wed	Virgo	Earth	Barren	4th
29 Thu	Virgo	Earth	Barren	4th
30 Fri 3:52 am	Libra	Air	Semi-fruitful	New 8:11 pm

September Aspectarian/Favorable & Unfavorable Days

Date	Sun	Mercury	Venus	Mars	Jupiter	Saturn	Uranus	Neptune	Pluto
1	C			Q		Q		O	T
2		C			C				
3			C			X			
4				X				O	Q
5									
6	X							T	X
7		X			X				
8			X			C		Q	
9	Q	Q		C			T		
10				Q					
11	T		Q					X	C
12		T			T		Q		
13						X			
14			T	X			X		
15						Q		C	X
16	O	O		Q					
17					O	T			
18			O	T			C		Q
19							X		
20	T	T							T
21					T	O	Q		
22		Q		O			X		
23	Q		T		Q			T	
24		X					Q		O
25	X		Q		X				
26						T			
27			T				T		
28			X			Q		O	T
29		C							
30	C				Q	C			

Date	Aries	Taurus	Gemini	Cancer	Leo	Virgo	Libra	Scorpio	Sagittarius	Capricorn	Aquarius	Pisces
1		f	u	f		F		f	u	f		U
2		f	u	f		F		f	u	f		U
3	U		f	u	f		F		f	u	f	
4	U		f	u	f		F		f	u	f	
5		U		f	u	f		F		f	u	f
6		U		f	u	f		F		f	u	f
7		U		f	u	f		F		f	u	f
8	f		U		f	u	f		F		f	u
9	f		U		f	u	f		F		f	u
10	u	f		U		f	u	f		F		f
11	u	f		U		f	u	f		F		f
12	u	f		U		f	u	f		F		f
13	f	u	f		U		f	u	f		F	
14	f	u	f		U		f	u	f		F	
15		f	u	f		U		f	u	f		F
16		f	u	f		U		f	u	f		F
17	F		f	u	f		U		f	u	f	
18	F		f	u	f		U		f	u	f	
19		F		f	u	f		U		f	u	f
20		F		f	u	f		U		f	u	f
21	f		F		f	u	f		U		f	u
22	f		F		f	u	f		U		f	u
23	u	f		F		f	u	f		U		f
24	u	f		F		f	u	f		U		f
25	f	u	f		F		f	u	f		U	
26	f	u	f		F		f	u	f		U	
27	f	u	f		F		f	u	f		U	
28		f	u	f		F		f	u	f		U
29		f	u	f		F		f	u	f		U
30	U		f	u	f		F		f	u	f	

October Moon Table

Date	Sign	Element	Nature	Phase
1 Sat	Libra	Air	Semi-fruitful	1st
2 Sun 3:43 pm	Scorpio	Water	Fruitful	1st
3 Mon	Scorpio	Water	Fruitful	1st
4 Tue	Scorpio	Water	Fruitful	1st
5 Wed 4:26 am	Sagittarius	Fire	Barren	1st
6 Thu	Sagittarius	Fire	Barren	1st
7 Fri 4:40 pm	Capricorn	Earth	Semi-fruitful	1st
8 Sat	Capricorn	Earth	Semi-fruitful	1st
9 Sun	Capricorn	Earth	Semi-fruitful	2nd 12:33 am
10 Mon 2:33 am	Aquarius	Air	Barren	2nd
11 Tue	Aquarius	Air	Barren	2nd
12 Wed 8:43 am	Pisces	Water	Fruitful	2nd
13 Thu	Pisces	Water	Fruitful	2nd
14 Fri 11:08 am	Aries	Fire	Barren	2nd
15 Sat	Aries	Fire	Barren	2nd
16 Sun 11:04 am	Taurus	Earth	Semi-fruitful	Full 12:23 am
17 Mon	Taurus	Earth	Semi-fruitful	3rd
18 Tue 10:30 am	Gemini	Air	Barren	3rd
19 Wed	Gemini	Air	Barren	3rd
20 Thu 11:28 am	Cancer	Water	Fruitful	3rd
21 Fri	Cancer	Water	Fruitful	3rd
22 Sat 3:34 pm	Leo	Fire	Barren	4th 3:14 pm
23 Sun	Leo	Fire	Barren	4th
24 Mon 11:16 pm	Virgo	Earth	Barren	4th
25 Tue	Virgo	Earth	Barren	4th
26 Wed	Virgo	Earth	Barren	4th
27 Thu 9:51 am	Libra	Air	Semi-fruitful	4th
28 Fri	Libra	Air	Semi-fruitful	4th
29 Sat 10:01 pm	Scorpio	Water	Fruitful	4th
30 Sun	Scorpio	Water	Fruitful	New 1:38 pm
31 Mon	Scorpio	Water	Fruitful	1st

October Aspectarian/Favorable & Unfavorable Days

Date	Sun	Mercury	Venus	Mars	Jupiter	Saturn	Uranus	Neptune	Pluto
1						X			Q
2				X			O		
3			C					T	X
4		X							
5					X				
6	X						C		Q
7		Q						T	
8					C	Q		X	C
9	Q		X					Q	
10		T				T			
11	T		Q				X	X	
12									
13				X		Q		C	X
14			T		O				
15		O		Q		T	C		Q
16	O								
17				T				X	T
18			O						
19		T			T	O	X	Q	
20	T								
21				O	Q			T	O
22	Q	Q						Q	
23			T		X	T			
24								T	
25	X	X	Q					O	
26				T		Q			T
27									
28			X		C	X			Q
29				Q			O		
30	C	C						T	
31				X					X

Date	Aries	Taurus	Gemini	Cancer	Leo	Virgo	Libra	Scorpio	Sagittarius	Capricorn	Aquarius	Pisces
1	U		f	u	f		F		f	u	f	
2	U		f	u	f		F		f	u	f	
3		U		f	u	f		F		f	u	f
4		U		f	u	f		F		f	u	f
5	f		U		f	u	f		F		f	u
6	f		U		f	u	f		F		f	u
7	f		U		f	u	f		F		f	u
8	u	f		U		f	u	f		F		f
9	u	f		U		f	u	f		F		f
10	f	u	f		U		f	u	f		F	
11	f	u	f		U		f	u	f		F	
12		f	u	f		U		f	u	f		F
13		f	u	f		U		f	u	f		F
14	F		f	u	f		U		f	u	f	
15	F		f	u	f		U		f	u	f	
16		F		f	u	f		U		f	u	f
17		F		f	u	f		U		f	u	f
18	f		F		f	u	f		U		f	u
19	f		F		f	u	f		U		f	u
20	u	f		F		f	u	f		U		f
21	u	f		F		f	u	f		U		f
22	u	f		F		f	u	f		U		f
23	f	u	f		F		f	u	f		U	
24	f	u	f		F		f	u	f		U	
25		f	u	f		F		f	u	f		U
26		f	u	f		F		f	u	f		U
27	U		f	u	f		F		f	u	f	
28	U		f	u	f		F		f	u	f	
29	U		f	u	f		F		f	u	f	
30		U		f	u	f		F		f	u	f
31		U		f	u	f		F		f	u	f

November Moon Table

Date	Sign	Element	Nature	Phase
1 Tue 10:43 am	Sagittarius	Fire	Barren	1st
2 Wed	Sagittarius	Fire	Barren	1st
3 Thu 11:05 pm	Capricorn	Earth	Semi-fruitful	1st
4 Fri	Capricorn	Earth	Semi-fruitful	1st
5 Sat	Capricorn	Earth	Semi-fruitful	1st
6 Sun 8:55 am	Aquarius	Air	Barren	1st
7 Mon	Aquarius	Air	Barren	2nd 2:51 pm
8 Tue 4:45 pm	Pisces	Water	Fruitful	2nd
9 Wed	Pisces	Water	Fruitful	2nd
10 Thu 8:45 pm	Aries	Fire	Barren	2nd
11 Fri	Aries	Fire	Barren	2nd
12 Sat 9:24 pm	Taurus	Earth	Semi-fruitful	2nd
13 Sun	Taurus	Earth	Semi-fruitful	2nd
14 Mon 8:23 pm	Gemini	Air	Barren	Full 8:52 am
15 Tue	Gemini	Air	Barren	3rd
16 Wed 7:57 pm	Cancer	Water	Fruitful	3rd
17 Thu	Cancer	Water	Fruitful	3rd
18 Fri 10:14 pm	Leo	Fire	Barren	3rd
19 Sat	Leo	Fire	Barren	3rd
20 Sun	Leo	Fire	Barren	3rd
21 Mon 4:34 am	Virgo	Earth	Barren	4th 3:33 am
22 Tue	Virgo	Earth	Barren	4th
23 Wed 2:42 pm	Libra	Air	Semi-fruitful	4th
24 Thu	Libra	Air	Semi-fruitful	4th
25 Fri	Libra	Air	Semi-fruitful	4th
26 Sat 3:01 am	Scorpio	Water	Fruitful	4th
27 Sun	Scorpio	Water	Fruitful	4th
28 Mon 3:46 pm	Sagittarius	Fire	Barren	4th
29 Tue	Sagittarius	Fire	Barren	New 7:18 am
30 Wed	Sagittarius	Fire	Barren	1st

November Aspectarian/Favorable & Unfavorable Days

Date	Sun	Mercury	Venus	Mars	Jupiter	Saturn	Uranus	Neptune	Pluto
1									
2					X	C		Q	
3			C				T		
4					Q			X	
5	X	X						Q	C
6			C						
7	Q				T	X			
8		Q	X				X		
9						Q		C	X
10	T	T	Q	X					
11					O	T			Q
12			T				C		
13			Q					X	T
14	O								
15		O		T	T	O		Q	
16							X		
17			O		Q			T	O
18	T							Q	
19		T		O					
20					X	T	T		
21	Q							O	
22		Q	T			Q			T
23	X								
24			Q	T	C				Q
25		X				X	O		
26								T	
27			X	Q					X
28									
29	C			X				Q	
30		C			X	C	T		

Date	Aries	Taurus	Gemini	Cancer	Leo	Virgo	Libra	Scorpio	Sagittarius	Capricorn	Aquarius	Pisces
1		U		f	u	f		F		f	u	f
2	f	U		f	u	f		F		f	u	
3	f	U		f	u	f		F		f	u	
4	u	f	U		f	u	f		F			f
5	u	f	U		f	u	f		F			f
6	f	u	f	U		f	u	f		F		
7	f	u	f	U		f	u	f		F		
8	f	u	f	U		f	u	f		F		
9		f	u	f	U		f	u	f		F	
10		f	u	f	U		f	u	f		F	
11	F		f	u	f	U		f	u	f		
12	F		f	u	f	U		f	u	f		
13		F		f	u	f	U		f	u	f	
14		F		f	u	f	U		f	u	f	
15	f	F		f	u	f		U		f	u	f
16	f	F		f	u	f		U		f	u	f
17	u	f	F		f	u	f		U		f	u
18	u	f	F		f	u	f		U		f	u
19	f	u	f	F		f	u	f		U		f
20	f	u	f	F		f	u	f		U		f
21	f	u	f		F		f	u	f		U	
22	f	u	f		F		f	u	f		U	
23	f	u	f		F		f	u	f		U	
24		f	u	f		F		f	u	f		U
25		f	u	f		F		f	u	f		U
26	U		f	u	f		F		f	u	f	
27	U		f	u	f		F		f	u	f	
28	U		f	u	f		F		f	u	f	
29	f	U		f	u	f		F		f	u	f
30	f	U		f	u	f		F		f	u	f

157

December Moon Table

Date	Sign	Element	Nature	Phase
1 Thu 3:52 am	Capricorn	Earth	Semi-fruitful	1st
2 Fri	Capricorn	Earth	Semi-fruitful	1st
3 Sat 2:44 pm	Aquarius	Air	Barren	1st
4 Sun	Aquarius	Air	Barren	1st
5 Mon 11:31 pm	Pisces	Water	Fruitful	1st
6 Tue	Pisces	Water	Fruitful	1st
7 Wed	Pisces	Water	Fruitful	2nd 4:03 am
8 Thu 5:15 am	Aries	Fire	Barren	2nd
9 Fri	Aries	Fire	Barren	2nd
10 Sat 7:41 am	Taurus	Earth	Semi-fruitful	2nd
11 Sun	Taurus	Earth	Semi-fruitful	2nd
12 Mon 7:41 am	Gemini	Air	Barren	2nd
13 Tue	Gemini	Air	Barren	Full 7:06 pm
14 Wed 7:09 am	Cancer	Water	Fruitful	3rd
15 Thu	Cancer	Water	Fruitful	3rd
16 Fri 8:15 am	Leo	Fire	Barren	3rd
17 Sat	Leo	Fire	Barren	3rd
18 Sun 12:52 pm	Virgo	Earth	Barren	3rd
19 Mon	Virgo	Earth	Barren	3rd
20 Tue 9:40 pm	Libra	Air	Semi-fruitful	4th 8:56 pm
21 Wed	Libra	Air	Semi-fruitful	4th
22 Thu	Libra	Air	Semi-fruitful	4th
23 Fri 9:32 am	Scorpio	Water	Fruitful	4th
24 Sat	Scorpio	Water	Fruitful	4th
25 Sun 10:19 pm	Sagittarius	Fire	Barren	4th
26 Mon	Sagittarius	Fire	Barren	4th
27 Tue	Sagittarius	Fire	Barren	4th
28 Wed 10:12 am	Capricorn	Earth	Semi-fruitful	4th
29 Thu	Capricorn	Earth	Semi-fruitful	New 1:53 am
30 Fri 8:29 pm	Aquarius	Air	Barren	1st
31 Sat	Aquarius	Air	Barren	1st

December Aspectarian/Favorable & Unfavorable Days

Date	Sun	Mercury	Venus	Mars	Jupiter	Saturn	Uranus	Neptune	Pluto
1								X	
2					Q		Q		C
3			C						
4	X								
5					C	T	X	X	
6		X						C	
7	Q					Q			X
8		Q	X						
9	T			X	O	T	C		Q
10			Q					X	
11		T	Q						T
12			T					Q	
13	O				T	O	X		
14				T				T	
15		O			Q		Q		O
16									
17			O		X	T	T		
18	T			O					
19		T						O	T
20	Q						Q		
21									
22		Q	T		C	X	O		Q
23	X			T					
24		X						T	X
25			Q						
26				Q				Q	
27			X		X	C	T		
28		C							
29	C			X				X	C
30					Q		Q		
31									

Date	Aries	Taurus	Gemini	Cancer	Leo	Virgo	Libra	Scorpio	Sagittarius	Capricorn	Aquarius	Pisces
1	u	f		U		f	u	f		F		f
2	u	f		U		f	u	f		F		f
3	u	f		U		f	u	f		F		f
4	f	u	f		U		f	u	f		F	
5	f	u	f		U		f	u	f		F	
6		f	u	f		U		f	u	f		F
7		f	u	f		U		f	u	f		F
8	F		f	u	f		U		f	u	f	
9	F		f	u	f		U		f	u	f	
10		F		f	u	f		U		f	u	f
11		F		f	u	f		U		f	u	f
12	f		F		f	u	f		U		f	u
13	f		F		f	u	f		U		f	u
14	u	f		F		f	u	f		U		f
15	u	f		F		f	u	f		U		f
16	f	u	f		F		f	u	f		U	
17	f	u	f		F		f	u	f		U	
18	f	u	f		F		f	u	f		U	
19		f	u	f		F		f	u	f		U
20		f	u	f		F		f	u	f		U
21	U		f	u	f		F		f	u	f	
22	U		f	u	f		F		f	u	f	
23		U		f	u	f		F		f	u	f
24		U		f	u	f		F		f	u	f
25		U		f	u	f		F		f	u	f
26	f		U		f	u	f		F		f	u
27	f		U		f	u	f		F		f	u
28	u	f		U		f	u	f		F		f
29	u	f		U		f	u	f		F		f
30	u	f		U		f	u	f		F		f
31	f	u	f		U		f	u	f		F	

2016 Retrograde Planets

Planet	Begin	Eastern	Pacific	End	Eastern	Pacific
Mercury	1/5/16	8:06 am	**5:06 am**	1/25/16	4:50 pm	**1:50 pm**
Jupiter	1/7/16	11:40 pm	**8:40 pm**	5/9/16	8:14 am	**5:14 am**
Saturn	3/25/16	6:01 am	**3:01 am**	8/13/16	5:50 am	**2:50 am**
Mars	4/17/16	8:14 am	**5:14 am**	6/29/16	7:38 pm	**4:38 pm**
Pluto	4/18/16	3:26 am	**12:26 am**	9/26/16	11:01 am	**8:01 am**
Mercury	4/28/16	1:20 pm	**10:20 am**	5/22/16	9:20 am	**6:20 am**
Neptune	6/13/16	4:43 pm	**1:43 pm**	11/19/16	11:38 pm	**8:38 pm**
Uranus	7/29/16	5:06 pm	**2:06 pm**	12/29/16	4:29 am	**1:29 am**
Mercury	8/30/16	9:04 am	**6:04 am**	9/21/16		**10:31 pm**
				9/22/16	1:31 am	
Mercury	12/19/16	5:55 am	**2:55 am**	1/8/17	4:43 am	**1:43 am**

Eastern Time in plain type, **Pacific Time in bold type**

Egg-Setting Dates

To Have Eggs by this Date	Sign	Qtr.	Date to Set Eggs
Jan 12, 6:53 pm–Jan 14, 9:48 pm	Pisces	1st	Dec 22, 2015
Jan 17, 12:48 am–Jan 19, 4:13 am	Taurus	2nd	Dec 27, 2015
Jan 21, 8:28 am–Jan 23, 2:21 pm	Cancer	2nd	Dec 31, 2015
Feb 9, 3:31 am–Feb 11, 4:55 am	Pisces	1st	Jan 19, 2016
Feb 13, 6:36 am–Feb 15, 9:35 am	Taurus	1st	Jan 23
Feb 17, 2:24 pm–Feb 19, 9:17 pm	Cancer	2nd	Jan 27
Mar 8, 8:54 pm–Mar 9, 2:40 pm	Pisces	1st	Feb 16
Mar 11, 2:44 pm–Mar 13, 5:03 pm	Taurus	1st	Feb 19
Mar 15, 8:57 pm–Mar 18, 3:54 am	Cancer	2nd	Feb 23
Mar 23, 1:23 am–Mar 23, 8:01 am	Libra	2nd	Mar 02
Apr 8, 2:10 am–Apr 10, 1:59 am	Taurus	1st	Mar 18
Apr 12, 4:07 am–Apr 14, 9:53 am	Cancer	1st	Mar 22
Apr 19, 7:24 am–Apr 21, 8:17 pm	Libra	2nd	Mar 29
May 6, 3:30 pm–May 7, 12:35 pm	Taurus	1st	Apr 15
May 9, 1:24 pm–May 11, 5:32 pm	Cancer	1st	Apr 18
May 16, 1:33 pm–May 19, 2:29 am	Libra	2nd	Apr 25
Jun 5, 11:41 pm–Jun 8, 2:47 am	Cancer	1st	May 15
Jun 12, 8:33 pm–Jun 15, 9:18 am	Libra	2nd	May 22
Jul 4, 7:01 am–Jul 5, 12:28 pm	Cancer	1st	Jun 13
Jul 10, 4:32 am–Jul 12, 4:52 am	Libra	1st	Jun 19
Aug 6, 12:57 pm–Aug 8, 12:51 am	Libra	1st	Jul 16
Sep 2, 8:55 pm–Sep 5, 8:38 am	Libra	1st	Aug 12
Sep 14, 10:23 pm–Sep 16, 3:05 pm	Pisces	2nd	Aug 24
Sep 30, 8:11 pm–Oct 2, 3:43 pm	Libra	1st	Sep 9
Oct 12, 8:43 am–Oct 14, 11:08 am	Pisces	2nd	Sep 21
Nov 8, 4:45 pm–Nov 10, 8:45 pm	Pisces	2nd	Oct 18
Nov 12, 9:24 pm–Nov 14, 8:52 am	Taurus	2nd	Oct 22
Dec 5, 11:31 pm–Dec 8, 5:15 am	Pisces	1st	Nov 14
Dec 10, 7:41 am–Dec 12, 7:41 am	Taurus	2nd	Nov 19

Dates to Hunt and Fish

Date	Quarter	Sign
Jan 3, 2:36 pm–Jan 6, 1:56 am	4th	Scorpio
Jan 12, 6:53 pm–Jan 14, 9:48 pm	1st	Pisces
Jan 21, 8:28 am–Jan 23, 2:21 pm	2nd	Cancer
Jan 30, 10:50 pm–Feb 2, 10:50 am	3rd	Scorpio
Feb 9, 3:31 am–Feb 11, 4:55 am	1st	Pisces
Feb 17, 2:24 pm–Feb 19, 9:17 pm	2nd	Cancer
Feb 27, 6:26 am–Feb 29, 6:56 pm	3rd	Scorpio
Feb 29, 6:56 pm–Mar 3, 5:01 am	3rd	Sagittarius
Mar 7, 2:08 pm–Mar 9, 2:40 pm	4th	Pisces
Mar 15, 8:57 pm–Mar 18, 3:54 am	2nd	Cancer
Mar 25, 2:09 pm–Mar 28, 2:46 am	3rd	Scorpio
Mar 28, 2:46 am–Mar 30, 1:45 pm	3rd	Sagittarius
Apr 4, 1:45 am–Apr 6, 2:46 am	4th	Pisces
Apr 12, 4:07 am–Apr 14, 8:53 am	1st	Cancer
Apr 21, 8:17 pm–Apr 24, 8:46 am	2nd	Scorpio
Apr 24, 8:46 am–Apr 26, 7:54 pm	3rd	Sagittarius
May 1, 10:33 am–May 3, 1:04 pm	4th	Pisces
May 9, 1:24 pm–May 11, 5:32 pm	1st	Cancer
May 19, 2:29 pm–May 21, 2:48 pm	2nd	Scorpio
May 21, 2:48 pm–May 24, 1:34 am	2nd	Sagittarius
May 28, 5:06 pm–May 30, 9:09 pm	3rd	Pisces
Jun 5, 11:41 pm–Jun 8, 2:47 am	1st	Cancer
Jun 15, 9:18 am–Jun 17, 9:34 pm	2nd	Scorpio
Jun 17, 9:34 pm–Jun 20, 7:55 pm	2nd	Sagittarius
Jun 24, 10:30 pm–Jun 27, 3:08 am	3rd	Pisces
Jun 27, 3:08 am–Jun 29, 6:03 am	3rd	Aries
Jul 3, 9:20 am–Jul 5, 12:28 pm	4th	Cancer
Jul 12, 4:52 pm–Jul 15, 5:14 am	2nd	Scorpio
Jul 15, 5:14 am–Jul 17, 3:33 pm	2nd	Sagittarius
Jul 22, 4:35 am–Jul 24, 8:33 am	3rd	Pisces
Jul 24, 8:33 am–Jul 26, 11:37 am	3rd	Aries
Jul 30, 5:09 pm–Aug 1, 9:12 pm	4th	Cancer
Aug 9, 12:51 am–Aug 11, 1:24 pm	1st	Scorpio
Aug 11, 1:24 pm–Aug 14, 12:11 am	2nd	Sagittarius
Aug 18, 12:34 pm–Aug 20, 3:18 pm	3rd	Pisces
Aug 20, 3:18 pm–Aug 22, 5:19 pm	3rd	Aries
Aug 26, 11:06 pm–Aug 29, 4:11 am	4th	Cancer
Sep 5, 8:38 am–Sep 7, 9:20 pm	1st	Scorpio
Sep 14, 10:23 pm–Sep 17, 12:22 am	2nd	Pisces
Sep 17, 12:22 am–Sep 19, 12:58 am	3rd	Aries
Sep 23, 4:33 am–Sep 25, 9:48 am	3rd	Cancer
Oct 2, 3:43 pm–Oct 5, 4:26 am	1st	Scorpio
Oct 12, 8:43 am–Oct 14, 11:08 am	2nd	Pisces
Oct 14, 11:08 am–Oct 16, 11:04 am	2nd	Aries
Oct 20, 11:28 am–Oct 22, 3:34 pm	3rd	Cancer
Oct 29, 10:01 pm–Nov 1, 10:43 am	4th	Scorpio
Nov 8, 4:45 pm–Nov 10, 8:45 pm	2nd	Pisces
Nov 10, 8:45 pm–Nov 12, 9:24 pm	2nd	Aries
Nov 16, 7:57 pm–Nov 18, 10:14 pm	3rd	Cancer
Nov 26, 3:01 am–Nov 28, 3:46 pm	4th	Scorpio
Dec 5, 11:31 pm–Dec 8, 5:15 am	1st	Pisces
Dec 8, 5:15 am–Dec 10, 7:41 am	2nd	Aries
Dec 14, 7:09 am–Dec 16, 8:15 am	3rd	Cancer
Dec 23, 9:32 am–Dec 25, 10:19 pm	4th	Scorpio

Dates to Destroy Weeds and Pests

Date	Sign	Qtr.
Jan 6, 1:56 am–Jan 8, 10:07 am	Sagittarius	4th
Jan 23, 8:46 pm–Jan 25, 10:46 pm	Leo	3rd
Jan 25, 10:46 pm–Jan 28, 9:59 am	Virgo	3rd
Feb 2, 10:50 am–Feb 4, 7:44 pm	Sagittarius	4th
Feb 7, 12:59 am–Feb 8, 9:39 am	Aquarius	4th
Feb 22, 1:20 pm–Feb 24, 5:41 pm	Virgo	3rd
Feb 29, 6:56 pm–Mar 1, 6:11 pm	Sagittarius	3rd
Mar 1, 6:11 pm–Mar 3, 5:01 am	Sagittarius	4th
Mar 5, 11:22 am–Mar 7, 2:08 pm	Aquarius	4th
Mar 28, 2:46 am–Mar 30, 1:45 pm	Sagittarius	3rd
Apr 1, 9:37 pm–Apr 4, 1:45 am	Aquarius	4th
Apr 6, 2:46 am–Apr 7, 7:24 am	Aries	4th
Apr 24, 8:46 am–Apr 26, 7:54 pm	Sagittarius	3rd
Apr 29, 4:47 am–Apr 29, 11:29 pm	Aquarius	3rd
April 29, 11:29 pm–May 1, 10:33 am	Aquarius	4th
May 3, 1:04 pm–May 5, 1:10 pm	Aries	4th
May 21, 5:14 pm–May 24, 1:34 am	Sagittarius	3rd
May 26, 10:27 am–May 28, 5:06 pm	Aquarius	3rd
May 30, 9:09 pm–Jun 1, 10:46 pm	Aries	4th
Jun 3, 11:01 pm–Jun 4, 11:00 pm	Gemini	4th
Jun 20, 7:02 am–Jun 20, 7:55 am	Sagittarius	3rd
Jun 22, 4:08 pm–Jun 24, 10:30 pm	Aquarius	3rd
Jun 27, 3:08 am–Jun 27, 2:19 pm	Aries	3rd
Jun 27, 2:19 pm–Jun 29, 6:03 am	Aries	4th
Jul 1, 7:44 am–Jul 3, 9:20 am	Gemini	4th
Jul 19, 11:10 pm–Jul 22, 4:35 am	Aquarius	3rd
Jul 24, 8:33 am–Jul 26, 11:37 am	Aries	3rd
Jul 28, 2:17 pm–Jul 30, 5:09 pm	Gemini	4th
Aug 1, 9:12 pm–Aug 2, 4:45 pm	Leo	4th
Aug 18, 5:27 am–Aug 18, 12:34 pm	Aquarius	3rd
Aug 20, 3:18 pm–Aug 22, 5:19 pm	Aries	3rd
Aug 24, 7:40 pm–Aug 24, 11:41 pm	Gemini	3rd
Aug 24, 11:41 pm–Aug 26, 11:06 pm	Gemini	4th
Aug 29, 4:11 am–Aug 31, 11:22 am	Leo	4th
Aug 31, 11:22 am–Sep 1, 5:03 am	Virgo	4th
Sep 16, 12:22 pm–Sep 18, 12:58 pm	Aries	3rd
Sep 21, 1:53 am–Sep 23, 4:33 am	Gemini	3rd
Sep 25, 9:48 am–Sep 27, 5:43 pm	Leo	4th
Sep 27, 5:43 pm–Sep 30, 3:52 am	Virgo	4th
Oct 15, 12:23 am–Oct 16, 11:04 am	Aries	3rd
Oct 18, 10:30 am–Oct 20, 11:28 am	Gemini	3rd
Oct 22, 3:34 pm–Oct 24, 11:16 pm	Leo	4th
Oct 24, 11:16 pm–Oct 27, 9:51 am	Virgo	4th
Nov 14, 8:23 pm–Nov 16, 7:57 pm	Gemini	3rd
Nov 18, 10:14 pm–Nov 21, 3:33 am	Leo	3rd
Nov 21, 3:33 am–Nov 21, 4:34 am	Leo	4th
Nov 21, 4:34 am–Nov 23, 2:42 pm	Virgo	4th
Nov 28, 3:46 pm–Nov 29, 7:18 am	Sagittarius	4th
Dec 13, 7:06 pm–Dec 14, 7:09 am	Gemini	3rd
Dec 16, 8:15 am–Dec 18, 12:52 pm	Leo	3rd
Dec 18, 12:52 pm–Dec 20, 8:56 pm	Virgo	3rd
Dec 20, 8:56 pm–Dec 20, 9:40 pm	Virgo	4th
Dec 25, 10:19 pm–Dec 28, 10:12 am	Sagittarius	4th

Time Zone Map

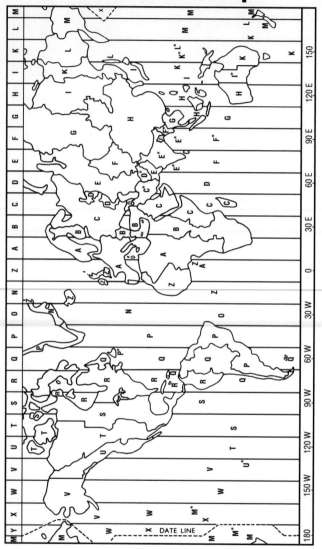

Time Zone Conversions

(R) EST—Used in book
(S) CST—Subtract 1 hour
(T) MST—Subtract 2 hours
(U) PST—Subtract 3 hours
(V) Subtract 4 hours
(V*) Subtract 4½ hours
(U*) Subtract 3½ hours
(W) Subtract 5 hours
(X) Subtract 6 hours
(Y) Subtract 7 hours
(Q) Add 1 hour
(P) Add 2 hours
(P*) Add 2½ hours
(O) Add 3 hours
(N) Add 4 hours
(Z) Add 5 hours
(A) Add 6 hours
(B) Add 7 hours
(C) Add 8 hours
(C*) Add 8½ hours

(D) Add 9 hours
(D*) Add 9½ hours
(E) Add 10 hours
(E*) Add 10½ hours
(F) Add 11 hours
(F*) Add 11½ hours
(G) Add 12 hours
(H) Add 13 hours
(I) Add 14 hours
(I*) Add 14½ hours
(K) Add 15 hours
(K*) Add 15½ hours
(L) Add 16 hours
(L*) Add 16½ hours
(M) Add 17 hours
(M*) Add 18 hours
(P*) Add 2½ hours

Important!

All times given in the *Moon Sign Book* are set in Eastern Time. The conversions shown here are for standard times only. Use the time zone conversions map and table to calculate the difference in your time zone. You must make the adjustment for your time zone and adjust for Daylight Saving Time where applicable.

Weather, Economic & Lunar Forecasts

Forecasting the Weather

by Kris Brandt Riske

Astrometeorology—astrological weather forecasting—reveals seasonal and weekly weather trends based on the cardinal ingresses (Summer and Winter Solstices, and Spring and Autumn Equinoxes) and the four monthly lunar phases. The planetary alignments and the longitudes and latitudes they influence have the strongest effect, but the zodiacal signs are also involved in creating weather conditions.

The components of a thunderstorm, for example, are heat, wind, and electricity. A Mars-Jupiter configuration generates the necessary heat and Mercury adds wind and electricity. A severe thunderstorm, and those that produce tornados, usually involve Mercury, Mars, Uranus, or Neptune. The zodiacal signs add their energy to the planetary mix to increase or decrease the chance of weather phenomena and their severity.

In general, the fire signs (Aries, Leo, Sagittarius) indicate heat and dryness, both of which peak when Mars, the planet with a similar nature, is in these signs. Water signs (Cancer, Scorpio, Pisces) are conducive to precipitation, and air signs (Gemini, Libra, Aquarius) to cool temperatures and wind. Earth signs (Taurus, Virgo, Capricorn) vary from wet to dry, heat to cold. The signs and their prevailing weather conditions are listed here:

Aries: Heat, dry, wind
Taurus: Moderate temperatures, precipitation
Gemini: Cool temperatures, wind, dry
Cancer: Cold, steady precipitation
Leo: Heat, dry, lightning
Virgo: Cold, dry, windy
Libra: Cool, windy, fair
Scorpio: Extreme temperatures, abundant precipitation
Sagittarius: Warm, fair, moderate wind
Capricorn: Cold, wet, damp
Aquarius: Cold, dry, high pressure, lightning
Pisces: Wet, cool, low pressure

Take note of the Moon's sign at each lunar phase. It reveals the prevailing weather conditions for the next six to seven days. The same is true of Mercury and Venus. These two influential weather planets transit the entire zodiac each year, unless retrograde patterns add their influence.

Planetary Influences

People relied on astrology to forecast weather for thousands of years. They were able to predict drought, floods, and temperature variations through interpreting planetary alignments. In recent years there has been a renewed interest in astrometeorology. A weather forecast can be composed for any date—tomorrow, next week, or a thousand years in the future. According to astrometeorology, each planet governs certain weather phenomena. When certain planets are aligned with other planets, weather—precipitation, cloudy or clear skies, tornados, hurricanes, and other conditions—are generated.

Sun and Moon

The Sun governs the constitution of the weather and, like the Moon, it serves as a trigger for other planetary configurations that result in weather events. When the Sun is prominent in a cardinal ingress or lunar phase chart, the area is often warm and sunny. The Moon can bring or withhold moisture, depending upon its sign placement.

Mercury

Mercury is also a triggering planet, but its main influence is wind direction and velocity. In its stationary periods, Mercury reflects high winds, and its influence is always prominent in major weather events, such as hurricanes and tornadoes, when it tends to lower the temperature.

Venus

Venus governs moisture, clouds, and humidity. It brings warming trends that produce sunny, pleasant weather if in positive aspect to other planets. In some signs—Libra, Virgo, Gemini, Sagittarius—Venus is drier. It is at its wettest when placed in Cancer, Scorpio, Pisces, or Taurus.

Mars

Mars is associated with heat, drought, and wind, and can raise the temperature to record-setting levels when in a fire sign (Aries, Leo, Sagittarius). Mars is also the planet that provides the spark that generates thunderstorms and is prominent in tornado and hurricane configurations.

Jupiter

Jupiter, a fair-weather planet, tends toward higher temperatures when in Aries, Leo, or Sagittarius. It is associated with high-pressure systems and is a contributing factor at times to dryness. Storms are often amplified by Jupiter.

Saturn

Saturn is associated with low-pressure systems, cloudy to over-cast skies, and excessive precipitation. Temperatures drop when Saturn is involved. Major winter storms always have a strong Saturn influence, as do storms that produce a slow, steady downpour for hours or days.

Uranus

Like Jupiter, Uranus indicates high-pressure systems. It reflects descending cold air and, when prominent, is responsible for a jet stream that extends far south. Uranus can bring drought in winter, and it is involved in thunderstorms, tornados, and hurricanes.

Neptune

Neptune is the wettest planet. It signals low-pressure systems and is dominant when hurricanes are in the forecast. When Neptune is strongly placed, flood danger is high. It's often associated with winter thaws. Temperatures, humidity, and cloudiness increase where Neptune influences weather.

Pluto

Pluto is associated with weather extremes, as well as unseasonably warm temperatures and drought. It reflects the high winds involved in major hurricanes, storms, and tornados.

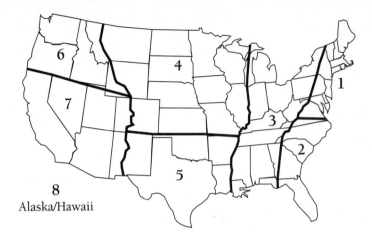

Weather Forecast for 2016

by Kris Brandt Riske

Winter

Winter precipitation in Zone 1 will be average to above along with temperatures ranging from seasonal to below. In Zone 2, winter weather will be mostly seasonal with average to below precipitation. Zone 3 will see average precipitation along with temperatures ranging from seasonal to below and windy conditions.

Abundant precipitation, which can lead to flooding, will be a prominent theme in Zones 4, 5, and 6, with low-pressure systems and notable winter storms, and temperatures ranging from seasonal to below. Precipitation in Zone 6 will be average to above along with seasonal temperatures. Western and central areas of Zone 7 will see average to above-average precipitation levels, while eastern parts of the zone will be drier; temperatures will range from seasonal to above.

In Zone 8, Alaskan temperatures will range from seasonal to below with average precipitation, and Hawaii will be windy with average precipitation and temperatures seasonal to above.

Fourth Quarter Moon, January 2–8

Zone 1: Temperatures are seasonal to below, northern areas see precipitation, some locally heavy later in the week, including a possible blizzard.

Zone 2: Northern areas see precipitation later in the week, possibly a blizzard, and much of the zone is cold with variably cloudy skies central and south.

Zone 3: Skies are partly cloudy to cloudy, eastern areas are cold and windy with precipitation, some locally heavy, and western and central areas are seasonal.

Zone 4: Northwestern parts of the zone are cold and stormy, other areas are fair to partly cloudy and seasonal to above, central areas are windy, and eastern parts of the zone see scattered precipitation.

Zone 5: Skies are mostly fair, eastern areas are windy, and temperatures are seasonal to above.

Zone 6: Much of the zone is stormy and overcast with abundant precipitation and temperatures seasonal to below.

Zone 7: Abundant precipitation in western areas moves into central parts of the zone, temperatures are seasonal to below, and northern mountain locations could see blizzard conditions.

Zone 8: Alaska—Windy as a front moves through central areas and into eastern parts of the state, western areas are fair, and temperatures range from seasonal to below. Hawaii—Mostly fair to partly cloudy with temperatures ranging from seasonal to above, and thunderstorms and windy conditions in central areas.

New Moon, January 9–15

Zone 1: Northern parts are cloudy with abundant precipitation, southern areas are partly cloudy and windy with scattered precipitation, and temperatures are seasonal to below.

Zone 2: The zone is mostly fair to partly cloudy, northern areas are seasonal to below with scattered precipitation, and central and southern parts are seasonal.

Zone 3: Skies are fair to partly cloudy and temperatures are seasonal to below.

Zone 4: Western parts of the zone are cloudy and windy with precipitation, some abundant, central and eastern areas are partly cloudy with a chance for precipitation, and temperatures are seasonal to below.

Zone 5: Temperatures are seasonal, western and central areas are windy and cloudy with precipitation, and eastern parts are partly cloudy.

Zone 6: Variably cloudy and seasonal, but cold and windy in the central area with precipitation later in the week, when western areas see scattered precipitation and eastern areas are windy with precipitation; central parts of the zone could see stormy conditions.

Zone 7: Skies are windy and fair to partly cloudy, temperatures are seasonal to above, and has a chance for precipitation.

Zone 8: Alaska—Variably cloudy and seasonal, western areas are fair, and central and eastern areas see precipitation, some abundant. Hawaii—Temperatures are seasonal, western and central parts of the state are partly cloudy, and eastern areas see precipitation, some locally heavy.

Second Quarter Moon, January 16–22

Zone 1: Windy, mostly cloudy, and seasonal with precipitation.

Zone 2: Temperatures are seasonal to above, much of the zone sees precipitation under variably cloudy skies, and some areas experience strong winds.

Zone 3: Western and central parts are stormy and windy, and some western areas could see strong thunderstorms with high winds and tornado potential, eastern areas are windy with scattered precipitation, and temperatures are seasonal.

Zone 4: Temperatures range from seasonal to below, western areas are windy with a chance for precipitation, and eastern areas are cold with storm potential.

Zone 5: A front moves through much of the zone, which is windy; central areas could see local heavy precipitation and strong thunderstorms and tornados, and eastern areas are cloudy with precipitation and storms later in the week.

Zone 6: Mostly cloudy and seasonal to below with precipitation.

Zone 7: Western, central, and northeastern parts are seasonal and windy with precipitation, and eastern desert areas are fair to partly cloudy and seasonal to above.

Zone 8: Alaska—Temperatures range from seasonal to below, western and eastern areas are fair to partly cloudy, and central areas are cloudy with precipitation. Hawaii—Seasonal, windy, and partly cloudy to cloudy with scattered showers and thunderstorms.

Full Moon, January 23–30

Zone 1: Temperatures are seasonal to below, skies are overcast, and zone sees precipitation, heaviest in the south.

Zone 2: Windy overcast skies and precipitation, some abundant central and south with flooding potential; northern areas are cold, and central and southern areas are seasonal.

Zone 3: Much of the zone sees precipitation with the heaviest central and east along with flood potential, conditions are windy, southern areas could see strong thunderstorms with tornados.

Zone 4: Skies are variably cloudy and much of the zone is windy with scattered precipitation; strong thunderstorms with tornado potential and heavy precipitation could result in flooding.

Zone 5: Temperatures range from seasonal to below, eastern areas could see strong thunderstorms with high winds and tornado potential, skies are variably cloudy, and western and central parts have a chance for precipitation.

Zone 6: Western skies are cloudy with precipitation, central and eastern areas are partly cloudy with scattered precipitation, eastern areas are windy with precipitation later in the week, and temperatures are seasonal.

Zone 7: Variably cloudy and windy with scattered precipitation west and a chance for precipitation and thunderstorms central and east, temperatures are seasonal to above.

Zone 8: Alaska—Eastern Alaska is windy and seasonal with precipitation, and western and central areas are fair to partly cloudy. Hawaii—Generally fair with temperatures ranging from seasonal to above and central areas see showers.

Fourth Quarter Moon, January 31–February 7

Zone 1: Cold, windy, and stormy with blizzard potential and heaviest precipitation in northern areas.

Zone 2: Northern areas are windy and stormy with blizzard potential, skies are cloudy, temperatures range from seasonal to below; central and southern areas see locally heavy precipitation.

Zone 3: Much of the zone is windy, central and eastern areas see precipitation, eastern parts have blizzard potential, western areas are mostly fair, and temperatures range from seasonal to below.

Zone 4: Western skies are cloudy with precipitation, central and eastern skies are fair to partly cloudy with a chance for precipitation, and temperatures are seasonal to above.

Zone 5: Skies are windy and fair to partly cloudy, and temperatures range from seasonal to above.

Zone 6: Much of the zone is windy and partly cloudy to cloudy, eastern areas are overcast with precipitation, some abundant with flood potential, and temperatures are seasonal to below.

Zone 7: Windy with abundant precipitation, cloudy skies, and temperatures ranging from seasonal to below.

Zone 8: Alaska—Western and central parts see precipitation under cloudy skies, eastern areas are fair, and temperatures range from seasonal to below. Hawaii—Partly cloudy to cloudy and seasonal to below with showers west and central.

New Moon, February 8–14

Zone 1: Temperatures range from seasonal to below and cloudy skies bring precipitation across the zone.

Zone 2: Skies are variably cloudy, northern areas see precipitation, central and southern parts see scattered precipitation; temperatures are seasonal, but warmer south.

Zone 3: Western and central parts are fair to partly cloudy, temperatures are seasonal, and eastern areas see precipitation followed by clearing and colder temperatures.

Zone 4: Much of the zone is cloudy with precipitation in central areas, some locally heavy, eastern parts are mostly fair, and temperatures range from seasonal to below.

Zone 5: Variably cloudy with a chance for precipitation in central areas, fair to partly cloudy east, more cloudiness west with precipitation later in the week, and temperatures are seasonal to above.

Zone 6: Eastern areas are windy with precipitation, some locally heavy with flood potential, temperatures are seasonal, and western and central parts are fair to partly cloudy.

Zone 7: Variably cloudy skies accompany windy conditions, seasonal temperatures, and precipitation in eastern areas.

Zone 8: Alaska—Temperatures are seasonal, eastern skies are fair, and western and central parts of the state see precipitation. Hawaii—Much of Hawaii is windy with showers, some locally heavy, skies are partly cloudy to cloudy, temperatures are seasonal.

Second Quarter Moon, February 15–21

Zone 1: Cloudy and windy with precipitation and temperatures ranging from seasonal to below.

Zone 2: Much of the zone is cloudy with precipitation and temperatures range from seasonal to below.

Zone 3: Skies are partly cloudy to cloudy with precipitation and a chance for thunderstorms; central areas could see flooding, and temperatures are seasonal to above.

Zone 4: Western and central parts are windy, central areas see precipitation, some abundant with flooding potential; temperatures are seasonal to above but colder east, which sees precipitation later in the week with flooding potential.

Zone 5: Western skies are windy and fair, central and eastern parts are variably cloudy with precipitation, some abundant with flooding potential, temperatures range from seasonal to above.

Zone 6: Central parts see scattered precipitation, skies are mostly fair to partly cloudy, and temperatures range from seasonal to above.

Zone 7: Windy and fair to partly cloudy with temperatures ranging from seasonal to above.

Zone 8: Alaska—Central Alaska is cold and windy with precipitation, eastern areas see precipitation, western skies are fair, and temperatures west and east are seasonal. Hawaii—Windy and partly cloudy with temperatures ranging from seasonal to above.

Full Moon, February 22–29

Zone 1: Windy and partly cloudy with temperatures ranging from seasonal to below, southern areas see scattered precipitation, and northern parts see precipitation later in the week.

Zone 2: Much of the zone is cloudy with temperatures ranging from seasonal to below and precipitation later in the week.

Zone 3: Western and central parts see abundant precipitation with flooding potential, eastern areas see precipitation later in the week, skies are mostly cloudy, and temperatures are seasonal.

Zone 4: Temperatures range from seasonal to below and skies are variably cloudy with precipitation, some abundant that could result in flooding in eastern areas.

Zone 5: Western parts are cloudy with abundant precipitation later in the week, central and eastern areas are windy and cloudy with precipitation and strong thunderstorms are possible, temperatures range from seasonal to below.

Zone 6: Partly cloudy to cloudy and windy with temperatures ranging from seasonal to below; some central and eastern areas see heavy precipitation with flooding potential.

Zone 7: Temperatures range from seasonal to below and the zone is windy with precipitation and variably cloudy skies, northeastern areas see heavy precipitation that could result in flooding, and eastern desert areas have a chance for showers.

Zone 8: Alaska—Windy with temperatures ranging from seasonal to below, western and central areas see precipitation, and eastern areas are fair. Hawaii—Seasonal and wind with showers.

Fourth Quarter Moon, March 1–7

Zone 1: Overcast skies are windy, temperatures are seasonal to below, and the zone sees precipitation from what could be a major storm.

Zone 2: Abundant precipitation and flood potential across the zone is heaviest north, along with variably cloudy skies and seasonal temperatures.

Zone 3: Temperatures range from seasonal to below, western parts of the zone see abundant precipitation, possibly from strong thunderstorms, skies are variably cloudy, and eastern areas see abundant precipitation later in the week that could cause flooding.

Zone 4: Skies are variably cloudy and windy, temperatures are seasonal to below, and front brings precipitation to western and central areas, some locally heavy.

Zone 5: Much of the zone sees precipitation, possibly from strong thunderstorms, skies are variably cloudy, and temperatures are seasonal to below.

Zone 6: Western parts are fair to partly cloudy, central areas are cloudy with abundant precipitation, eastern areas are partly cloudy with precipitation, and temperatures are seasonal to below.

Zone 7: Northeastern parts see precipitation early in the week, temperatures are seasonal, skies are partly cloudy to cloudy, and western and central areas see precipitation later in the week with a chance in the east.

Zone 8: Alaska—Central Alaska is fair, eastern and western areas see precipitation, some locally heavy, skies are variably cloudy, and temperatures are seasonal. Hawaii—Fair to partly cloudy and seasonal with scattered showers.

New Moon, March 8–14

Zone 1: Windy, mostly cloudy, and seasonal to below, and a low pressure system brings stormy conditions with heavy precipitation later in the week.

Zone 2: Much of the zone sees precipitation, some locally heavy with flooding potential, temperatures are seasonal, central and southern areas see strong thunderstorms with tornado potential.

Zone 3: Temperatures are seasonal to below, western and central areas see strong storms with high winds and tornado potential, abundant precipitation in the east could result in flooding.

Zone 4: Skies are fair to partly cloudy west and central, eastern areas are cloudy and could see strong thunderstorms with tornado potential and heavy precipitation; temperatures are seasonal but colder east.

Zone 5: Much of the zone is fair to partly cloudy and seasonal to above, eastern areas see locally heavy precipitation along with potential for strong thunderstorms with tornados.

Zone 6: Western and central parts are cloudy with precipitation, some abundant that could result in flooding, eastern areas are partly cloudy with a chance for precipitation, and temperatures range from seasonal to below.

Zone 7: Temperatures are seasonal to below, western and central parts are cloudy with abundant precipitation, and eastern areas are fair to partly cloudy with a chance for precipitation.

Zone 8: Alaska—Fair to partly cloudy and seasonal with more cloudiness and precipitation east.

Second Quarter Moon, March 15–22

Zone 1: Skies are variably cloudy and temperatures are seasonal to below with precipitation.

Zone 2: Much of the zone sees scattered precipitation, including thunderstorm potential in central and southern areas, temperatures are seasonal, and skies are variably cloudy.

Zone 3: Abundant precipitation and thunderstorms with tornado potential could result in flooding in western and central parts of the zone, eastern skies are fair to partly cloudy, and temperatures range from seasonal to below.

Zone 4: Much of the zone is windy and seasonal, western areas are partly cloudy, eastern areas see scattered thunderstorms and showers along with potential flooding.

Zone 5: Abundant precipitation is possible in western parts of the zone, strong thunderstorms with tornado potential are possible in eastern areas, skies are variably cloudy, and temperatures are seasonal.

Zone 6: Western areas are fair to partly cloudy, central and eastern parts see more cloudiness along with precipitation, some locally heavy, and temperatures are seasonal.

Zone 7: Much of the zone is partly cloudy, northern coastal areas see scattered precipitation, eastern parts are variably cloudy with locally heavy precipitation northeast, and temperatures are seasonal to above.

Zone 8: Alaska—Variably cloudy and windy with scattered precipitation and seasonal temperatures. Hawaii—Temperatures range from seasonal to above, skies are variably cloudy, and the state sees scattered showers and thunderstorms.

Spring

Zones 1 is windy this spring with temperatures ranging from seasonal to below with above-average precipitation. Northern parts of Zone 2 will experience similar weather, while central and southern areas will be warmer with precipitation ranging from seasonal to above. Western and central parts of Zone 3 will see abundant precipitation and cool temperatures along with a high potential for flooding; eastern areas will be seasonal with average precipitation.

Although all of Zones 4 and 5 have potential for flooding, eastern areas have an increased tendency along with strong thunderstorms and tornados; temperatures will range from seasonal to below. Zone 6 will tend toward dryness with temperatures ranging from seasonal to above. In Zone 7 precipitation and temperatures will be seasonal in western areas, but precipitation will be below average and temperatures above average in the central and east areas.

Alaska will be seasonal with below-average precipitation, except in eastern areas where more precipitation and cooler temperatures will prevail. Temperatures in Hawaii will range from seasonal to above with periods of high winds and precipitation levels below average.

Full Moon, March 23–30

Zone 1: Cold temperatures and variably cloudy skies accompany precipitation; potential for a major storm.

Zone 2: Northern areas are cold with precipitation, possibly a major storm, central and southern areas are seasonal to below with precipitation, and potential for stormy conditions.

Zone 3: Eastern parts could see storm conditions, western areas are windy, and an advancing front brings precipitation to much of the zone, and temperatures range from seasonal to below.

Zone 4: Precipitation in the west moves into central parts, bringing locally heavy downfall under cloudy skies, eastern areas are partly cloudy with precipitation later in the week, and temperatures range from seasonal to below.

Zone 5: Much of the zone is cloudy with precipitation, some abundant along with a chance for strong thunderstorms with tornado potential, and temperatures are seasonal to below.

Zone 6: Skies are variably cloudy and windy, temperatures are seasonal to below, and much of the zone sees precipitation.

Zone 7: Eastern parts see precipitation, western and central areas are windy and fair to partly cloudy with a chance for precipitation, and temperatures are seasonal to above.

Zone 8: Alaska—Much of Alaska is cloudy with precipitation, which is heaviest in central areas, and temperatures are seasonal. Hawaii—Fair to partly cloudy, temperatures are seasonal, and central and eastern parts of the state see showers.

Fourth Quarter Moon, March 31–April 6

Zone 1: Temperatures range from seasonal to below along with cloudy skies and precipitation, some locally heavy and possibly from a major storm.

Zone 2: Much of the zone is windy with precipitation and partly cloudy to cloudy skies, temperatures are seasonal to below; strong thunderstorms with tornado potential are possible in the central and south.

Zone 3: Temperatures are seasonal to below, western areas see scattered precipitation, central areas could see strong thunderstorms with tornado potential, eastern areas are windy with locally heavy precipitation and possible stormy conditions.

Zone 4: Western areas see scattered precipitation, central and eastern parts could see strong thunderstorms with tornado potential, temperatures are seasonal to below, and skies are variably cloudy.

Zone 5: Fair to partly cloudy with a chance of precipitation in the

west; thunderstorms with locally heavy precipitation and tornado potential central and east, and seasonal temperatures.

Zone 6: Much of the zone is cloudy with temperatures seasonal to below and locally heavy precipitation.

Zone 7: Temperatures are seasonal to above under fair to partly cloudy skies, and western parts have a chance for precipitation.

Zone 8: Alaska—Partly cloudy to cloudy and seasonal with precipitation central and east later in the week. Hawaii—Skies are variably cloudy, temperatures are seasonal, and central and eastern areas see showers.

New Moon, April 7–12

Zone 1: Temperatures are seasonal to below, skies are partly cloudy to cloudy, and much of the zone sees precipitation.

Zone 2: Northern areas are cloudy with precipitation, central and southern parts are windy with thunderstorms, some strong with tornado potential and locally heavy precipitation, temperatures are seasonal to below.

Zone 3: Western and central parts are windy with scattered showers and thunderstorms, some strong with tornado potential and locally heavy precipitation, eastern areas are windy and cloudy with precipitation, temperatures are seasonal to below.

Zone 4: Skies are cloudy in the west and then clearing and colder; precipitation in central areas moves into eastern parts, temperatures are seasonal to below and skies are variably cloudy.

Zone 5: The zone is partly cloudy to cloudy with precipitation and seasonal temperatures.

Zone 6: Much of the zone sees precipitation, some locally heavy with possible flooding in central areas, temperatures are seasonal.

Zone 7: Skies are partly cloudy to cloudy with scattered showers and thunderstorms, along with locally heavy precipitation, temperatures range from seasonal to above.

Zone 8: Alaska—Variably cloudy with temperatures ranging from seasonal to below and central areas are windy with precipitation that moves into eastern parts of the state. Hawaii—Partly cloudy to cloudy and windy with temperatures ranging from seasonal to below and scattered showers and thunderstorms, some strong.

Second Quarter Moon, April 13–21

Zone 1: Much of the zone sees precipitation under partly cloudy to cloudy skies and temperatures ranging from seasonal to below.

Zone 2: Northern areas are partly cloudy to cloudy with precipitation, temperatures are seasonal, central and southern parts see thunderstorms, possibly strong with tornado potential.

Zone 3: Skies are variably cloudy and temperatures are seasonal but cooler east; central parts could see strong thunderstorms with locally heavy precipitation and tornado potential.

Zone 4: Temperatures range from seasonal to below and skies are variably cloudy with showers and thunderstorms with tornado potential; locally heavy precipitation in the central area could result in flooding.

Zone 5: Showers and thunderstorms across the zone, some with tornado potential, accompany seasonal temperatures and variably cloudy skies.

Zone 6: Windy with precipitation central and east, scattered precipitation west, seasonal temperatures, and partly cloudy to cloudy skies.

Zone 7: Skies are fair to partly cloudy, temperatures are seasonal to above, and eastern areas have a chance for precipitation.

Zone 8: Alaska—Central areas of the state are windy and cloudy with precipitation, western and eastern areas are fair to partly cloudy, temperatures are seasonal. Hawaii—Windy, seasonal, and variably cloudy with showers central and east.

Full Moon, April 22–28

Zone 1: Temperatures range from seasonal to below and skies are partly cloudy to cloudy with scattered precipitation.

Zone 2: Much of the zone is partly cloudy to cloudy and seasonal with scattered showers.

Zone 3: Western and central areas see precipitation, some locally heavy, along with potential for strong thunderstorms with tornados, temperatures are seasonal to below, skies are variably cloudy and windy, and eastern areas see scattered precipitation.

Zone 4: Much of the zone is cloudy with precipitation and temperatures ranging from seasonal to below; precipitation is heaviest in eastern areas along with flooding potential, stormy conditions, and strong thunderstorms with tornados.

Zone 5: Western parts are windy with scattered thunderstorms and fair to partly cloudy skies, eastern areas could see strong thunderstorms with tornados and locally heavy precipitation along with more cloudiness; temperatures range from seasonal to below.

Zone 6: Much of the zone is overcast with precipitation, some locally heavy, temperatures range from seasonal to below.

Zone 7: Abundant precipitation is possible in western and central parts, which are cloudy and windy; eastern areas are partly cloudy, temperatures range from seasonal to above.

Zone 8: Alaska—Windy with precipitation, some locally heavy in central areas, temperatures are seasonal to below. Hawaii—Partly cloudy to cloudy with precipitation and seasonal temperatures.

Fourth Quarter Moon, April 29–May 5

Zone 1: Temperatures range from seasonal to below and skies are windy and partly cloudy with scattered precipitation.

Zone 2: Skies are partly cloudy to cloudy with showers and scattered thunderstorms, some strong with tornado potential in central parts of the zone, and temperatures are seasonal.

Zone 3: Partly cloudy to cloudy with scattered showers and thunderstorms and seasonal temperatures.

Zone 4: Central and eastern parts are fair to partly cloudy with scattered thunderstorms, some with locally heavy precipitation that could result in flooding, temperatures are seasonal, and western areas are cloudy with precipitation.

Zone 5: Western skies are cloudy with abundant precipitation and flooding potential, central and eastern areas have potential for strong thunderstorms with tornados and locally heavy precipitation, temperatures range from seasonal to below.

Zone 6: Temperatures are seasonal, skies are variably cloudy and windy, and much of the zone sees scattered precipitation with potential for strong thunderstorms in eastern areas.

Zone 7: Windy with temperatures ranging from seasonal to above, western and central areas could see strong storms, and eastern areas see locally heavy precipitation from storms.

Zone 8: Alaska—Temperatures range from seasonal to below, skies are fair to partly cloudy and windy in the west, and central and eastern areas see precipitation. Hawaii—Variably cloudy and windy with temperatures ranging from seasonal to above; some areas see strong thunderstorms.

New Moon, May 6–12

Zone 1: Variably cloudy and seasonal with precipitation.

Zone 2: Northern areas are variably cloudy with precipitation, temperatures are seasonal, central and southern areas see more cloudiness along with locally heavy precipitation and possible strong thunderstorms with tornados.

Zone 3: Eastern parts are fair to partly cloudy with a chance for precipitation, temperatures are seasonal, western and central areas are partly cloudy to cloudy with locally heavy precipitation and flooding potential along with possible strong thunderstorms with tornados.

Zone 4: Western areas are windy and fair to partly cloudy with showers later in the week, temperatures are seasonal, central and eastern areas see more cloudiness and precipitation, some locally heavy with flooding potential.

Zone 5: Western and central parts are windy and fair, temperatures are seasonal to above, and strong thunderstorms with tornado potential are possible in eastern areas.

Zone 6: Precipitation moves across the zone during the week with the heaviest in eastern areas, temperatures are seasonal, and skies are partly cloudy to cloudy.

Zone 7: Windy and variably cloudy with temperatures ranging from seasonal to above and showers in central areas.

Zone 8: Alaska—Much of the state sees precipitation under variably cloudy skies, temperatures are seasonal. Hawaii—Fair to partly cloudy with scattered showers west and central; temperatures range from seasonal to above.

Second Quarter Moon, May 13–20

Zone 1: Skies are mostly fair, temperatures are seasonal, northern areas have a chance for thunderstorms.

Zone 2: Southern areas see showers and thunderstorms, northern and central parts are fair, and temperatures range from seasonal to above.

Zone 3: Variably cloudy and windy with seasonal temperatures, showers, and scattered thunderstorms.

Zone 4: Precipitation across the zone is heaviest in the west and central areas, skies are variably cloudy, and temperatures range from seasonal to below.

Zone 5: Skies are fair to partly cloudy, temperatures are seasonal to above, central areas could see abundant precipitation, and eastern parts have a chance for scattered thunderstorms.

Zone 6: Eastern parts have a chance for thunderstorms, skies are partly cloudy, temperatures range from seasonal to above.

Zone 7: Temperatures range from seasonal to above, skies are fair to partly cloudy, and eastern areas have a chance for storms.

Zone 8: Alaska—Western and eastern Alaska see precipitation, which is abundant east, central areas are fair to partly cloudy, and temperatures range from seasonal to above. Hawaii—Fair to partly cloudy and seasonal with showers in western areas.

Full Moon, May 21–28

Zone 1: Skies are fair to partly cloudy, conditions are humid, temperatures range from seasonal to above, and a chance for thunderstorms.

Zone 2: Humid with temperatures ranging from seasonal to above, skies are partly cloudy, much of the zone has a chance for showers and thunderstorms.

Zone 3: Western and central areas see thunderstorms, some strong with tornado potential, eastern areas are humid and cloudy, and temperatures range from seasonal to above.

Zone 4: Skies are fair to partly cloudy, temperatures range from seasonal to above, central parts have a chance for showers; eastern areas could see strong thunderstorms with tornado potential.

Zone 5: Temperatures range from seasonal to above under mostly fair skies, eastern areas are partly cloudy with scattered showers, central and eastern parts are humid with scattered showers and thunderstorms.

Zone 6: Partly cloudy with temperatures ranging from seasonal to above, and chance for precipitation in western areas.

Zone 7: Northern coastal areas see showers, eastern areas have a chance for precipitation, and the zone is mostly fair with temperatures ranging from seasonal to above.

Zone 8: Alaska—Partly cloudy and seasonal, windy in central areas, central and eastern parts of the state see scattered precipitation. Hawaii—Partly cloudy and windy with temperatures ranging from seasonal to above.

Fourth Quarter Moon, May 29–June 3

Zone 1: Skies are fair to partly cloudy, and temperatures are seasonal to above.

Zone 2: Fair with temperatures ranging from seasonal to above.

Zone 3: Western and central parts see abundant precipitation with flooding potential under cloudy skies, eastern areas are partly cloudy, and temperatures are seasonal to below.

Zone 4: Much of the zone is fair with temperatures ranging from seasonal to above, and eastern areas are cooler with locally heavy precipitation and flooding potential.

Zone 5: Skies are partly cloudy, temperatures range from seasonal to above, eastern areas are partly cloudy; western and central see precipitation, some abundant later in the week, along with strong thunderstorms with tornado potential and possible flooding.

Zone 6: Partly cloudy to cloudy with seasonal temperatures, central and eastern areas are windy with precipitation, some locally heavy with flooding potential.

Zone 7: Skies are fair to partly cloudy and windy, temperatures range from seasonal to above, and eastern areas have a chance for precipitation.

Zone 8: Alaska—Windy and fair to partly cloudy with temperatures ranging from seasonal to above. Hawaii—Temperatures seasonal to above and skies are windy and partly cloudy.

New Moon, June 4–11

Zone 1: A front brings precipitation across the zone under partly cloudy to cloudy skies with temperatures ranging from seasonal to below.

Zone 2: The zone is variably cloudy and humid with scattered thunderstorms central and south, and temperatures ranging from seasonal to above.

Zone 3: Much of the zone has a chance for showers and thunderstorms under generally partly cloudy skies with humidity, and temperatures ranging from seasonal to above.

Zone 4: Eastern areas see scattered thunderstorms, skies are fair to partly cloudy, and temperatures range from seasonal to above.

Zone 5: Variably cloudy skies, humidity, and temperatures ranging from seasonal to above accompany scattered thunderstorms in eastern areas, some strong with locally heavy precipitation.

Zone 6: Western skies are fair, temperatures range from seasonal to above, and central and eastern parts see more cloudiness with precipitation.

Zone 7: Partly cloudy with temperatures ranging from seasonal to above, and eastern areas have a chance for scattered thunderstorms.

Zone 8: Alaska—Precipitation in central parts of the state moves into eastern areas, western skies are fair, and temperatures are seasonal. Hawaii—Central and eastern Hawaii are windy with scattered thunderstorms, western areas are fair, and temperatures are seasonal.

Second Quarter Moon, June 12–19

Zone 1: Northern areas are cloudy with precipitation, some heavy later in the week, southern areas are partly cloudy with scattered showers, and temperatures are seasonal.

Zone 2: Skies are variably cloudy in the north with scattered precipitation, central and southern areas are partly cloudy to cloudy and humid with showers.

Zone 3: Temperatures range from seasonal to above, central and southern areas see scattered showers and thunderstorms, some strong with heavy precipitation that could result in flooding.

Zone 4: Skies are fair to partly cloudy, temperatures are seasonal to above, and central areas see scattered thunderstorms.

Zone 5: The zone is variably cloudy with temperatures ranging from seasonal to above and scattered thunderstorms.

Zone 6: Seasonal temperatures and variably cloudy skies accompany showers across the zone as the week progresses; precipitation in western areas is locally heavy.

Zone 7: Western and central parts see showers and scattered thunderstorms with a chance in eastern areas later in the week, and temperatures are seasonal to above.

Zone 8: Alaska—Partly cloudy to cloudy skies yields precipitation, some abundant in the west and central, eastern skies are fair to partly cloudy, and temperatures are seasonal to below. Hawaii—seasonal and partly cloudy to cloudy with showers in eastern areas.

Summer

Temperatures in Zones 1 and 2 will range from seasonal to above, along with a tendency toward dryness. Gulf coast areas of Zones 3 and 5 are prone to hurricanes this summer, and western and central areas of Zone 3 will be generally cooler and wetter with above-average potential for strong thunderstorms, locally heavy precipitation, and tornados. Eastern areas of Zone 3 will be seasonal with below-average precipitation. Zones 4 and 5 will experience above-average temperatures, as well as periods of dryness, and weeks with strong thunderstorms. Temperatures in Zone 6 will be seasonal with average precipitation in most areas.

Zone 7 will be generally seasonal with average precipitation, as will Alaska and Hawaii in Zone 8.

Full Moon, June 20–26

Zone 1: Humid and variably cloudy with temperatures ranging from seasonal to above, and showers and thunderstorms.

Zone 2: Skies are partly cloudy and the zone is humid with temperatures seasonal to above, and showers and thunderstorms.

Zone 3: Much of the zone is humid with showers and thunderstorms, some strong with tornado potential, western and central areas see locally heavy downfall with flooding potential, skies are variably cloudy, eastern areas are seasonal to above, western and central parts of the zone are cooler, and a tropical storm or hurricane is possible.

Zone 4: Western areas are fair to partly cloudy and seasonal to above with scattered thunderstorms, central and eastern parts are humid with strong thunderstorms with tornado potential and locally heavy downfall that could result in flooding, central and eastern areas are cooler with more cloudiness, and a tropical storm or hurricane possible.

Zone 5: Temperatures are seasonal to above with scattered thunderstorms west and central, eastern areas are humid with showers and thunderstorms, some strong with tornado potential and locally heavy downfall that could result in flooding, western and central parts are fair to partly cloudy, eastern areas are partly cloudy to cloudy, and a tropical storm or hurricane possible.

Zone 6: The zone is partly cloudy to cloudy, central areas see precipitation, some locally heavy, eastern areas windy with scattered thunderstorms, and temperatures are seasonal.

Zone 7: Eastern areas are humid with potential for strong thunderstorms, temperatures are seasonal, skies are partly cloudy to cloudy, and western and central parts have a chance for showers.

Zone 8: Alaska—Variably cloudy with precipitation, some locally heavy in the west and central, eastern areas are mostly fair, and temperatures are seasonal. Hawaii—Much of the state is humid with showers and thunderstorms, and temperatures are seasonal.

Fourth Quarter Moon, June 27–July 3

Zone 1: Humid, partly cloudy to cloudy, seasonal to above with showers and scattered thunderstorms.

Zone 2: Skies are variably cloudy, temperatures range from seasonal to above, and the zone sees scattered thunderstorms and showers later in the week.

Zone 3: Temperatures are seasonal to above, skies are partly cloudy and windy, and humid with showers and thunderstorms; especially in the west.

Zone 4: Skies are fair to partly cloudy and windy, temperatures are seasonal to above, and eastern parts see showers and thunderstorms, some possibly strong with high winds.

Zone 5: Fair to partly cloudy, temperatures range from seasonal to above, and eastern areas are windy with scattered thunderstorms, some possibly strong.

Zone 6: Western areas are cloudy and cool with locally heavy precipitation, central and eastern areas are partly cloudy to cloudy with temperatures seasonal to above and chance for precipitation.

Zone 7: Western and central parts are variably cloudy with scattered precipitation, eastern areas are fair to partly cloudy, and temperatures are seasonal to above.

Zone 8: Alaska—Fair to partly cloudy and seasonal with scattered precipitation; eastern areas are windy. Hawaii—Fair to partly cloudy and temperatures are seasonal.

New Moon, July 4–10

Zone 1: Humid, partly cloudy to cloudy, temperatures range from seasonal to above; northern areas see precipitation.

Zone 2: Skies are windy and partly cloudy to cloudy, temperatures are seasonal to above, and showers and scattered thunderstorms.

Zone 3: Temperatures are seasonal to above, conditions are humid, skies are fair to partly cloudy and windy, and eastern areas see precipitation later in the week.

Zone 4: Western parts are cloudy with precipitation, some locally heavy, central and eastern areas are fair to partly cloudy with scattered thunderstorms, and temperatures are seasonal to above, but cooler in the west.

Zone 5: Skies are partly cloudy to cloudy, temperatures range from seasonal to above, eastern areas have a chance for scattered thunderstorms, and western parts see precipitation; some locally heavy later in the week.

Zone 6: The zone is fair to partly cloudy with temperatures ranging from seasonal to above and chance for precipitation in the east.

Zone 7: Western areas have a chance for scattered showers and thunderstorms, the zone is fair to partly cloudy and temperatures are seasonal to above.

Zone 8: Alaska—Variably cloudy and seasonal with precipitation in central areas. Hawaii—Windy; central and eastern areas are partly cloudy to cloudy with showers and thunderstorms, western areas are fair, and temperatures are seasonal.

Second Quarter Moon, July 11–18

Zone 1: Temperatures are seasonal to above and the zone is humid and fair to partly cloudy with showers and thunderstorms later in the week.

Zone 2: Skies are variably cloudy, temperatures range from seasonal to above, and central and southern areas have a chance for scattered showers and thunderstorms.

Zone 3: Fair to partly cloudy with temperatures ranging from seasonal to above, and a chance for precipitation.

Zone 4: Variably cloudy skies, humidity, and seasonal to above temperatures accompany thunderstorms, some strong with tornado potential in central parts, and eastern areas see scattered showers.

Zone 5: Temperatures range from seasonal to above, western parts are fair, and central and eastern areas are partly cloudy to cloudy with showers and thunderstorms; some possibly strong with tornado potential.

Zone 6: The zone is humid, partly cloudy to cloudy, temperatures ranging from seasonal to above, and scattered showers and thunderstorms.

Zone 7: Skies are mostly fair and temperatures are seasonal to above, northern coastal areas see showers, and central and eastern areas have a chance for precipitation later in the week.

Zone 8: Alaska—Windy, seasonal, and fair to partly cloudy with scattered precipitation central and east. Hawaii—Windy and fair to partly cloudy with temperatures ranging from seasonal to above, and scattered showers and thunderstorms.

Full Moon, July 19–25

Zone 1: The zone is fair to partly cloudy and seasonal.

Zone 2: Temperatures range from seasonal to above, and the zone is fair to partly cloudy.

Zone 3: Variably cloudy skies accompany temperatures ranging from seasonal to above with a chance for showers and thunderstorms.

Zone 4: Skies are partly cloudy, temperatures are seasonal to above, and humid with a chance for showers and thunderstorms.

Zone 5: Fair to partly cloudy with temperature seasonal to above, and eastern areas have a chance for showers and thunderstorms.

Zone 6: Temperatures are seasonal to above, eastern areas are fair, and western and central parts are partly cloudy with precipitation; some locally heavy.

Zone 7: Western and central areas see showers, skies are partly cloudy to cloudy, eastern areas have a chance for precipitation, and temperatures are seasonal to above.

Zone 8: Alaska—Fair to partly cloudy and seasonal with precipitation central and east. Hawaii—Temperatures are seasonal and skies are mostly fair.

Fourth Quarter Moon, July 26–August 1

Zone 1: Temperatures are seasonal, skies are fair to partly cloudy, and the zone sees scattered showers and thunderstorms later in the week.

Zone 2: The zone is humid with temperatures ranging from seasonal to above, and central and southern areas have a chance for thunderstorms with locally heavy precipitation.

Zone 3: Temperatures ranging from seasonal to above accompany humidity, variably cloudy skies, and scattered showers.

Zone 4: Skies are fair to partly cloud, and temperatures are seasonal to above; chance for thunderstorms.

Zone 5: Fair to partly cloudy with temperatures ranging from seasonal to above and a chance for thunderstorms.

Zone 6: Skies are mostly fair, temperatures are seasonal to above, and western areas have a chance for showers.

Zone 7: Temperatures are seasonal to above, and skies are fair to partly cloudy.

Zone 8: Alaska—Eastern areas are windy with precipitation, western and central parts are fair to partly cloudy, and temperatures are seasonal. Hawaii—Humid, partly cloudy, and seasonal.

New Moon, August 2–9

Zone 1: The zone is fair to partly cloudy with temperatures ranging from seasonal to above.

Zone 2: Skies are mostly fair and temperatures are seasonal to above.

Zone 3: Conditions are humid, temperatures are seasonal, and eastern areas are fair to partly cloudy; western and central areas are partly cloudy to cloudy with precipitation, some locally heavy, with potential for strong thunderstorms with tornados.

Zone 4: Thunderstorms across much of the zone bring locally heavy downfall to some areas, especially west; temperatures are seasonal, and skies are variably cloudy.

Zone 5: A front moves through bringing locally heavy precipitation and potential for strong thunderstorms with tornados west and central; eastern areas see precipitation later in the week, and temperatures are seasonal to above.

Zone 6: Western parts are partly cloudy, central and eastern areas see more cloudiness with precipitation, eastern areas are windy, and temperatures are seasonal.

Zone 7: Temperatures are seasonal to above, central and eastern areas see showers and thunderstorms, western parts are fair, and the zone is variably cloudy and windy in the east.

Zone 8: Alaska—Temperatures are seasonal, central areas are windy with precipitation that moves into eastern parts, and western areas are fair. Hawaii—Mostly fair to partly cloudy and windy, temperatures seasonal to above, and scattered showers and thunderstorms.

Second Quarter Moon, August 10–17

Zone 1: Temperatures are seasonal and zone sees abundant precipitation later in the week under cloudy skies.

Zone 2: Northern areas are cloudy with precipitation, central and southern areas have a chance for thunderstorms, and temperatures are seasonal to above.

Zone 3: Mostly fair with temperatures seasonal to above; eastern areas are cloudy with locally heavy precipitation.

Zone 4: Partly cloudy skies and temperatures ranging from seasonal to above accompany a chance for scattered precipitation.

Zone 5: Skies are fair to partly cloudy, temperatures are seasonal to above, and the zone has a chance for showers and thunderstorms.

Zone 6: The zone is seasonal, windy, and variably cloudy with precipitation central and east.

Zone 7: Northern coastal areas are fair to partly cloudy, southern coastal and central areas are cloudy with precipitation, some locally heavy, possibly from a tropical storm or hurricane, and temperatures are seasonal to below; eastern parts are seasonal to above, humid, and partly cloudy with a chance for thunderstorms.

Zone 8: Alaska—Western Alaska sees precipitation, central and eastern areas are fair to partly cloudy, and temperatures are seasonal. Hawaii—Fair with temperatures seasonal to above.

Full Moon, August 18–23

Zone 1: Scattered thunderstorms accompany temperatures seasonal to above, and the zone is windy and fair to partly cloudy.

Zone 2: Much of the zone is windy with scattered showers and thunderstorms under variably cloudy skies, and temperatures are seasonal to above.

Zone 3: Partly cloudy to cloudy and seasonal with showers and thunderstorms, some with tornado potential and locally heavy downfall; possibly from a tropical storm or hurricane.

Zone 4: Temperatures are seasonal to above and the zone is humid and partly cloudy to cloudy with scattered showers and thunderstorms, some strong with tornado potential.

Zone 5: Western skies are fair, central and eastern skies are partly cloudy to cloudy with scattered thunderstorms, some strong with tornado potential, possibly from a tropical storm or hurricane, and temperatures are seasonal to above.

Zone 6: Locally heavy precipitation in the west could cause flooding, temperatures are seasonal to above, skies are variably cloudy, and central and eastern areas are windy as a front moves through bringing cooler temperatures.

Zone 7: Central and eastern areas are windy, precipitation in the west moves into central areas, eastern areas have a chance for precipitation, skies are partly cloudy, and temperatures are seasonal, but warmer east.

Zone 8: Alaska—Central and western Alaska are partly cloudy to cloudy with precipitation, eastern areas are fair, and temperatures are seasonal. Hawaii—Windy, fair to partly cloudy, and temperatures are seasonal to above with scattered thunderstorms.

Fourth Quarter Moon, August 24–31

Zone 1: Temperatures are seasonal, skies are partly cloudy, and the zone sees scattered showers and thunderstorms.

Zone 2: Fair to partly cloudy skies, and seasonal temperatures accompany scattered showers and thunderstorms.

Zone 3: The zone is variably cloudy and humid with temperatures ranging from seasonal to above, thunderstorms with tornado potential west and central, and showers in the east.

Zone 4: Western parts are windy with precipitation, some locally heavy, central and eastern areas are humid with scattered thunderstorms with tornado potential, skies are variably cloudy and windy, and temperatures are seasonal to above.

Zone 5: Temperatures range from seasonal to above, and the zone is humid and partly cloudy with scattered thunderstorms, some strong with tornado potential.

Zone 6: The zone is very windy, temperatures are seasonal to above, western and central areas see showers, and eastern parts are fair.

Zone 7: Northern coastal areas see showers, the zone is mostly fair and very windy, and eastern areas are humid with thunderstorms; temperatures range from seasonal to above.

Zone 8: Alaska—Fair to partly cloudy and seasonal, with precipitation in the west later in the week. Hawaii—Temperatures are seasonal to above, skies are windy and fair to partly cloudy with a chance for showers and thunderstorms.

New Moon, September 1–8

Zone 1: Showers across the zone accompany partly cloudy to cloudy skies and temperatures ranging from seasonal to above.

Zone 2: The zone is variably cloudy and humid with showers and thunderstorms; temperatures range from seasonal to above.

Zone 3: Partly cloudy to cloudy skies yield showers and thunderstorms, and humid with seasonal to above temperatures.

Zone 4: Humid and partly cloudy to cloudy with temperatures ranging from seasonal to above and locally heavy precipitation from thunderstorms.

Zone 5: Windy and variably cloudy skies, temperatures seasonal to above accompany precipitation in the west and central; some locally heavy from thunderstorms.

Zone 6: Central and eastern skies are windy and partly cloudy to cloudy with precipitation, western areas are fair, and temperatures are seasonal.

Zone 7: Western parts are fair, eastern areas see precipitation, temperatures are seasonal, and central and eastern areas are partly cloudy to cloudy.

Zone 8: Alaska—Most of the state is fair to partly cloudy and seasonal, with precipitation in central areas. Hawaii—Temperatures are seasonal to above, skies are fair to partly cloudy, and the state sees scattered showers.

Second Quarter Moon, September 9–15

Zone 1: The zone is fair and temperatures are seasonal to above.

Zone 2: Temperatures are seasonal to above, northern areas are fair, and central and southern areas see thunderstorms with hail potential.

Zone 3: Eastern areas are fair, western and central parts see thunderstorms and showers, and temperatures range from seasonal to above.

Zone 4: Western and Plains areas are cloudy with precipitation, some locally heavy with flooding potential, eastern areas see thunderstorms, and temperatures are seasonal to above.

Zone 5: Western parts are fair with temperatures ranging from seasonal to above, central and eastern areas are cloudy with locally heavy precipitation, possibly from a tropical storm or hurricane; and temperatures are seasonal to below.

Zone 6: Skies are fair to partly cloudy, temperatures are seasonal to above, and eastern areas see showers.

Zone 7: The zone is mostly fair and windy with temperatures seasonal to above and a chance for showers.

Zone 8: Alaska—Central and eastern Alaska are partly cloudy to cloudy with precipitation, western areas are fair, and temperatures are seasonal. Hawaii—Much of the state sees showers and thunderstorms, and temperatures range from seasonal to above.

Full Moon, September 16–22

Zone 1: Skies are fair and windy, and temperatures are seasonal with a chance for showers in the south later in the week.

Zone 2: Partly cloudy to cloudy and seasonal with precipitation, some abundant, possibly from a tropical storm or hurricane.

Zone 3: Western and central areas are windy, central and eastern areas see precipitation, some locally heavy, skies are variably cloudy, and temperatures are seasonal to below.

Zone 4: Temperatures range from seasonal to below with scattered precipitation, and the zone is windy.

Zone 5: The zone is windy and fair to partly cloudy with temperatures seasonal to above and precipitation in the west.

Zone 6: Skies are variably cloudy with precipitation west and central, some abundant, and temperatures are seasonal to below.

Zone 7: Much of the zone is windy and partly cloudy to cloudy with precipitation, thunderstorms in the east, and temperatures seasonal to below.

Zone 8: Alaska—Much of the state is windy and seasonal with precipitation under variably cloudy skies. Hawaii—Windy and fair with temperatures ranging from seasonal to above.

Autumn

Cooler, cloudy weather will dominate in Zone 1 with some periods of fair skies. In Zone 2, the trend is much the same with heavy precipitation at times in central areas. Cool temperatures and precipitation, some abundant, and windy conditions will prevail in Zone 3.

Zones 4 and 5 will experience the heaviest precipitation with increased flood potential, as well as low-pressure systems and temperatures from seasonal to below. Seasonal temperatures and average precipitation will be the norm in Zone 6, although there will be periods of notable downfall.

Zone 7 will be generally seasonal to above, with precipitation levels ranging from average to below. Temperatures in Zone 8 will be seasonal to above with average precipitation.

Fourth Quarter Moon, September 23–29

Zone 1: Chance for showers and thunderstorms, skies fair to partly cloudy, and temperatures are seasonal to above.

Zone 2: Temperatures are seasonal to below with showers and thunderstorms.

Zone 3: Western areas are fair, central parts are partly cloudy to cloudy with showers and thunderstorms, eastern areas have a chance for precipitation, and temperatures are seasonal to below.

Zone 4: Temperatures are seasonal to above while skies are fair to partly cloudy with a chance for thunderstorms.

Zone 5: Skies are fair to partly cloudy, temperatures range from seasonal to above, and eastern areas are windy with storms.

Zone 6: Western and central parts see precipitation as a front moves through under partly cloudy to cloudy skies; temperatures are seasonal to below, but warmer in the east.

Zone 7: Northern coastal areas see precipitation, southern coastal and central parts have a chance for precipitation, conditions are windy, and temperatures are seasonal to above under variably cloudy skies.

Zone 8: Alaska—Western and central Alaska are windy with precipitation, eastern areas are mostly fair, and temperatures are seasonal with variable cloudiness. Hawaii—Fair with temperatures ranging from seasonal to above.

New Moon, September 30–October 8

Zone 1: The zone is windy, partly cloudy to cloudy, and seasonal temperatures with thunderstorms.

Zone 2: Northern areas see precipitation, central and southern areas are fair to partly cloudy with a chance for thunderstorms, and temperatures are seasonal to above.

Zone 3: Much of the zone is partly cloudy, eastern areas see more cloudiness, wind, and precipitation; and temperatures are seasonal.

Zone 4: Temperatures range from seasonal to above, skies are fair to partly cloudy, and western and central areas see thunderstorms.

Zone 5: The zone is partly cloudy with scattered thunderstorms, and temperatures seasonal to above.

Zone 6: Western areas are cloudy with precipitation, central and eastern areas are fair to partly cloudy, and temperatures are seasonal.

Zone 7: Fair to partly cloudy skies accompany temperatures ranging from seasonal to above, and northern coastal areas see precipitation.

Zone 8: Alaska—Seasonal and partly cloudy to cloudy with precipitation central and east. Hawaii—Much of Hawaii sees showers under partly cloudy to cloudy skies, and temperatures are seasonal.

Second Quarter Moon, October 9–15

Zone 1: Partly cloudy and windy with seasonal temperatures and a chance for precipitation.

Zone 2: Temperatures range from seasonal to above under variably cloudy skies, and much of the zone is windy with storms.

Zone 3: Skies are partly cloudy and much of the zone sees scattered thunderstorms, and temperatures are seasonal to above, but cooler in the east.

Zone 4: Temperatures range from seasonal to above, conditions are cooler in the west and western Plains, skies are variably cloudy, and a chance for showers and storms.

Zone 5: Western parts are cloudy with precipitation, central and eastern areas have a chance for thunderstorms, and temperatures are seasonal to above.

Zone 6: Windy with partly cloudy skies and temperatures ranging from seasonal to above, and precipitation in west and central parts.

Zone 7: Partly cloudy to cloudy skies yield precipitation in northern coastal areas, central and eastern areas are mostly fair, and temperatures are seasonal to above.

Zone 8: Alaska—Western Alaska sees precipitation, skies are generally fair to partly cloudy, and temperatures are seasonal. Hawaii—Partly cloudy and seasonal.

Full Moon, October 16–21

Zone 1: Fair to partly cloudy and seasonal with precipitation and colder temperatures later in the week in northern areas.

Zone 2: Conditions are windy across the zone with precipitation and thunderstorms, some strong with tornado potential central and south; temperatures are seasonal to above and then cooler.

Zone 3: Western and central areas are windy, central parts see storms with tornado potential, and eastern areas see precipitation as a front moves through bringing cooler temperatures.

Zone 4: Partly cloudy to cloudy skies accompany precipitation west and central, most of the zone is windy, temperatures are seasonal to below, and eastern areas are generally fair with a chance for thunderstorms.

Zone 5: The zone is fair to partly cloudy with temperatures seasonal to above, and eastern areas have a chance for thunderstorms.

Zone 6: Temperatures are seasonal, the zone is variably cloudy, and central and eastern areas see precipitation.

Zone 7: Much of the zone sees precipitation under partly cloudy to cloudy skies, and temperatures are seasonal to above.

Zone 8: Alaska—Temperatures are seasonal to below, skies are partly cloudy to cloudy, and central areas see precipitation. Hawaii—Western and central areas see showers, skies are variably cloudy, and temperatures are seasonal to above.

Fourth Quarter Moon, October 22–29

Zone 1: Abundant precipitation under cloudy skies accompanies seasonal temperatures.

Zone 2: Northern areas are cloudy with precipitation, southern and central parts are mostly fair, and temperatures are seasonal to above.

Zone 3: Much of the zone is fair to partly cloudy with more cloudiness in the east with precipitation; temperatures are seasonal to above in the west and central, and cooler in the east.

Zone 4: Western and central parts are cloudy with precipitation and temperatures below seasonal, and eastern areas are partly cloudy and seasonal.

Zone 5: Western and central areas are partly cloudy to cloudy with precipitation, eastern parts are fair to partly cloudy, and temperatures are seasonal to below, but warmer in the east.

Zone 6: Eastern and central areas are cloudy with precipitation, some locally heavy, western areas are windy and partly cloudy, and the zone is windy with seasonal temperatures.

Zone 7: Much of the zone sees precipitation, some locally heavy in the mountains, under partly cloudy to cloudy skies, and temperatures range from seasonal to below.

Zone 8: Alaska—Western and central Alaska are windy with precipitation, eastern areas are mostly fair, and temperatures are seasonal to below. Hawaii—The area is humid and cloudy with locally heavy precipitation, possibly from a tropical storm or hurricane, and temperatures are seasonal to below.

New Moon, October 30–November 6

Zone 1: The zone is fair to partly cloudy with temperatures ranging from seasonal to below.

Zone 2: Seasonal to below temperatures accompany partly cloudy skies.

Zone 3: Western and central areas see scattered precipitation, eastern areas are fair, and temperatures are seasonal to below.

Zone 4: Windy conditions accompany partly cloudy to cloudy skies, scattered precipitation, and temperatures ranging from seasonal to below.

Zone 5: Skies are partly cloudy to cloudy, temperatures are seasonal to below, conditions are windy, and eastern areas see scattered precipitation.

Zone 6: The zone is partly cloudy and seasonal with a chance for precipitation in the east.

Zone 7: Seasonal temperatures accompany fair to partly cloudy skies.

Zone 8: Alaska—Mostly fair and seasonal. Hawaii—Skies are fair and temperatures are seasonal to above.

Second Quarter Moon, November 7–13

Zone 1: Skies are fair to partly cloudy, temperatures are seasonal to above, and southern areas see precipitation later in the week.

Zone 2: Much of the zone is partly cloudy to cloudy with precipitation and seasonal temperatures, central and southern areas are windy.

Zone 3: Cloudy skies yield precipitation across the zone, storm potential west and central, and temperatures range from seasonal to below.

Zone 4: Western and central parts are fair to partly cloudy, eastern areas are cloudy with precipitation and storm potential, and temperatures are seasonal to below.

Zone 5: Eastern areas see precipitation, some locally heavy, along with storm potential, and skies are partly cloudy to cloudy with temperatures ranging from seasonal to below.

Zone 6: The zone is variably cloudy and windy with precipitation, and temperatures seasonal to below.

Zone 7: Skies are windy and partly cloudy to cloudy with seasonal temperatures and precipitation in the central and east areas.

Zone 8: Alaska—Partly cloudy to cloudy and seasonal with precipitation in the west. Hawaii—Windy, fair, and seasonal.

Full Moon, November 14–20

Zone 1: Temperatures are seasonal to below, and conditions are windy.

Zone 2: Partly cloudy to cloudy skies yield precipitation across the zone, and the zone is windy with seasonal temperatures.

Zone 3: Skies are variably cloudy, temperatures are seasonal, western areas are windy, and central and eastern parts see precipitation; some locally heavy.

Zone 4: Western areas are windy and cloudy with precipitation that moves into central areas where it is locally heavy, eastern areas are windy and partly cloudy with a chance for precipitation, and temperatures are seasonal.

Zone 5: Much of the zone is windy with precipitation, which is locally heavy central and east, skies are cloudy, and temperatures are seasonal.

Zone 6: The zone is variably cloudy with temperatures seasonal to below along with scattered precipitation.

Zone 7: Temperatures are seasonal, skies are partly cloudy, conditions are windy, and western and central areas see scattered precipitation.

Zone 8: Alaska—Windy with temperatures seasonal to below and fair to partly cloudy skies, and western areas see more cloudiness with precipitation. Hawaii—Temperatures are seasonal to above, and skies are fair to partly cloudy and windy.

Fourth Quarter Moon, November 21–28

Zone 1: The zone is cloudy, stormy, and windy with precipitation, some locally heavy, and temperatures are seasonal to below.

Zone 2: Locally heavy precipitation accompanies cloudy skies and potential for stormy conditions; temperatures are seasonal to below and windy.

Zone 3: Eastern areas are stormy, much of the zone sees precipitation, some locally heavy, skies are cloudy, and temperatures range from seasonal to below.

Zone 4: Western and central parts are fair and seasonal, eastern areas are cloudy and windy with precipitation, and temperatures are seasonal.

Zone 5: The zone is fair with temperatures ranging from seasonal to above, and western areas are windy.

Zone 6: Cloudy skies prevail across the zone yielding precipitation, some abundant in the central and east, and temperatures range from seasonal to below.

Zone 7: Much of the zone sees precipitation and cloudy skies, some locally heavy in the central and east, conditions are windy, and temperatures are seasonal to below.

Zone 8: Alaska—Windy, partly cloudy, and seasonal with scattered precipitation. Hawaii—Temperatures are seasonal and much of the state sees precipitation under partly cloudy to cloudy skies.

New Moon, November 29–December 6

Zone 1: The zone is windy and variably cloudy with precipitation, and then colder.

Zone 2: Northern areas are windy, central and southern areas see precipitation, skies are partly cloudy to cloudy, and temperatures are seasonal to below.

Zone 3: Much of the zone sees precipitation, which is abundant in western areas, eastern areas are windy, and temperatures range from seasonal to below under variably cloudy skies.

Zone 4: Temperatures are seasonal to below, skies are partly cloudy to cloudy, and eastern and central parts see precipitation; some abundant.

Zone 5: Partly cloudy to cloudy skies accompany temperatures seasonal to below, and precipitation in the central and east; some abundant.

Zone 6: The zone is fair to partly cloudy with temperatures seasonal to below.

Zone 7: Temperatures range from seasonal to above, conditions are windy, and skies are fair to partly cloudy.

Zone 8: Alaska—Windy in the west and central, partly cloudy and seasonal. Hawaii—Partly cloudy and seasonal.

Second Quarter Moon, December 7–12

Zone 1: Skies are partly cloudy to cloudy, temperatures are seasonal to below, and the zone is windy with precipitation.

Zone 2: Much of the zone sees precipitation later in the week, temperatures are seasonal, and skies are variably cloudy.

Zone 3: Western and central areas are cloudy with precipitation, some abundant, eastern areas are partly cloudy, and temperatures are seasonal.

Zone 4: Skies are partly cloudy to cloudy with precipitation in the east, scattered precipitation in the west and central, and temperatures are seasonal to below.

Zone 5: The zone is cloudy with precipitation, some abundant; and temperatures are seasonal to below.

Zone 6: Temperatures are seasonal, skies are partly cloudy to cloudy with scattered precipitation, and central and eastern parts are windy.

Zone 7: Skies are windy and fair to partly cloudy, temperatures are seasonal, and western areas see scattered precipitation.

Zone 8: Alaska—Generally partly cloudy with more cloudiness and precipitation in the east; temperatures are seasonal. Hawaii—Temperatures are seasonal to above, and fair to partly cloudy.

Full Moon, December 13–19

Zone 1: The zone is windy and cloudy; stormy in the north, precipitation in the south, and temperatures are seasonal to below.

Zone 2: Skies are partly cloudy to cloudy, conditions are windy, temperatures are seasonal to below with scattered precipitation; and strong storms are possible in the central and south areas.

Zone 3: Western and central areas are windy with precipitation, skies are partly cloudy to cloudy, temperatures are seasonal to below, and eastern areas see scattered precipitation.

Zone 4: The zone is variably cloudy with a chance for precipitation in the west, temperatures seasonal to below, and precipitation and wind in the central and eastern parts.

Zone 5: Temperatures are seasonal, skies are fair to partly cloudy, and with more cloudiness and precipitation, some locally heavy, in eastern areas.

Zone 6: Much of the zone is windy with precipitation and seasonal temperatures, and skies are partly cloudy to cloudy.

Zone 7: Fair to partly cloudy with temperatures seasonal to above, and scattered precipitation in the east.

Zone 8: Alaska—Temperatures are seasonal to below, skies are partly cloudy to cloudy, and central areas see precipitation. Hawaii—Windy and variably cloudy with precipitation, and temperatures ranging from seasonal to below.

Fourth Quarter Moon, December 20–28

Zone 1: Temperatures range from seasonal to below, and the zone is partly cloudy to cloudy with precipitation.

Zone 2: The zone is variably cloudy, and temperatures are seasonal with precipitation in the central and north.

Zone 3: Skies are partly cloudy to cloudy with precipitation across the zone, and temperatures are seasonal.

Zone 4: Skies are variably cloudy and temperatures range from seasonal to below, and western and eastern areas are windy with precipitation.

Zone 5: Western parts are very windy with precipitation, central and eastern areas are partly cloudy to cloudy with a chance for thunderstorms, and temperatures are seasonal.

Zone 6: Seasonal temperatures accompany variably cloudy skies with a chance for precipitation in central areas.

Zone 7: The zone is seasonal and partly cloudy to cloudy with precipitation in the west and central; eastern areas are windy with precipitation later in the week.

Zone 8: Alaska—Much of the state sees precipitation under variably cloudy skies, and temperatures are seasonal to below. Hawaii—Windy, seasonal temperatures, and partly cloudy to cloudy with showers and thunderstorms.

New Moon, December 29–January 4, 2017

Zone 1: Partly cloudy skies and seasonal temperatures accompany windy conditions with scattered precipitation.

Zone 2: Skies are partly cloudy, central and southern areas see scattered precipitation and thunderstorms, some strong with tornado potential; and temperatures are seasonal to above.

Zone 3: Windy, partly cloudy to cloudy, and seasonal temperatures with precipitation in the western and central areas, including potential for strong thunderstorms with tornados.

Zone 4: Temperatures are seasonal to above, skies are partly cloudy to cloudy, western and central parts see precipitation, and a possibility for strong thunderstorms with tornado potential in the southeast.

Zone 5: Precipitation across the zone under partly cloudy to cloudy skies, includes a chance for thunderstorms in central areas, and temperatures are seasonal to above.

Zone 6: Western and central parts are cloudy with scattered precipitation, eastern areas are mostly fair, and temperatures are seasonal.

Zone 7: Much of the zone is partly cloudy to cloudy with a chance for precipitation, eastern areas are mostly fair, and temperatures are seasonal to below.

Zone 8: Alaska—Precipitation across much of the state is locally heavy in some areas, skies are cloudy and windy, and temperatures are seasonal to below. Hawaii—Temperatures are seasonal to below, and the state is windy with showers and thunderstorms.

About the Author

Kris Brandt Riske is the executive director and a professional member of the American Federation of Astrologers (AFA), the oldest US astrological organization, founded in 1938; and a member of the National Council for Geocosmic Research (NCGR). She has a master's degree in journalism and a certificate of achievement in weather forecasting from Penn State. Kris is the author of several books, including Llewellyn's Complete Book of Astrology: The Easy Way to Learn Astrology; Mapping Your Money; Mapping Your Future; *and she is coauthor of* Mapping Your Travels and Relocation *and* Astrometeorology: Planetary Powers in Weather Forecasting. *Her newest book is* Llewellyn's Complete Book of Predictive Astrology. *She also writes for astrology publications and does the annual weather forecast for* Llewellyn's Moon Sign Book. *In addition to astrometeorology, she specializes in predictive astrology. Kris is an avid NASCAR fan, although she'd rather be a driver than a spectator. In 2011 she fulfilled her dream when she drove a stock car for twelve fast laps. She posts a weather forecast for each of the thirty-six race weekends (qualifying and race day) for NASCAR drivers and fans. Visit her at www.pitstopforecasting.com. Kris also enjoys gardening, reading, jazz, and her three cats.*

Economic Forecast for 2016

by Christeen Skinner

New and Full Moons do not occur on the same date and therefore are not on the same zodiacal degrees each year. They are part of a much larger cycle lasting almost two decades. Within the course of any year, there will be a minimum of two solar eclipses (which you can think of as sophisticated New Moons) and a maximum of five. These may or may not be accompanied by a lunar eclipse, which always take place around a Full Moon.

Each degree of the zodiac seems to carry its own story, and the financial astrologer is particularly interested in those degrees on which an eclipse (either Sun or Moon) occurs. In 2016 during the months of March and September, there are solar eclipses accompanied by lunar eclipses, affording important punctuation marks for the financial astrologer.

The March 9 solar eclipse marks the anniversary of a low on Wall Street that echoed across many industries. Anniversary dates seem to have powerful, though often unconscious, messages. Yet it is to some still a little surprising that extreme movements take place at these times. March 9, 2009, also marked a major low. It is not necessarily the case that there will be a recurrence in 2016, but at the very least, this date should mark a significant turning point. In this instance it is perhaps most likely that a high will form that date and be followed by a drop into mid-April.

This particular solar eclipse occurs at a highly significant degree—opposing Mars in a chart commonly used for the New York Stock Exchange. It should be appreciated that there is never one singular chart for any company or entity. Over time, stock exchanges and companies are taken over, re-formed, and re-incorporated. This does not render earlier charts useless, but brings into play new degrees that over time subsume the power of earlier ones. Whatever time of day is used for the NYSE (which is recorded as opening on May 17, 1792) the planet Mars is positioned mid-Virgo. Throughout the twentieth century, major transits over or opposed to this point have coincided with sharp movement in Wall Street indices. March 9, 2016, is unlikely to prove an exception.

The March 9 solar eclipse is followed by a lunar eclipse two weeks later on March 23. This date is close to the Spring Equinox and although the lunar eclipse does not align exactly with this powerful degree, it is probable that March 20–23 will be a highly eventful period in stock markets across the world, possibly as a result of political struggle. Though the eclipses themselves highlight the potential for volatility, it is the coincidence with two other major cycles that underscore the likelihood of extreme movement.

The planetoid Chiron is often described as the Wounded Healer and is certainly high profile in the charts of medical personnel and at times of unease. In the world of finance, it may be viewed as an appraiser or auditor identifying errors. Chiron aligns with the lunar south node within days of the Spring Equinox, indicating a cosmically significant wealth-check moment.

This same period witnesses the fourth quarter phase of the Jupiter-Saturn cycle: yet another signal that this could be a period of commercial stress with resistance levels tested. Should markets be in decline, reversal of trend is unlikely until mid-April.

The September eclipse is accompanied by two lunar eclipses. The first precedes the solar eclipse by two weeks, taking place on August 18. The second occurs after the solar eclipse and takes place on September 16. This four-week period should prove as eventful as the March period, once again bringing considerable volatility. Whereas the March eclipse takes place at 18 degrees Pisces, the September eclipse takes place at 9 degrees Virgo, which is another interesting degree to the financial astrologer.

Though there is no singular birth chart for any particular commodity, it can be shown that the zodiacal axis of 9 degrees Virgo and Pisces is a sensitive zodiac area for silver. Silver may be much in the news over this four-week period, which would be keeping with the crest of another, much-longer cycle. Volatility in the silver price should be expected. Given the phase relationships of various other planetary cycles in early September, it seems reasonable to forecast that after the solar eclipse, and in the days leading into the lunar eclipse on September 16, the price could rise.

While eclipse periods themselves offer the basic punctuation marks for the year, no less significant is the monthly New and Full Moon rhythm and the interaction with other planetary cycles. A bank study in the early 1990s showed that using a basic trading strategy of buying on the New Moon and selling on the Full Moon over the course of a decade would have yielded a far greater reward than simply placing money on deposit in the bank. This simple system does not work for every index; however, as some indices fare better between the Full Moon and fourth quarter. What seems to be the case is that when a New or Full Moon coincides with a planetary station, turning points are reached.

Planetary Stations/Retrogrades

As viewed from Earth, each of the planets in our solar system experience retrograde motion relative to Earth's own orbit. The dates on which the relevant planet appears to stand still are known as *stations*. Mercury provides several of these important turning points each year. Venus and Mars are generally retrograde every couple of years, while Jupiter, Saturn, Uranus, Neptune, and Pluto have at least one annual station. Research shows that though the stations of the slower-moving planets do not generally coincide with large-scale market movement, that is not the case when the inner planets of Mercury and Venus are involved, particularly when these station points coincide with the New or Full Moon phases.

Mercury stations within twenty-four hours of the January 24 Full Moon. Mercury is the planet associated with commerce, and at this stage in its cycle, it will be in the fourteenth degree of Capricorn—opposing the solar position on the chart for the United States (July 4, 1776). This could be a date of importance on Wall Street. Capricorn is the sign associated with banking and major corporations, so it may be these stocks that hit the headlines in the closing week of January. A further possibility; however, is that this period will see unusual movement in foreign exchange markets. It can be shown that the Australian dollar/Euro relationship is particularly sensitive to lunation cycles, with trend reversals often coinciding with Full Moons.

Mercury's direct station on May 22 coincides with another Full Moon (May 21). This Full Moon takes place in the opening degrees of the Gemini-Sagittarius axis. Note that Mercury is said to rule Gemini, so that any coincidental effect is likely to be marked as a result. In this instance, the sectors likely to be affected are travel, airlines, and publishing, whose stock prices could reach turning points that day.

A review of the remaining New and Full Moons of 2016 shows no coincidence with a planetary station until the very end of the year when the New Moon on December 29 coincides with a Uranus's station. Though a Uranus station does not normally coincide with particular market movement, this station could be an exception. It would be entirely normal for indices across the world to experience incline in the very last days of any calendar year. The alignment of Uranus (planet of the unexpected) with the New Moon on December 29 suggests that any spike in prices could be larger than usual.

Mercury

In 2016, Mercury, whose orbit is at an incline of 7 degrees to that of Earth, transits the face of the Sun. This major transit can only occur in either May or November in a year when Mercury's orbit intersects the ecliptic. These relatively rare May events have happened within recorded stock market history—in May 2003 and May 1970. In 2003 within a week of this major transit, the Dow Jones Index broke through an important resistance level and continued an upward trajectory. In May 1970, the reverse was true: the Dow Jones Index fell sharply over a period of three weeks. The point to make is that in both cases there was clear reaction. The financial astrologer would not find this surprising, given that Mercury is the planet of commerce.

As viewed from Earth, Mercury appears retrograde on at least three occasions in any year. At this point in its cycle, it seems to go back over degrees already transited before arriving at another station (where it appears to stand still) and then returning over these same degrees once more. It is only when Mercury finally crosses the degree of its first (pre-retrograde) station that its speed seems to increase and it once more appears in direct motion.

As with New and Full Moons, Mercury's retrograde periods, though they form a pattern over a period of around two decades, do not occur in the same zodiacal degrees every year. The actual area of the zodiac through which Mercury is retrograde is of great importance to the financial astrologer. Some astrologers feel that such periods coincide with times of miscommunication and general disconnect. Not all Mercury retrograde periods are equal. It seems that aberrant reaction is more common when Mercury is moving through the signs it is said to rule (Gemini and Virgo) and their opposites (Sagittarius and Pisces). It is perhaps also the case that when Mercury stations in an air sign, lines of communication become crossed.

Mercury first stations and moves retrograde on January 5 in an early degree of Aquarius. As we shall shortly see, this area of the zodiac is worthy of special attention between now and the end of the decade. We may well see the focus of commercial attention falling on the foreign exchange markets and the new currencies that have developed in recent years. It is entirely possible that until the planet returns to Capricorn (an earth sign) on January 8, there will indeed be ample evidence of things going wrong. These would not be good days to sign business deals.

Mercury appears to retreat all the way to the mid-degrees of Capricorn where, as mentioned above, it stations with the Full Moon on January 24/25 before appearing to once again move forward. It reaches the early degrees of Aquarius once more on February 13, when it is entirely possible that deals that have been stuck since January once again gain momentum.

Mercury is then in direct motion from February 13 through the end of April. This should be seen as a commercially active period where fresh ideas gather momentum. Those seeking investment may find that with Mercury direct and the Sun in Aries until April 20, their ideas capture imaginations and funds become available.

The next Mercury retrograde period begins on April 28 in the sign of Taurus. It is possible that those born under this sign—or indeed any of the fixed signs of the zodiac (Taurus, Leo, Scorpio, or Aquarius)—will find that their cash flow is subject to disruption and that repairs impair their ability to balance the books by the end of May. However, this ought not to be an especially difficult Mercury retrograde period.

That definition ought to be reserved for the next Mercury retrograde period, which begins on August 30 and continues throughout the September eclipse period. Recall that this will be a long eclipse period as the solar eclipse is accompanied by lunar eclipses two weeks on either side. Add in Mercury's retrograde status in Virgo (one of the signs Mercury is said to rule) and this could be a highly eventful period in the world of commerce.

To conclude our view of 2016 through the lens of Mercury's position, we must now consider those periods when the planet is said to be *combust*. Mercury is combust when it appears very close to the Sun, or near conjunction. The reaction of traders and investors over these dates is perhaps to experience a peculiar form of commercial seduction. Whereas normally they might apply due diligence in their analysis of a company's trading position, these same individuals are more likely to be seduced into thinking something is a good bet during Mercury combust period. However, it is equally possible that even the most experienced trader and market tactician will make errors of judgement during these times.

There is not total agreement on the length of a combust period. Some argue that when Mercury is approximately 8.5 degrees either side of its conjunction with the Sun is the combust period. Others argue for 8.5 degrees prior to the conjunction and double that distance after the conjunction (17 degrees). Even highly experienced traders may later find that information employed between this time is in some way false or misguided.

Venus

No less important are the cycles of Venus and their connections with those of the Sun and Moon. Venus does not go through a retrograde period in 2016, so it forms just one conjunction of the Sun. This occurs on June 6 at 16 degrees Gemini and is special in that it is actually an occultation of Venus by the Sun. Many high-tech companies have planets at this degree or at right angles to it. This suggests one of two possibilities: Such stocks may fall out of favor with traders in early June, and that until Venus is clear of the conjunction with

the Sun, the value of these stocks may fall. On the other hand, the opposite may be true in that traders could fall for these stocks and see their value rise sharply as a result. Astrology alone does not define the direction—technical analysis would also be required.

Hints that this sector might be highlighted in 2016 are provided by other, earlier aspects between the Sun and Venus and by another aspect occurring not too long after the September eclipse: The Sun and Venus are just 30 degrees apart on February 7, with the Sun in Aquarius and Venus in Capricorn, and on September 27 with the Sun in Libra and Venus in Scorpio.

Note that the three Sun signs involved in these aspects all belong to the air triplicity. It would be in keeping with these aspects if investors were initially to experience a love affair with stocks thought to be connected with air signs. Air is all about the transmission of ideas and products and thus encompasses travel stocks, the dissemination of news and items, and (relatively new on the scene) the developing robotic industry as well as those companies embracing computer technology. It is probable that the latter industry and related stocks will enjoy a peak in value in the early part of February.

Venus will then be 30 degrees behind the Sun, so that the Sun will be in technology-related Aquarius while Venus moves through earthy but ambition-oriented Capricorn. It is not unreasonable to imagine that companies working in suggested sectors will experience a peak in volume of trade and high prices in the early days of February.

It is said that conjunctions mark seed moments and the alignments of the Sun with Venus through the various signs seems to concur with investors falling for companies working in the associated sectors. Though Venus does not transit the face of the Sun in 2016 (and indeed will not do so until the end of the century), Venus is combust (near conjunction with the Sun) from June 3–10. To the investor or shopper, one of the positive features of a combust Venus is that there is generally confusion about values during these periods. This can be a bargain hunter's dream, when it is entirely possible that mis-priced items are on sale, allowing what is potentially precious to go for a song.

The Sun-Venus conjunction in Gemini in June 2016 occurs just a few weeks after a Mercury retrograde phase, when (as suggested earlier) telecommunication and transport stocks could experience lows. It might take until after Venus leaves its combust period for these same stocks to come back into favor—and it's entirely possible that their price will rise as Venus moves to trine. This aspect takes place on September 12. Traders might want to red mark this date as a potential turning point.

The last Sun-Venus aspect of 2016 is a semi-square on December 14 when the Sun is moving through Sagittarius and Venus is in Aquarius. Note now that it is Venus that takes up position in an air sign after the solar position domination of the air triplicity earlier in the year. This date could mark a low point for the robotic industry stocks that may have reached a high back in February.

Venus, as with the other planets, does not keep a regular distance from the Sun. In 2016, Venus is in aphelion (farthest from the Sun) on March 20 and is in perihelion (nearest to the Sun) on July 10. The former date may be highly significant in that the period around the Spring Equinox has already been identified as one of singular cosmic activity and patterning.

Tracing Venus's aphelion positions since 2000, we find that on only one occasion was there an exception to the rule that within two weeks of aphelion, the Dow Jones experienced a downturn. This is further evidence to suggest that the Spring Equinox this year will witness negative trading that will not recover until mid-April. The perihelion position, held on July 10, provides a similar picture. Again it seems reasonable to expect markets to close lower that month than at its start.

There is an occultation of Venus by the Moon on both April 6 and September 3. These special eclipses last only a short time as the faster-moving Moon blocks the view of Venus for a short time. These events may coincide with movements in sugar prices, which are apt to fall for a few hours before recovering. Obviously this effect needs to be studied against the backdrop of longer cycles, but it is an interesting phenomenon.

Mars

It is thought that there are more than 1.6 million pieces of "stuff" orbiting the Sun. Some appear as fragments, while the recognized and known planets are much larger and have very particular orbits. Earth travels between the orbits of Venus and Mars, who are often viewed as a pair. Though they are written about in connection with affairs of the heart, no less important are affairs of money where alliances are formed for the good of both parties.

Mars is retrograde from April 17 (a possible market turning point) through June 29 (another significant date). Within that time frame it opposes Venus on May 24. Analysis of the FTSE index through the twentieth century shows the importance of Mars's retrograde periods and of the dates of its station. The fact that Venus opposes Mars in May suggests that one of the issues that might unsettle markets may be an alliance that appears in jeopardy.

Mars and Venus oppose one another across the first degrees of Gemini and Sagittarius. These signs profile travel companies, distribution networks, and publishing. Once again we have a cosmic clue as to which sectors could experience particular volatility in May.

Mars has two other high-profile roles to play this year. On August 24 Mars appears within two degrees of the fixed star Antares. Antares is the fifteenth brightest star in the sky. It is a red star found deep in the heart of the constellation of Scorpio (not to be confused with the tropical sign of the same name). This star has a bad reputation and is associated with danger and passion. Mars of course is known for adding heat to any situation, so it is entirely possible that this will prove to be a war-torn period that has considerable effect on stock markets worldwide. While this may augur well for armament and military suppliers, the nerves of traders could be frazzled around this date, leading to a few days of overreaction and volatility.

Mars is high profile again on October 29, when it is at perihelion within twenty-four hours of the Scorpio New Moon, whose chart contains a conjunction of Venus and Saturn. Again it seems reasonable to anticipate a day of marked activity. As the asteroid Vesta is in square aspect to the New Moon, greatest volatility may be seen on foreign exchange markets, where fluctuation could be above average.

Virtual Currencies and Financial Instruments

In a journey of approximately nineteen years, the nodes of the Moon move through all twelve signs of the zodiac, traversing these in reverse order. It has been recognized that as the nodes move from Aquarius through to Leo, the business cycle trend is upward. Once the sign of Leo is reached, a downturn begins. This nodal cycle is not so different from the accepted twenty-year business cycle, which has correlations with the Jupiter-Saturn cycle. An understanding of both the lunar nodal and Jupiter-Saturn cycles is imperative for the would-be Astro-investor.

Jupiter and Saturn form a conjunction every twenty years. Their last alignment was in May 2000, just weeks after the spectacular dot-com crash in April 2000. This conjunction was part of a new baseline and the beginning of a new cycle. The two planets form their next conjunction in 2020. This conjunction, as with that of the early 1980s, is in one of the air signs. The conjunction of 1981 and the development of that particular cycle offers many hints as to how the Jupiter-Saturn business cycles of the twenty-first century will develop. As with the Libra conjunction of 1981, all the Jupiter-Saturn conjunctions of the twenty-first century will be in air signs.

The 1980s saw the advance of yuppies and the development of financial algorithms and practices that have since been described as weapons of mass financial destruction. Essentially, all these developments were based on ideas that were difficult for even some of the most seasoned financiers to understand. These ideas have not gone away, and they may well revive during the next business cycle.

Already, virtual currencies have captured the imaginations of some. In the case of the Bitcoin, an exchange rate is in existence.

Whether or not this particular currency survives, it seems likely that similar forms of virtual currency will come into being in the coming years.

The next Jupiter-Saturn conjunction takes place in a very early degree of Aquarius. As planets pass this zodiacal degree between now and 2020, there are likely to be hints as to which of the new currencies will gain momentum. These periods are likely to occur in the opening months of each year as Mercury, Venus, and the Sun each make their Aquarius ingress. In 2016, the key dates are January 2 and 20, and February 13 and 17.

Jupiter and Saturn

Jupiter is the faster moving of the two planets and, since its conjunction with Saturn in 2000, it has completed an entire cycle of the zodiac (whereas Saturn does not complete a cycle for almost three decades). Jupiter begins 2016 in the sign of Virgo while Saturn is in Sagittarius: both mutable signs of the zodiac. They are at right angles in the fourth quarter phase of their cycle in late March (close to the Spring Equinox) and again on May 26.

A smoothed curve of the angular relationship of these two planets as compared with the Dow Jones Index movements shows that this particular angular relationship coincides with a rise in this index value. This rise is halted when the two planets are approximately 285 degrees from one another. If history repeats, it is entirely possible there will be a rise in stock market values from late May into the September eclipse period.

Jupiter aligns with the lunar node in the last week of January and again at the summer solstice on June 20. It is reasonable to expect that around both periods, markets across the world will experience highs. A general and very marked downturn should not be expected until after the lunar North node reaches the sign of Leo in the early part of 2017. 2016 then could see something of a last hurrah for many indices before a period of difficulty.

The sectors most likely to enjoy buoyancy during 2016 are those related to the sign of Virgo. This is the sign generally associated with the service and health industries. Gains and progress here could be remarkable. Indeed, companies working in these fields should enjoy particular success in the first six months of the year.

But the sign of Virgo does not confine itself to just service and health. Those working in the fields of data management, precision engineering, the production of earth-moving equipment, and those involved in infrastructure projects should also experience a period of high workload with commensurate reward

The manufacturing industries—particularly those involved in the production of foodstuffs, ready meals, and dietary management—should also find the first six months of the year to be a period of expansion even if their shares suffer in March when all indices could be down.

Of course, a steady incline in share prices would be abnormal. The solar eclipse on March 9 and at 18 degrees Pisces is also a Super Moon. At this point the Moon will be extremely close to Earth (perigee). An eclipse on its own tends to coincide with marked market reaction; with a Super Moon, any effect is likely to be heightened. As explained earlier, this particular degree area has been shown to be Wall Street sensitive. Going back nineteen years to the last solar eclipse near this degree, we find that immediately following the eclipse, the Dow Jones Index fell from a high of 7112 on the eclipse date to a low of 6391 in April. Having reached this level close to a Mercury retrograde station, this index then soared to reach a high of 8300 in August of that year. History never repeats exactly, but it does seem likely that there will be major market movement in 2016.

On December 10, Uranus and Chiron will be just 30 degrees apart from one another. This aspect has coincided with market turbulence in the past. That same day, the Sun aligns with Saturn (in Sagittarius) as Mercury is at greatest elongation. A few hours earlier, on December 9, the Moon, aligned with Uranus, is opposed by Jupiter, with both planets at right angles to Pluto—thus forming an important T-square pattern.

Pluto entered the sign of Capricorn in 2008, when markets across the world were brought to the brink of collapse. Since then there have been tranches of quantitative easing to keep banks afloat. It is probable that until Pluto leaves this sign, the financial difficulties besetting governments and major institutions will continue to require attention. December 9 may prove a key date in this respect. Once again there may be signs that a major international institution is on the brink of collapse, prompting a major sell-off of shares that day and a weekend of considerable stress to the world's financiers. The unravelling of corporate or government debt will surely cause great aggravation to many. Given that there are hints of recovery in the last days of December, presumably solutions will be found looking ahead to 2017, these troubles may only be temporary.

Visions, Technical Development, and Investment

In 2016, Jupiter and Uranus will be in septile aspect to one another on February 8 and again on September 1. Jupiter will hold a late degree of Virgo whilst Uranus will still be moving through Aries. They will therefore be three-sevenths the zodiac apart.

These two planets could be termed the "dynamic duo" and are often in major aspect when scientific breakthroughs are made. The fact that the aspect this time involves sevenths of a cycle suggest that these breakthroughs will be inspired. Septiles are said to coincide with inspired thinking. It is also very likely that these breakthroughs will not be made by experts in particular fields but by amateurs who happen on something that is most like a "message from the Gods."

Investors should keep a close eye on unusual news stories in the weeks following these two dates. Following their trail could lead to extraordinary innovations. It might be possible to get in on the ground floor and reap fast monetary reward.

No less important are two septiles made between Saturn and

Chiron on June 14 and September 9. Through 2016 Saturn travels through Sagittarius and Chiron through Pisces. It is reasonable to anticipate that these "inspired developments" will in some way be related to these two signs, both of which come from the mutable or multifaceted group of signs.

A reasonable image for Saturn in Sagittarius is of a well-established university. Whereas the combination of Jupiter with Uranus suggests quick and sudden breakthrough, Saturn and Chiron work at a much slower pace. It may be work that has been in progress for over a decade finally yields results that are at once simple and easy to implement (there is an ease about septile aspects). Given Chiron's involvement, it is probable that developments will have health benefits. Saturn is associated with old age, so it may be that thanks to the inspired thinking of someone who has been laboring long and hard for years, a simple and effective treatment for unease associated with old age will be found.

While this might not bring a miracle cure, it would no doubt have a profound effect on expenditure and may be a product or service that yields wealth to those who invest in it.

Astro-economists and financial astrologers will be keeping a close eye on services and products brought to market around these septile dates.

About the Author

Christeen Skinner is the author of Financial Universe *(2004) in which she forecast the banking crisis. She works in London and has a broad clientele—from city traders to entrepreneurs to private investors. She taught for the Faculty of Astrological Studies for a half-nodal cycle, was chair of the Astrological Association of Great Britain, and is a trustee of Urania Trust.*

New and Full Moon Forecasts for 2016

by Sally Cragin

When I present seminars on how to use the phases of the Moon in life, I always begin by explaining that every culture on the planet creates a story about the phases of the Moon, from new to second quarter to full to fourth quarter to new again. And even though the Plains Indians of North America may not have interacted with Europeans or Chinese or Aztecs, every single culture agrees that during the waxing Moon, you plant. During the waning Moon you harvest. During the Full Moon, everything happens. During the New Moon, much is hidden.

The idea of the Moon influencing behavior is also a cross-cultural theme. Do you feel more outgoing when the Moon is full? Do you feel anxious when the Moon is new? Bear in mind that the word *lunatic* has the root word *luna*—another word for Moon. So when the Moon is full—yes, it may bring out a lunatic side. And not just in humans—see whether your pets are a little more agitated than normal. I am writing as the Moon is nearly new, and I need to keep removing my cat, Wendle, as he wants to be between the computer screen and my eyes!

We are not machines—we have a variety of emotions, so when the Moon is transitioning to a full phase, or back to new, on some endocrinal level we are registering this. But what if we can't tell what the Moon is doing? Or, we look out at the night and can't decide if it's waxing or waning. My suggestion is to take your datebook and mark the dates of the new and Full Moons for this year. That's just twenty-four or so little marks, and the first step to understanding the phases. So here's the formula: when the Moon is light on the right, it's waxing. When it's dark on the left, it's waning.

The new and Full Moons account for just a few days of a 29.5 day orbit. Most of the time, the Moon is either growing or diminishing, depending on where the shadow of the earth is falling. Divide the month in two, and you have two weeks of moving forward and two weeks of retreat. Some of my clients find they're at their most effective when the Moon is new and things are less hectic, while others prefer that week before the Full Moon and the days afterward. They feel as if they have more energy to handle whatever life brings their way.

Most cultures view the Moon as female and the Sun as male, and the Greeks created Artemis, the goddess of the hunt and her brother Apollo, who drove the sun chariot across the sky to explain the varied movements of these two stellar entities. And of course, the term *moon* comes from the word *mens*, from which we derive *month* as well as *menstrual*. The Moon shapes our year even more than the month, given that most of the world organizes our days into groups that add up to twelve months (although usually thirteen Full Moons).

As you are planning your year, consider scheduling social gatherings for the time of the Full Moon, and downsizing your obligations for the New Moon and the week preceding. Staying in tune with the Moon is something our great (times twenty) grandparents understood and would undoubtedly approve of!

Waning Moons

The waning Moon phase is easy to overlook or underutilize. Specifically, the days following a Full Moon are excellent for implementing and simplifying a plan that emerged just before the Full Moon and for developing and deepening relationships that may have been fraught or confused during the time of the Full Moon.

Waning Moons could bring hidden motives to the surface as well, and if Venus and Mars are at odds to one another (making a 90- or 180-degree angle), that waning Moon could bring a sense of hopelessness to resolving an emotional situation.

Venus and Mars will be happily relating to one another on April 5–16 and July 3–11. This will facilitate love and work relationships and help us to see one another with more interest, kindness, and tolerance.

Venus and Mars will be out of synch to one another on March 10–20, May 21–28, and July 31–August 16. This doesn't mean that all love affairs go awry—just that patience, irritation, and delusion are more likely. This could also be a time when one gets infatuated with something very short-term—a mullet haircut or wearing uncomfortable high heels.

Waxing Moons

Most people seem to be aware of the constantly shifting lunar phases as the Moon goes from new to full, and especially from just past the crescent phase to nearly full. I'm an astrologer who gives much credence to the three-day rule—the Full Moon period and most dramatic effects will encompass the day before, the day of, and the day after. Waxing Moons can be invigorating and exciting, and Full Moons on election days can definitely assist the underdog candidate. If you've put off some vital project, waiting until the time of the Full Moon can give you the muscle to see something to the finish line.

As I was starting to learn about astrology, I found that thinking about the phases and signs in relationship to the Moon made a lot of sense and seemed logical. Something simple to start with is that the Full Moon will always be in the opposite sign the Sun is in. So if the Sun is in the sign of Leo (as it is for most of August), the Full Moon will be in the opposite sign of Aquarius (which it will be on August 18).

The Moon and Love

"Who is the best person for me?" is a question I hear frequently when teaching astrology classes, doing tarot readings, or trying to change the subject at a cocktail party once my profession is divulged (invariably, not by me!). The weeks between new and Full Moon definitely will assist a fledgling relationship, although when you get close to the Full Moon, you may find a relationship emerges in lots of busy chatter, not smoldering glances.

Yes, more weddings take place in June than in any other month, and with the Moon going from new to full for most of the first two thirds of the month in 2016, there will be plenty of hopefulness and optimism accompanying our June brides and grooms. But remember that marriage has roots that go way back, and the reason that many weddings were traditionally held in June was because the European May feasts and festivals (Beltane) celebrated the wedding of the gods. So we mortals waited until a month later.

Special note for female readers—It's no accident that fertility cycles follow a 28–30-day cycle on average, which means that ovulation, or time of greatest fertility will follow 14 days after your cycle. This means that if you bleed on the New Moon, you'll ovulate on the Full Moon, and no matter what you are using for birth control, your body and brain (at least the primitive part) is screaming *Party! Party! PARTY!!* So if the Full Moon is a time of increased socializing, you may find yourself dressing more provocatively during this ovulation period.

However, if you bleed on the Full Moon, that means you ovulate on the New Moon. And it also means that you may have PMS just before the Full Moon, which could bring a short temper and emotionality. Having PMS before the New Moon could bring more of a feeling of depression, helplessness, and futility. Yes, isn't it lovely to have all these female hormones, plus Luna up above, helping to guide their passage through our bodies?

The Moon and Work

This is one of my favorite topics to discuss in groups, and one that people new to astrology immediately understand after a brief conversation. Work is such a broad term. Some of us work in an office from nine to five; others work in sites that range from outdoors to hospitals to schools to places where you need a certain uniform. And the number of people I know making a living as pet-sitters has tripled in the past three years.

No matter what you do and where you do it, chances are you work with others and for others. Keeping track of the lunar phases and signs can be a helpful addition to helping you get through the day, the week, the month, and the year. Knowing when to take action or when to lie low should make your work environment more comfortable, and help you succeed at what you do.

Bearing in mind some of the simple principles regarding the Moon's phases, consider how you can conduct your business depending on the phase of the Moon. For example, is a deadline at the Full Moon or New Moon easier to reach? The Full Moon can be a frantic time, which means if a number of people are engaged in a task and the leadership is not clear, a Full Moon could bring more complications. However, if leadership is clear, getting over the biggest hump could be what occurs during the Full Moon.

If your deadline is a personal one, or one where you are the only responsible party, aiming to finish a task during that waning Moon phase might be more successful. But the only way to see how you function during a lunar month is to keep track of what you are doing—and how you are feeling—plus your general energy levels. When the Full Moon occurs at the end of a week, you'll find everything is a blur between Monday and Thursday. When the New Moon occurs at the end of a week, you may find that your activities either stall or stop being attended to.

Saturday, January 9, New Moon in Capricorn
The original "Capricornus" was a sea-goat—so you got the horns, plus a mermaid tail. Much more creative than just the goat, and this New Moon can be a time of practical creativity. Libra, Aries, Leo, Gemini, and Cancer are tempted to take a stand, no matter what the consequences. Capricorn, Taurus, Virgo, Scorpio, Sagittarius, Aquarius, and Pisces may need to take things slowly but will find everything slotting into place if they do. Remember that Mercury is in retrograde, so communication will probably be a little crazy!

Saturday, January 23, Full Moon in Leo
The sign of the lion coming on a weekend says party hearty! Leo Moons are super for celebrating. After all, January is nearly over—that's certainly worth raising a glass to. However, Leo Moons can also bring out the actor in us all. If someone seems less than sincere, figure it's Luna messing with their head. Scorpio, Taurus, Aquarius, Capricorn, and Pisces are subject to impulsiveness,

which could get them in trouble. Leo, Sagittarius, Aries, Virgo, Libra, Gemini, and Cancer—this is no time to be a wallflower.

Monday, February 8, New Moon in Aquarius

The sign of the water carrier can be capricious. Changing your mind, looking for a way to help humanity. These are all themes of this particular New Moon. Aquarius Moons are excellent for coming at a problem from another direction, as well as reaching out to faraway friends. Taurus, Leo, Scorpio, Virgo, and Cancer—as much as you like to be loyal, today is super for starting a new project or starting over and not looking back. Aquarius, Libra, Gemini, Sagittarius, Capricorn, Pisces, and Aries—impulsiveness could bring you someplace fabulous. Give in to your whims.

Monday, February 22, Full Moon in Virgo

The Virgin isn't just an indolent lass—she's associated with Ceres, the goddess of the harvest, and this Full Moon is about taking care of health and work matters that you may have overlooked. Being fussy and meticulous is a perfectly fine way to launch your week, even if others may not get on board with perfectionism. Pisces, Sagittarius, Gemini, Aries, and Aquarius—take your time no matter how much others rush you. Virgo, Capricorn, Taurus, Libra, Scorpio, Leo, and Cancer—physical movement will restore you if you've been exercising your opinions instead of your body.

Tuesday, March 8, New Moon in Pisces

The sign of the fish swimming in two directions is the most Zen image in our pantheon of astrological signs. What does that mean? Stasis? Indecision? Definitely introspection, and with the New Moon, the psychic abilities latent in us definitely get a boost. All twelve signs should make time for meditation, particularly Cancer, Pisces, Scorpio, Aries, Taurus, Aquarius, and Capricorn (all thoughtful types anyway). Virgo, Gemini, Sagittarius, Libra and Leo—take a hint from the caterpillar in Alice in Wonderland and find a comfy couch and settle in.

Wednesday, March 23, Full Moon in Libra

The sign of the scales has some similarities with fellow air sign Gemini, and water sign Pisces, in that it's easy to start sentences with "on the one hand…" Finding the merits in both sides of a situation comes easily, particularly for Libra, Gemini, Leo, Virgo, Scorpio, Sagittarius, and Aquarius. Aries, Capricorn, Cancer, Pisces, and Taurus—you may be bubbling over with great ideas and random follow-through.

Thursday, April 7, New Moon in Aries

The first sign of the zodiac is the happy ram, horns down, marching along. With the New Moon, shortcuts appeal, as does completing tasks quickly. Since Aries rules the head, consider buying a fabulous new spring hat or getting your hair cut. Cancer, Capricorn, Libra, Virgo, and Scorpio will resist being rushed. Aries, Leo, Sagittarius, Taurus, Gemini, Pisces, and Aquarius—fresh starts, particularly for friendships or a job should be pursued. If you've heard it before, walk out the door.

Friday, April 22, Full Moon in Scorpio

This sign rules sex, death, and other people's money. This can also translate to romance, spiritual transformation, and credit cards! In any event, having a weekend Full Moon in Scorpio definitely adds up to sensuousness and spring awakenings, and could definitely perk up your life. Scorpio, Cancer, Pisces, Libra, Sagittarius, Virgo, and Capricorn—excellent ingredients for an erotic adventure, or a full-bodied immersion in (fill in the blank!). Taurus, Aquarius, Leo, Gemini, and Aries may find it easy to take offense over trifles. Stick with what feels good.

Friday, May 6, New Moon in Taurus

The sign of the bull brings responsibility and stubbornness. It's a fine day for antique hunting or for attending concerts. Try to make some time today or tomorrow to review financial matters or resources. Taurus, Virgo, Capricorn, Gemini, Cancer, Pisces, Aries—creativity is your salvation, and things may be more simple than you think. Leo, Scorpio, Aquarius, Libra, and Sagittarius—if you've put off repairing or refurbishing something in your abode, go to it.

Saturday, May 21, Full Moon in Scorpio

Yes, another Scorpio Full Moon—Full Moons in the same sign twice occasionally happens in the course of a year. So, if you didn't indulge yourself in deep thoughts or deep relationships, you get another opportunity. But remember, Scorpio also rules surgery, so you may find something needing to be removed that was just fine a moment ago! Scorpio, Cancer, Pisces, Libra, Sagittarius, Virgo, and Capricorn—skepticism isn't always comfortable but will make a lot of sense today. Taurus, Aquarius, Leo, Gemini, and Aries—focus on making something grow. Even those with the blackest of thumbs might find planning a garden rewarding.

Saturday, June 4, New Moon in Gemini

The sign of the twins helps us to see at least two angles—although if you know any Geminis, you'll know that they have way more than two personalities! Writing, communicating, or having quick conversations are all highly pleasurable, particularly for Gemini, Libra, Aquarius, Taurus, Aries, Leo, and Cancer. For Sagittarius, Pisces, Virgo, Capricorn, and Scorpio—the quickest decision might bring unwelcome consequences. Be cautious versus impulsive.

Monday, June 20, Full Moon in Sagittarius

Were Bottom and Snout performing "Pyramus and Thisbe" tonight in *A Midsummer's Night Dream,* they could use available Moonlight easily. With the Moon in the side of the jovial archer, jokes, journeys, and justice are the themes. The wildest ideas sound plausible, and even the most conservative folks could share some surprising personal information. Having a blast will be Sagittarius, Leo, Aries, Libra, Scorpio, Capricorn, and Aquarius. Definitely looking for drama may be Pisces, Virgo, Gemini, Taurus, and Cancer.

Monday, July 4, New Moon in Cancer

The sign of the crab governs baking, ceramics, and massage. Cancer New Moons are about molting, which means you may need solitude for a good long while. This water sign can bring out everyone's sensitive side, so if you are starting a project or relationship (work or otherwise), tentativeness should be the theme. Cancer, Scorpio, Pisces, Virgo, Leo, Gemini, and Taurus—your insights are deep, but having faith in your abilities to evaluate is more than half the battle. Aries, Capricorn, Libra, Aquarius, and Sagittarius—you could be caretaking for someone else, when in fact, that care and attention should be self-directed.

Tuesday, July 19, Full Moon in Capricorn

The sign of the goat is helpful for bringing out the workaholic side—even during these summer months when one's impulse is to kick back. Long-term financial planning plus construction should be on the agenda for many, and Capricorn Moons bring out the thoughtful, versus impetuous side. Capricorn, Taurus, Virgo, Aquarius, Pisces, Sagittarius, and Scorpio—patience will be rewarded, and if you take the time to build a structure, the rest will fall into place. Cancer, Libra, Aries, Leo, and Gemini—are you feeling impatient with outspoken or childish companions? You could surprise yourself by feeling more mature, if only for the day!

Tuesday, August 2, New Moon in Leo

The sign of the lion is all about children's activities and public events. If you feel like dressing like a kid or pouring your change into a gumball machine, this Moon could be to blame. However, exaggeration could come easily to some, and as much as Leo can bring gaiety and good times, impatience with ego-trips could come with this phase, particularly for Scorpio, Aquarius, Taurus, Pisces, and Capricorn.

Thursday, August 18, Full Moon in Aquarius

The water-carrier represents electricity and mass movements, so if you're feeling like following a trend, you'll have lots of company. Conversations that cover a wider range of topics or concerns about humanitarianism definitely take precedence on this Full Moon. If you help a charity or nonprofit, go full steam ahead with the marketing and fund-raising. Aquarius, Libra, Gemini, Pisces, Aries, Capricorn, and Sagittarius—those in the neighborhood may not understand you, but faraway friends have your number. Call them first. Taurus, Scorpio, Leo, Virgo, and Libra—you may feel like taking apart something that seems solid.

Thursday, September 1, New Moon in Virgo

The Virgin oversees matters concerning work, health, and service. Doing for others is a smart use of your time, as is assessing your career. Starting a project that enhances your professional abilities is a fine investment, particularly for Virgo, Taurus, Capricorn, Libra, Scorpio, Leo, and Gemini. Getting caught up in minutia, or being super fussy could be a downfall for Pisces, Gemini, Sagittarius, Aries, and Aquarius.

Friday, September 16, Full Moon in Pisces

The sign of the fish rules the feet, and if you haven't treated your toes in a while, today is excellent for shoe shopping. Look at photographs, explore what has been concealed from you, evaluate from the core, and appreciate the fact that people are more complicated than we can understand (which is why we have pets!). Virgo, Gemini, Sagittarius, Libra, and Leo—you may feel, "less than," or overwhelmed by your inability to keep things simple. Give yourself a break! Pisces Moons are complicated.

Sunday, October 16, Full Moon in Aries

The sign of the ram loves a fresh start, and with the Moon in its full phase this could mean that a project that's gone forward suddenly changes direction or is seen as needing more work. Yes, it's the Harvest Moon so additional light is shining in every direction. Aries, Sagittarius, Leo, Taurus, Gemini, Aquarius, and Pisces—be tolerant of those who have a bee in their bonnet about something that wasn't in the plans. Chances are, they'll burn themselves out, and things can go back to how they were. Cancer, Libra, Capricorn, Scorpio, and Virgo—you could be persuaded by those who express themselves loudly versus clearly.

Sunday, October 30, New Moon in Libra

The sign of the scales promotes a spirit of justice or even-handedness. All risks taken will be calculated, and partnerships get a focus. So you can explore what's missing from your relationship, or get into the spirit of the holiday. Put on costumes and have some fun as someone else! Libra, Gemini, Aquarius, Scorpio, Sagittarius, Virgo, and Leo—look for opportunities to mesh or to complement someone. Libra Moons are about harmony, so

2015 © rolffimages image from BigStockPhotc.com

pursue those with whom you make beautiful music. Cancer, Capricorn, Aries, Pisces, and Taurus—changing your mind could be frustrating, but could be a safe move overall.

Monday, November 14, Full Moon in Taurus

The sign of the bull and the Full Moon focuses on practical matters. The acquisition of wealth? The beautification of your home or yourself? Taurus is a pretty straightforward sign, so hearing the real deal is highly likely. Some folks prefer their information prettied up, but stick to the facts and you won't get into trouble. Taurus, Virgo, Capricorn, Gemini, Cancer, Pisces, and Aries—slow and steady wins the race. Scorpio, Aquarius, Leo, Libra, and Sagittarius—this is a terrible time to hold a grudge, or to control matters that others need to handle. Step back.

Tuesday, November 29, New Moon in Sagittarius

The sign of the archer encourages higher education and exploration of other cultures. Plan some long travel and look for opportunities to sample different cultures and skip steps in procedures. Find something to laugh about and share the humor with others. Sagittarius, Leo, Aries, Scorpio, Libra, Capricorn, and Aquarius—you're incredibly persuasive right now. Use those powers for good! Gemini, Virgo, Pisces, Taurus, and Cancer—you could be rushing, when caution and patience makes more sense.

Tuesday, December 13, Full Moon in Gemini

The sign of the twins encourages us to find alternatives or to consider the opposition. This is a useful exercise if you are working with a SWOT chart (strengths, weaknesses, opportunities, and threats). Gemini Moons help to keep everything moving along. There's little likelihood of getting bogged down in precision—broad strokes carry the day. Gemini, Libra, Aquarius, Taurus, Gemini, Leo, and Cancer—this is a friend-making time. Put yourself out there. Sagittarius, Virgo, Pisces, Scorpio, and Capricorn—an impulse to be all things to everyone could tax your versatility. Think of the stress the chameleon feels when put on a background of plaid.

Thursday, December 29, New Moon in Capricorn

Having a New Moon coincide with the year's end will encourage those who are inclined to make New Year's resolutions. Making small but lasting changes comes more easily during the New Moon. However, slow and steady will win the race, and the sign of the goat is very, very patient. This is also a time when some folks may be blunt without being aware of the impact that they are having. Libra, Cancer, Aries, Leo, and Gemini—try not to take offense if others' comments are insensitive. Taurus, Capricorn, Virgo, Aquarius, Pisces, Sagittarius, and Scorpio—be firm and don't be talked out of something you care about.

About the Author

Sally Cragin is a teacher and the author of Astrology on the Cusp *for people whose birthdays are at the end of one Sun sign or the beginning of the next. Her first book was* The Astrological Elements, *and both titles were published with Llewellyn Worldwide. She has written the astrological forecast "Moon Signs" for the* Boston Phoenix, *syndicated throughout New England. Re-elected to the Fitchburg, MA, School Committee, she is the only professional astrologer holding elected office in New England. She also provides forecasts for clients that are "cool, useful, and accurate." More at Moonsigns.net.*

2016
Moon Sign Book
Articles

Astrology of Garden Icons

By Robin Ivy Payton

S mall and private or large and public, a balanced garden invites
you in and instantly gives you a feeling of comfort or discovery. You may gravitate to places and not know why a certain
garden holds such magic and inspiration! The flora, color, shapes,
and features are somehow just right. The blend of yin and yang
in a garden appeals to the senses, evoking feelings of both peace
and connection.

Just as you can cultivate a balance of strong and vulnerable traits
in your personality or home, your garden can express serenity and
invite activity. Your outdoor sanctuary can become a yin place to
meditate and read, and also a yang spot for entertaining and play!
Introduce contrasting energies with foliage and flowers, or elements such as water, wood, stones, arrangements, or statues. Their
form and expression evoke feelings and reflect personality.

Garden features relate to the elements of water, earth, air/wind, fire, and also the zodiac signs. Yang is the fire and air signs: Aries, Gemini, Leo, Libra, Sagittarius, and Aquarius. Water and earth are yin and include Taurus, Cancer, Virgo, Scorpio, Capricorn, and Pisces. Regardless of your Sun sign, your gardening style reflects your preferences and may lean in one direction. Yang with bright, long, and tall; or yin with low, cool, and curvaceous. We'll explore the energies of some popular statues through element and Sun sign correlations for a new perspective on gardens.

Perfectly Yin

Ponds, birdbaths, and fountains are physical representations for the water element of Cancer, Scorpio, and Pisces. The life force of water is nourishment for all beings. Healthful water generally moves and flows as in a fountain or waterfall, though even quiet water attracts and provides for the birds and insects inhabiting the garden. Water can also be incorporated on an energetic level with statues representing qualities of compassion, spirituality, and flow.

Buddha is yin and a water element. Representing peace and contentment, a Buddha in the garden lends a restful quality. Often with eyes closed and a subtle smile, Buddha is calming and welcomes us to sit and rest. Buddha with one hand raised and the other holding a bowl represents healing and compassion, and is sometimes called the medicine Buddha. Others are full of expression, smiling or laughing with arms open. These happy Buddhas gestures signify abundance, also connected to the water element. Whether reclining, seated, or walking, male or female, Buddha aligns with the astrological energy of Pisces. Empathetic, connected to a higher purpose and a reminder that peace comes from within, Buddha softens the garden energy.

Frogs symbolize fertility and rebirth, and also bring yin to the landscape. Frog statues hold the mutable energy of Pisces, and as frogs are amphibious, it represents the ability to transform and adapt. Long associated with water, frogs are seen as rainmakers in some native cultures and are an offering for cooling and nourishment. Energetically, the frog is connected to the Moon and our emotions and allows for release of anger, fear, or other feelings containing heat or yang. Place a frog in the garden to balance spiky plants, columns, tall structures or bushes, and things that project.

Moon man or Moon goddess epitomizes the yin concept. Representing night, cool, the subconscious, and dreams, any Moon statue brings the spirit of night to a place in the Sun. Lunar vibes can be childlike too, especially the Moon man with a smile who acts as a protector. The comfort of Moon energy in the garden embodies Cancer, a sign of fertility and nurturing. A Moon garden that blooms at night complements your daytime landscape, and a physical lunar element brings yin presence that can be enjoyed all hours of the day.

The yin of earth, ever present outdoors, can be introduced to the garden as a stabilizing force. As water flows, earths grounds. Some common earth statues include animals like rabbits and deer, saints in their human form, gnomes and trolls, and the green man.

The Green Man symbolizes oneness between humans and nature. His energy is renewal and the cycles of life. Some cultures use Green Man totems to encourage successful crops, so he also signifies abundance. Placing Green Man in your landscape is a way of honoring the earth and offering healing for any imbalances humans have created in the environment. Astrologically, Green Man (along with trolls, gnomes, and some fairies) relates to Taurus, Virgo, and Capricorn. An old man or crone image leans toward Capricorn ruled by Saturn, while a more youthful creature has the spirit of strong Taurus or graceful Virgo. Rootedness, receptivity, rebirth, and regeneration make the garden feel like a nourishing and protected place. The spirit of Green Man and other earth elementals are nourishing and protective.

Deer and rabbits are common animals introduced to garden

areas in statue form. Both represent the yin aspect of fauna and are gentle totems. Deer, known for their grace, are totems of understanding and intuition. In Celtic and Native American lore, deer are said to lead humans to the best medicinal herbs. Deer bring Virgo qualities of service and sensitivity to the garden. Tune in and listen to the energy of deer. The rabbit brings gentle and feminine energy. Known as a fertility totem, rabbits also help us move through fear with quick thinking and instinctive movement. Several cultures have associated rabbits with the Moon, and, like deer, rabbits tell us to pause, tune in, and listen. In Western astrology, rabbit's fertility aspect is most typified by earthy Taurus, and her gentility aligns with Virgo. Added to the yin aspect of the garden, rabbit statues calm the busy mind and are symbols of good fortune.

Uplifting Yang

Gardens are for relaxation and enjoyment of nature, and ideally you are recharged and inspired by the landscape and its structures. The yang element is represented with warm and hot colors, high or spiky trees and flowers, and representations of the fire and air elements—Aries, Gemini, Leo, Libra, Sagittarius, and Aquarius. Fire-sign energy comes with statues that embody courage or defenders of the territory like lions, gods, or sphinxes. Air elements include all things with wings and carry the spirit of messengers, birds, and even music. Where yin statues have a quiet, receptive quality, yang has a more forceful presence, whether that's something propelling, imposing, or extending. The statues themselves do not have to move to exert yang energy. Some, like an angel or a girl and boy duo, may have both a yin and yang dynamic. The Victorian boy and girl might best represent Gemini, since this is the sign of siblings and also duality. The angel has the spiritual aspect of the water sign Pisces, yet her wings and role as a messenger lend air-sign qualities of Libra, Gemini, and

Aquarius. Feel the balance of yin and yang intuitively, and pair statues that complement each other as well as the land and water features of the garden. When seeking to add yang energy think light, playful, or bold!

The fire side of yang might be described as royal, strong, or wild. Lions or sphinx often sit at garden entries as a protective influence. They are both guardian totems, connected to the solar deities, and therefore Leo. From Egyptian, Greek, or Asian traditions, the sphinx is generally recognized for ferocity, a connection to royalty, and may be depicted with or without wings. This mythical beast stands up to violent or evil forces and is a formidable guardian of property and its inhabitants. The lion is the earthly version with the same symbolism and energy, and both represent strength.

A dragon is another way to incorporate the fire element. Dragons can be of earth, water, or air, yet the dragon's fierce protection and bravery characterizes fire. A force of transformation, transmutation, and creation, the dragon represents power. Bring this in to connect you to other worlds or as a totem of achievement and success. Regardless of physical traits, a dragon is a strong yang presence in the landscape.

Birds inhabit our gardens bringing air energy, so an owl is often introduced as a fixture. Sometimes owl statues are displayed to scare away small mammals that may be pests. The owl is a bird of prey, and as a garden totem is another protector. On a spiritual level, an owl is like the air sign Libra with the art of discernment and sharp senses. Connected to Athena, the owl replaces or balances emotion with knowledge. The owl is also a messenger, as are all creatures with wings. Both logical and intuitive, owls bring intellect and good judgment, and they may be a complement to the emotional qualities of frogs.

Fairies and angels are contrasts in the air element, as one suggests magic and the other divinity. With wings to transport them, they travel between the realms and have the yang of movement and communication associated with Libra, Aquarius, and Gemini. Angels receive and transport prayers and deliver messages. Various types of angels have the common traits of guarding the faithful and stirring the soul with information, ideas, and prayer. They are a symbol of spiritual connection.

Fairies, on the other end of the air spectrum, are not always winged, and have been described as between human and angel. Usually winged when displayed in modern gardens, fairies are known for mischief and magic. Playful energy is introduced to the garden with fairy figures. They insinuate that anything can happen, including spontaneous fun or trickery. Fairies remind us of mystery and things that exist beyond the physical realm. Uplifting spirits is a fairy's gift to the garden! Their yang air energy may complement the earthy groundedness of a deer or rabbit statue.

Have It All

A popular figure amid flowers and birdbaths is St. Francis. Sources cite a Libra birth date and his church feast day is in early October, however, St. Francis best embodies the earth element. He is noted for his love and kindness to all creatures and has been called the saint of ecology and the environment. He honored the sacredness of all living creatures and his story includes imprisonment, illness, and military service, yet his message is to live simply and respect the animal world, nature, and the heavenly bodies. His statue can add peace and acceptance to your garden. His strong connection to the birds may attract more air energy as well! The St. Francis statue seems to bring a yin/yang balance all its own and is a fit for many gardens.

Gargoyles provide quite a different feeling to the outdoor sanctuary. Their architectural purpose was to divert water from rooftops, but gargoyles are often found grounded on the earth or on stairways and walls. Astrologically, gargoyles bring both water and dragons into the garden, and they represent Scorpio as well. Many resemble lions or chimera and can be the underbelly of the Leo. Gargoyles give protection from negative forces and can be placed in the garden as a warning against intruders. Gargoyles might be described as yang on the surface and yin below.

It's Up to You

Walk around the neighborhood and note the feeling of garden statues you see. Your response to their presence is an indicator of the qualities they might bring to your landscape. Whether you build around one theme or add a new feature to an outdoor space, the vibration of garden statues will contribute to the feeling of the area. An element of strength, surprise, and lightness comes with your yang selections, while softness, nourishment, and flow are the yin effect. A mix of high and low, light and shade, warm and cool blooms, open areas and private spots lends grace and juxtaposition to the outdoor space. Your statues and structures are the finishing touch.

About the Author

Robin Ivy Payton is a yoga instructor specializing in yoga therapy, prenatal yoga, and her brand RoZoYo, an astrology based yoga practice. As creator and proprietor of Robin's Zodiac Zone online, she has been writing and broadcasting daily astrology forecasts following the aspects of Moon, Sun, and planets since 1999. Her forecasts air daily on WCYY and WHOM out of Portland, Maine. Robin began writing for Llewellyn in 2003. Find her at www.RoZoYo.com, facebook.com/RobinsZodiacZone, or twitter.com/robinzodiacyoga.

2015© yuris010 Image from BigStockPhoto.com

Lasagna Gardening

By Charlie Rainbow Wolf

I will admit I am a lazy gardener. So when someone said that they knew a way to make fertile beds that needed little digging or weeding, I was all ears. Lasagna gardening isn't a Mediterranean plot where Italian food ingredients are grown—although you can grow just about anything in one. The term gets its name from the way organic matter is layered, much like the ingredients in lasagna are layered, one on top of the other.

This method has other names too. You may have heard it called a no-dig garden, a compost bed garden, or even sheet composting. Whatever the name, the results are the same. This lasagna recipe makes rich soil right where you want to grow your vegetables, so there is no need for digging, correcting poor soil, or other tedious preparation. Layer it right and you'll have a very rich bed where it is unnecessary to do a lot of digging, fertilizing, or weeding.

These gardens can be created all at once, but I found more success building it up over time. I was lucky. I had fairly good soil to begin with. I started with a straw bale garden, and the next year I used the rotting straw as one of the layers in my lasagna garden.

Building the Garden

If you're starting from scratch, the best thing to do is outline where you want the garden to go. I actually spray painted the lines on the grass so that I knew where to fill in with the layers. There's no need to remove the grass or break the turf for this type of garden bed—nature will do that for you. It is best if you don't have a load of stubborn weeds or high grass when starting though. A trip with the lawnmower or weed whacker should do the trick.

The first layer to put on the measured area is thick paper or cardboard. I always use newspaper or plain brown cardboard (any packaging labels or tape removed) because I'm never sure the effect the colored inks might have on the bed. The shiny magazine-type paper doesn't seem to do as well as newspaper. You'll probably find that you use much more paper than you originally estimate. Ask at your local newspaper if they have any back issues that you can have. You may have to remove the flyers or glossy inserts.

I've found it's best to wet the paper before placing it. Not only does this stop it from blowing away, but it also makes a more impenetrable barrier. Don't be afraid to pile this on thickly. This is your weed barrier, and it will stop weeds and grass from coming through into your bed. Use several sheets, wet, and overlap the edges so that there's a good, uninterrupted cover.

It's quite possible to stop here for the first season. As I mentioned, this is what I did. I planted, used the wet paper and decomposing straw for the mulch that year, and then built on the top of it the next year.

If you're in a hurry to get started, place your wet newspaper in late autumn or early spring and cover it with thick black plastic for several weeks. This will help to heat up the paper and start the decomposition to be ready for the next stage in the process. Autumn is my preferred time to start simply because of the leaves and other readily available rotting organic matter that can be added to the layers to help build the rich soil for the spring.

Just like layering lasagna with both noodles and filling, the garden bed has to have both brown and green plant-based material so that it will cook properly. Nearly anything you'd throw into a compost heap can be thrown into a no-dig bed, just remember to alternate the brown ingredients with the green. Brown ingredients are leaves, junk mail, evergreen waste, and wood chippings. Green ingredients are things like kitchen waste (excluding meat), grass clippings, and garden trimmings. A rule of thumb is the brown layers should be up to twice as thick as the green layers, but it's not an exact science. Thoroughly wet the layers before adding the next one. Making a lasagna garden in autumn has the advantages of the autumn rains and the winter snowfalls to help keep the layers moist and aid in breaking down nicely.

Over time this will break down and make the bed on its own, but if you're in a hurry, you'll have to add some ingredients so that you'll be able to plant in the spring. If this is the case, add a layer of topsoil or peat to the recipe and just keep layering, finishing with soil as the top layer. You will be able to plant in the bed if you finish it off with a layer of about four inches of soil—which is why it is best to start in the autumn, and let the bed make its own soil. The bottom ingredients will settle as they break down.

Planting the Garden

So what can you plant in your lasagna garden? Just about anything! There's very little that falls under a right or wrong way to do this. Nature is very forgiving, fortunately for us! I mostly transplant young seedlings in the lasagna beds, so I just loosen the soil with a trowel and add the plant, disturbing the surrounding area as little as possible. After you plant, keep adding layers. Weeding will be light, and if you find that you're getting overrun, add another layer of paper as a barrier around your seedlings and start building things up again. It's that simple.

I'm very fond of using a lasagna bed for annual vegetables, but it will support flowers and perennials as well. Herbs also do well in lasagna gardens. The great thing about this is that once you've assessed the amount of sunlight exposure it will get, you can customize your garden to any size or shape to meet your requirements. Get creative with it!

Because there is no need for digging or tilling, your plants can be placed closer together. That greatly reduces the need for weeding because the seedlings will grow and help to form their own barrier. The soil is nice and fertile, and any weeds that try to grow can quickly be pulled out and turned into part of the recipe, provided they haven't gone to seed.

When autumn brings the end of the harvest, the stalks and deadheads of anything that had been grown in that bed can be turned into layers for the next decomposition. No moving things to the compost heap, no putting the garden away for the winter. It's right there! Layer it up with additional greens or browns, and you're done until next spring. Be mindful of anything gone to seed though. You don't want volunteer plants—especially weeds—popping up in your garden! A general rule of thumb is that if you would chuck it in your compost heap, you can layer it in your lasagna garden.

Container Gardens

This method of layering can be used in container gardens as well, which makes it ideal for those who want to garden but have no soil to plant in. Containers can be placed on patios or balconies. If you've already got boxes for your raised beds, this is a wonderful way to add the soil and compost all in one process. The size of the container doesn't matter. Lasagna gardening can be done anywhere, in whatever sized area meets your needs.

Start the container garden the same way as you would a lasagna bed, with the layers of wet newspaper placed over the drainage holes in the pot. If the pots are very small, use unbleached coffee filters. If the container is exceptionally deep, rocks, empty soda cans, or plastic bottles can be put in the bottom before the paper is added. This lifts up the base, so not as many layers are needed to make the topsoil where you'll be planting. Once the bottom layer is in place, keep layering the green and brown layers as you would if you were working a larger area. Make sure that every layer is thoroughly moistened before adding the next one.

In addition to the wide array of beautiful bedding plants that can be grown in containers, many vegetables can also be grown this way. Determinate (bush) tomatoes, peppers, and bush beans may seem the obvious choices, but with a bit of imagination there are other, less obvious selections that also do well. Indeterminate (vining) tomatoes can be grown in a container as long as some kind of cage or other support system is used, and cucumbers can be grown in a similar fashion. Even baby melons and pie pumpkins do well in larger containers either with a support system or gracefully hanging over the sides. Seasonal dwarf trees can be planted in this manner too, with the container being brought into the greenhouse or other sheltered area for colder winters.

Other Perks

There are so many advantages to lasagna gardening this way! There's no need to till, so no expensive equipment is necessary. If you have a garden spade, a shovel, a fork, and maybe a wheelbarrow or cart, you have all the tools needed to start a lasagna garden. Finally, because you create the lasagna garden exactly where you want it, the plot can be any size or any shape.

If you have ever wanted to try your hand at gardening but the thought of digging, weeding, and the expense put you off, let lasagna gardening entice you to try. Start small, maybe a deep container or small plot in your yard. Only bite off what you think you can comfortably chew (unlike yours truly). You're likely to find that it is easy, economical, and most of all, fun!

For More Reading

Bartholomew, Mel. *Square Foot Gardening: A New Way to Garden in Less Space With Less Work*. Nashville, TN: Cool Springs Press, 2005.

Lanza, Patricia. *Lasagna Gardening: A New Layering System for Bountiful Gardens: No Digging, No Tilling, No Weeding, No Kidding!* Emmaus, PA: Rodale Press, 1998.

Warren, Spring. *The Quarter-Acre Farm: How I Kept the Patio, Lost the Lawn, and Fed My Family for a Year*. Berkely, CA: Seal Press, 2011.

About the Author

Charlie Rainbow Wolf is happiest when she's creating something, especially from items that others have cast aside. She is passionate about writing, and deeply intrigued by astrology, tarot, runes, and other divination oracles. Knitting and pottery are her favorite hobbies, although she happily confesses that she's easily distracted by all the wonderful things that life has to offer. Charlie is an advocate of organic gardening and cooking, and lives in the Midwest with her husband and her special needs Great Danes. www.charlierainbow.com

Understanding the Moon Signs of Others

An excerpt from *Astrology & Relationships*

By David Pond

The sign your Moon was in at your birth describes your habits, comfort zones, the way you respond to your emotional needs, and how you express yourself emotionally. In relationships the Moon is just as important as the Sun. These two parts of your character must be integrated for you to experience the best with others. The sign of your Moon gives definition to the unconscious habit patterns that are expressed through your personality as a response to what is going on around you.

Consider the needs of your Sun sign and think of your Moon sign as the emotional support system you need to sustain the strength of the Sun. While your Sun sign describes how you project yourself to the world, your Moon sign describes how you retreat to rejuvenate yourself and what habit patterns of comfort you develop. Knowing the Moon sign of others will give you clues as to how to better understand and relate to their emotional needs.

Aries

These people have a bright, intense emotional character that responds to the moment. You will always know how they feel and will need to learn to deal with issues right when they come up. They prefer the "intense confrontation and then be done with it" approach to emotional encounters rather than a drawn-out solution. Their feelings can be easily hurt, and to protect themselves they usually become defensive. Allow them to vent pent-up anger and frustration. Venting is healthy. Just don't allow yourself to be a target.

Moon in Aries individuals are very inspirational and motivational. They possess a "can do" philosophy about life that will motivate you to become all that you can become. They are at their best in a very active relationship, so passive activities are usually not tolerated. They love to be surprised by spontaneous plans, however, there are times when it is best to just leave them alone and let them go at their own pace. These people change moods very quickly, so be prepared. They need to be recognized and appreciated; yet they want you to support their independence.

Taurus

Moon in Taurus individuals have a down-to-earth practicality about the way they respond to life. They usually know where they stand on emotional issues and are not easily influenced. You can rely on these sturdy individuals, as they like to follow through on all commitments. Realize ahead of time that their first response to change is resistance. You cannot force these individuals to change; if they are going to make a change in their lives it will be because they have already decided it was the right thing to do. Continuity allows them to steer a steady course in life, but also makes it difficult to adapt to disruptions in their plans. Give them plenty of advance notice and don't expect spontaneous changes in plans to be appreciated. Along with wanting a comfortable life, Moon in Taurus individuals want an uncomplicated emotional life. Not at ease with the uncertainty of intrigue, they prefer to relate to those who are clear and direct.

In intimate relationships, these people need to feel secure about your love and concern for them. They know how to enjoy life, and through their heightened awareness of the senses, you can become much more appreciative of life's simple pleasures as well. Highly affectionate, these individuals are soothed through simple touch like holding hands, hugs, and massage. No need for pretense with Moon in Taurus individuals. They appreciate genuineness and naturalness above all else.

Gemini

Be prepared to listen to what is going on with these individuals. They need to talk, share, and relate endless details about their lives, even to the extent of talking their way through emotional situations as a way of coming to terms with their feelings. The interaction is what they find exciting and satisfying. Keep your expectations of how they should respond or react to a minimum, and they will trust you. Your mental rapport is going to have to be very strong for bonding to occur, and you will have to understand their need for variety and change. You may feel that their many interests come before their feelings for you, but try not to read too much into their spontaneous reaction to life. It's just their nature; they don't want to miss anything. You will not get bored with these inquisitive souls, but you will certainly be tested in your flexibility because they will change plans often.

Cancer

Emotional security is likely to be much more of an issue with these people than first appears. Expect to move slowly in establishing your bonds of friendship and trust. They are cautious and reserved, but that does not mean that they do not care about you. They will stand back and observe you and feel out where they can best fit into your world. Much of how they relate to the world, and to you, is through their feelings that can overwhelm them, so they pull back and again watch and wait. Encourage them to talk about their feelings, and yet know that much of what is going on for them is not easily translatable into words. Their insecurities will surprise you. They appear strong on the outside, but on the inside, they are extremely sensitive. They will protect their vulnerability until they trust your loyalty, and then express tremendous warmth and caring for you. Realize that they are likely to respond to the emotional undercurrents of any situation, not just the presentation. They are responding to how you feel, not what you say. Once accepted into their close circle, you become family and their loyalty is unfaltering.

Leo

These people can be fun, warm, and lovable. They express their emotions with heartfulness and dignity. There seems to be something royal and regal about these individuals. They are big-hearted folks, and if they are secure in the heart you will see the best of them. However, if their heart requirements are not being met, their tremendous need for attention and recognition are likely to lead to a strong competitive nature. Then they can seem self-serving and demanding. They do not want their relationships to be ordinary in any way. They feel they are special people and want their relationships to reflect this. They want the very best. Moon in Leo individuals are likely to be just as proud of you as they want you to be of them. In intimate relationships they need to be the center of attention. They do not deal well as an appendage to someone else's life. They will give just as much as they expect in love relationships, which is considerable. They do not adapt to change well so always introduce changes in plans slowly.

Virgo

These people are very rational in their emotional expression, or at least try to be. They hold themselves to very exacting standards, are very thoughtful, and rarely act out of character. Moon in Virgo individuals seek appreciation for their efforts, and this is one area you can't overdo it. They need a great deal of reassurance about the role they play in your life. They want to be adding something significant to its overall quality, and seem to always work themselves into a position of being indispensable. This placement leads to a tendency to look at life through the lens of a current problem. Problem sharing and problem solving can be techniques for closeness between you and a Virgo Moon friend. They crave interaction and involvement on their work issues so don't be afraid to get involved. Conversely, don't be afraid to remind them that there is more to life than work. They are typically overcoming their excessively self-critical nature. Your feedback and support will speed along this process, as their primary emotional need is to feel appreciated. If you value sincerity and integrity more than flamboyance, this is the type for you.

Libra

There is a certain sense of style and class in these people that will motivate you to put your best foot forward. Their natural refinement is also expressed in the emotional realm and they are quite uncomfortable with unpleasantness of any sort. You can expect them to be fair, just, and diplomatic in all of their dealings with others. Moon in Libra individuals think before they act, so give them time to go through their evaluating process rather than push for immediate decisions. Do not expect them to be overly emotional and syrupy, as they are more comfortable with some distance from their feelings. This does not mean that they do not care about you. They are simply concerned about refined expression. They probably do not handle anger well so you will have to watch for the subtle signals and help them express their real feelings. They really do believe that emotional issues and differences could best be solved if people would simply deal with differences in a clear, calm, and rational way. Of course this is unrealistic, but realize that it is their ideal nonetheless and you will be better able to understand them.

Scorpio

Emotions for these people run strong, deep, and intense. There is a mysterious quality about their souls that keeps you feeling that more is going on with them than meets the eye. Moon in Scorpio people are excellent about getting you to reveal your secrets, but you will realize they share their innermost feelings only after trust has been established. As they begin to share their private side with you treat it as special, privileged information not to be shared with others. They are uncanny at knowing your true moti-

2015 © scol22 Image from BigStockPhoto.com

vations and intentions, and are not easily fooled by presentations. They are often much more expressive in silence than they are with words. Silent looks and glances to and from these individuals can communicate volumes of information.

The paradox of these individuals lies in their craving for emotional intimacy, yet their emotional world is often guarded and protected with the barbs of past memories. Forgiveness does not come easy to these psychologically complex individuals. Never assume that time itself will heal wounds with them. It doesn't. It is best to deal directly and in the moment with emotional issues to keep the air clean. Those with Moon in Scorpio have a need for some privacy and prefer one-to-one, intimate sharing to large social functions. Trust is something that you will develop together. Your own emotional growth will be sped up through the closeness of this friendship.

Sagittarius

These people are optimistic, outgoing, and fun loving. Decidedly positive, they want to believe in the best. They like a fast-paced life with plenty of mental stimulation. The enthusiasm of Sagittarius is infectious and it is easy to feel more positive in their presence. The excitement of anticipating future potential is one of the main types of emotional experiences they enjoy, so indulge their dreams, plans, and goals as this keeps them at their best.

Moon in Sagittarius is looking for an adventure, an opportunity to grow and expand, and if that can happen through you, you will win your companion's love. Allow lots of room to change, as these people need a variety of forms through which to express. They are honest and sincere, so you will not have to be threatened by their need to occasionally spend time by themselves. They need to occasionally connect with their urge for freedom by following their own momentum without considering other people's expectations. Give them this freedom and you have won a warm-hearted, enthusiastic friend. Although good-natured naturally, these fiery folks can turn competitor and occasionally need a good philosophical argument just for the sport of it. Without an adventure to plan or a goal to pursue, they can feel quite hemmed in.

Capricorn

For these people, the theme of respect is of central importance in all of their relationships. Moon in Capricorn individuals are responsible to the nth degree. Trust them. Commitment is like a solemn bond. If they promised something, they will deliver. Of course they will expect the same accountability from you. They want your recognition for their accomplishments along with the person behind the work. You will have to respond to both of these needs. They identify with their work so much that they need to share this part of their life with their partners.

They need their relationships to take some definite form so the more clearly you can define your expectations, the more comfortable they will become. When they are in one of their broody, introspective moods it is best to leave them to their work. They want your support concerning some of the hardships and difficulties they have endured. These people respect competence; yet they need to feel useful in your life to feel secure so don't fear asking them for assistance.

They are comfortable in a providing role. They are not sentimentalists, but when they have someone in their life who sees through the mountain of strength and recognizes their sensitivity, they become very loyal and loving friends. Their appreciation for quality and their high standards of excellence are just as important to them in relationships as everywhere else in life.

Aquarius

These highly independent individuals are sure to keep you guessing as to how they will respond next, because they refuse to conform to convention or the expectations of others. They are friendly, outgoing, and open to sharing their ideas. Often altruistic and inclined toward larger social issues, they love to deal with abstractions. They question authority at every turn and are advocates for individual rights. Don't expect them to pamper your emotional sensitivities—they won't. It is not their expertise, nor their interest. It is not that they are hiding their emotions. It's just that they are mistrustful and completely unsure of that arena of expression.

To bring out their best in working situations give them the freedom to fulfill their responsibilities in their own way. They view life from a far removed vantage point, which gives them a unique perspective. They will provoke your thinking, as the clarity of their insights is often shocking. Keep things light, friendly, and impersonal to best get along with these people. Share your ideals and hopeful thoughts on how life could be improved. Encourage them to talk about their ideals and frankly let them know when they have walked on your feelings. Tell them how that feels to you. They really do not know unless you confront them with it. Their matter-of-fact-ness can be annoying and you will need to let them know when they are being insensitive. They have an abstract sense of humor that is a true pleasure to share. Expect a fresh original point of view when you ask their opinion.

Pisces

These deep feeling individuals are most often governed by their emotions. They will react to even the slightest emotional shift in your feelings toward them so be aware that your nonverbal communication will be more loudly heard than your verbal ones. They are naturally compassionate and have a knack for drawing out your deepest, personal feelings. Move slowly with them because much of who they are is hidden, and only time will bring it to the surface. They will respond to the purest and deepest spiritual connection from you. They are understanding and caring by nature, and you can trust that any revelations that you share with them concerning your sensitivities will be handled in the gentlest of ways.

Moon in Pisces people enjoy the poetic, romantic approach. The imaginative, the magical, and the mystical hold their interest. Their emotional cycles may appear confusing to you, as they periodically need to go to a place inside themselves that words cannot convey. When you have their attention, there are none more sensitive and understanding, but there are times when they need to be alone to connect with the depths of their emotional character. Without quality alone time they become overwhelmed by the worries and concerns of others. When you establish an emotional bond with these people, the reward is a truly caring and compassionate friendship.

About the Author

David is an internationally recognized astrologer, author, and workshop leader. He has been a practicing professional astrologer for over 35 years and has a Master of Science degree in "Experimental Metaphysics" from Central Washington University. His many books on metaphysical topics include: Astrology and Relationships, Chakras for Beginners, *and* The Pursuit of Happiness. *David's greatest love remains working with clients, one-to-one, exploring how their astrology can be helpful in their lives. David@Davidpond.com or www.Davidpond.com*

Hemp: Herb of Many Uses

By Bruce Scofield

Nearly four hundred years ago Nicholas Culpeper, physician, astrologer, and author of *The Complete Herbal*, wrote that hemp required no description because every housewife knew what it looked like. He designated it as an herb of Saturn and organized its uses. The seeds boiled in milk were a remedy for a hot, dry cough, and as a blend it was good for treating jaundice or easing colic and bowel problems. It was good for easing pains in the joints and for gout, and juice made from the root and mixed with oil was good for treating burns. Culpeper's description is very much in line with the symbolism of Saturn, which is traditionally associated with the skin, dense matter, and the need for order. Jaundice visible in the skin, colic which requires calming, and gout which is caused by the crystallization of uric acid would have been understood by a seventeenth-century physician as ailments requiring a Saturn-ruled herb.

Today this herb is used medicinally for side effects from chemo-therapy, chronic neurological pain, rheumatoid arthritis, and a number of other ailments. Many find that it aids in calming the mind for better sleep, stimulates the appetite, and focuses the mind. Again, the symbolism of Saturn seems appropriate because these are all conditions that benefit from calming the nervous system.

Common Uses

The use of cannabis as a medicinal plant has a long history, as hinted at above. In China, an early treatise on pharmacology and medicine written by Emperor Shen Nung contains references to the herb. Called *ma* in Chinese, cannabis was considered a remedy for gout, rheumatism, and absentmindedness. There are also references to cannabis in ancient Indian writings, where it was used in traditional medicine as a sedative and anti-inflammatory agent as well as a hallucinogen. There are also references to it in ancient Eastern and Asian cultures. Writing in fifth century BCE, Greek historian Herodotus described customs of the Scythians living near the Black Sea. They used wild and cultivated hemp fiber to make garments and the seeds to make an aromatic vapor bath. The procedure placed seeds on hot stones in a closed room, which produced a powerful smoke that they regarded as cleansing. Herodotus also described another culture of the region that would throw a plant (presumably cannabis) on a fire and breath in the smoke, inspiring them to sing and dance. Hemp was also known to be used in similar medicinal ways in Africa. It was not known in the Americas until the Spanish and Portuguese brought it.

Hemp has long been an important plant for reasons other than medical. It was a major source of fiber and was of particular importance in making rope needed for ship rigging, and it as therefore vital to trade. International trade in hemp was extremely important for hundreds of years, and this trade was a motivating force for colonization where growing areas were sought. In addition to rope, hemp fiber was, and still is, used for clothing, textiles, paper, and building materials. Hemp seed is used for making oil, which biofuels, paints, and plastics are made from. The seed is also a component of bird food. The leaves are edible and can be added to salads, the oil is about 80 percent essential fatty acids, and the seeds are protein-rich. Over the past century, the use of hemp declined considerably for various reasons, but now it is returning as one of humanity's most useful plants on the planet.

In India the use of cannabis evolved in ways more complex than anywhere else. There are at least three grades for how the herb is prepared for intoxication purposes. Bhang is composed of leaves and flowers consumed as a beverage, though it is considered to be weak. Ganja includes the resins from the flowers, is more potent, and is smoked. Charas, also known as hashish, is also usually smoked. This is the resin in its most potent form, perhaps five to eight times stronger than Bhang.

Before the restriction of cannabis, the medical establishment used it as an important ingredient in remedies that targeted specific ailments. More than a hundred years ago, the manufacturing of tablets containing high concentrations of herbs and other substances was a major trend in the medical community. A tablet to treat spasmodic croup contained extracts of *Cannabis indica*, Hyoscyamus, opium, benzoic acid, camphor, oil of anise, ipecac syrup, extract of licorice, milk-sugar, and acacia mucilage. A formula for nerve pain included Hyoscyamus, Conium fruit, ignatia, opium, aconite, *Cannabis indica*, Stramonium seed, and Belladonna in a base of starch, milk-sugar, and yellow dextrin. Both of these are designed to tone down the nervous system—confirmation that hemp is, as Culpeper wrote, an herb of Saturn.

Origins

Hemp is one of several strains of Cannabis, also known as marijuana, weed, pot, and many more colorful names. What is called hemp, or sometimes industrial or commercial hemp, has a tall stalk (10–15 feet) that is the source of fiber and produces seeds used to make hemp seed oil. The name comes from the Greek name for the plant, derived from the Scythian or Thracian name. It is related to the Persian word *kanab* and also survives in the word *canvas*, which was made of hemp fiber. *Marijuana* is a relatively recent term that was used as part of the propaganda campaign against hemp in the early twentieth century. In general, the name hemp refers to the plant when it is grown for fiber or other practical uses. The name cannabis is probably the best name to use when the plant is used for medical, recreational, or spiritual purposes.

Hemp is a flowering plant in the Cannabaceae family and is related to hops and hackberry. It originated in the mountains of central Asia, but aided by humans has now spread around the globe. The evolution of its psychoactive properties is thought to have been a strategy to deter consumption by predators, and also as a response to the high levels of ultraviolet light found at high elevations of its native environment. Many varieties of cannabis exist, including sativa, which is tall and used for both fiber and medicine; indica, which is shorter with some chemical differences; and ruderalis, the original plant that is better conditioned to grow in cold climates. There are some issues concerning the technical classification of cannabis and its varieties. Some would call sativa, indica, and ruderalis species of the genus Cannabis, while others regard them as subspecies of *Cannabis sativa*. Cannabis grows in both male and female forms. The male plants tend to be taller and produce pollen, while females are bushier and produce flowers.

The chemistry of hemp is quite complex. The plant itself contains nearly five hundred individual chemical compounds, at least sixty being cannabinoids. Tetrahydrocannabinol (THC) and cannabidiol (CBD) are more abundant than the others. THC is the psychoactive compound that accounts for stronger effects, while CBD blocks the actions of THC on the nervous system. The relative amounts of these primary cannabinoids vary according to species, though higher CBD seems to both dampen and extend the effects of the herb. Because the brain and other parts of the body have built-in cannabinoid receptors that are involved in pain sensation, mood, appetite, and memory, humans are strongly responsive to the chemical compounds in cannabis. It is thought by many that the cannabinoid system in the body plays a major role in maintaining homeostasis, therefore suggesting that claims for the wide range of healing properties claimed for cannabis may be valid and that it is truly a holistic herb.

Contraband

Hemp was considered a legitimate healing herb when the 1937 Congressional hearings on its prohibition took place. At these hearings, a representative of the American Medical Association testified that the organization opposed prohibition and argued that Cannabis was a respected medicine that was on sale at many pharmacies and was an ingredient in many medicinal products. Articles in medical journals also opposed prohibition and criticized assertions in the proposed legislations that the herb was dangerous. But the bill to prohibit hemp was passed and those behind it harassed doctors, including taxing and the deletion of the herb from the United States Pharmacopeia, so most stopped prescribing it.

Why did hemp become prohibited? This is a fascinating and very dark story in our nation's history, and a bit too complex to be fully recounted here. The short version is that when the Eighteenth Amendment was passed banning the sale and use of alcohol, many people took to smoking cannabis as an alternative. This was amplified by imports of cannabis into New Orleans, from which it found its way to Chicago and beyond. When the Twenty-First Amendment was passed restoring the legality of alcohol, the enforcement units of alcohol probation morphed into the Federal Bureau of Narcotics, a direct predecessor of today's Drug Enforcement Administration (DEA). One former prohibition enforcer, Harry J. Anslinger, almost single-handedly ran an anti-hemp propaganda campaign during the 1930s. He effectively used the name marijuana to draw attention to the plant's sources south of the border, and by 1937 had managed to scare Congress into passing the Marijuana Tax Act of 1937, which for the most part made it illegal. This act was also supported by the logging and synthetic fiber industries, both of which benefited by the outlaw of hemp growing, and therefore the production of natural hemp fiber.

Today the situation regarding the legality of hemp in the United States is changing. It is becoming apparent to farmers that hemp for fiber, oil, and construction materials could be a benefit. Other countries allow industrial hemp to be grown—China, France, and Chile are major producers. Cannabis as a medicine is now legal in many states, and its legality for recreational purposes is growing as well. There is still considerable resistance to legalization coming primarily from law enforcement agencies, particularly the DEA, for reasons that are probably best summarized as inertia, not because of reason or science.

It is possible to view the current movement from prohibition to legalization of hemp as the beginning of a return to the respectability of herbalism. During the twentieth century most modern medicine became based almost entirely on surgery and pharmaceuticals, the latter produced by a few large corporations. Doctors are trained in drugs produced by pharmaceutical companies and are given vast amounts of samples to provide familiarity with these products. What doctors don't know about is traditional medicine that is largely based on herbs. Of course some therapeutic components of herbs have been synthesized and used in drugs, willow bark and acetylsalicylic acid (aspirin) being prime examples. But the mixing of herbs as targeted remedies is carried on today by only a few herbalists who operate on a relatively small scale, so their remedies are not widely available and are not handled by insurance companies. With the ongoing legalization of cannabis as a medicine, doctors will have to learn more about this multipurpose herb, and perhaps this will lead to a better understanding of other herbs and their uses.

References

Brecher, Edward. *Licit and Illicit Drugs*. Boston: Little, Brown & Co., 1973.

Conrad, Chris. *Hemp for Health*. Rochester, VT: Healing Arts Press, 1997.

Culpeper, Nicholas. *Culpeper's Complete Herbal*. London: Foulsham, 1994.

Drake, William Daniel. *The Connoisseur's Handbook of Marijuana*. San Francisco: Straight Arrow Books, 1971.

Herer, Jack. *The Emperor Wears No Clothes*. Van Nuys, CA: Ah Ha Publishing, 2010.

Wood, Joseph R. *Tablet Manufacture*. Philadelphia: Lippincot Company, 1906.

About the Author

Bruce Scofield holds a PhD in geoscience and is the author of fifteen books and numerous articles on astrology, science, archaeology, hiking, and travel. He maintains a private practice as an astrological consultant, speaks at conferences, and teaches for Kepler College.

Strawberries

By Mireille Blacke, MA, RD, CD-N

As a Registered Dietitian I can advise you about the impact certain foods might have on your health in a logical and scientific manner. I can also explain the Moon phases and how they impact your life, in a logical and practical way.

During arduous weeding and pruning of the overgrown and secluded gardens I now maintain, I unearthed a surprise: a lone strawberry within a seemingly dormant patch. With some diligence and care, this strawberry patch flourished. Anticipating tasty rewards, my efforts were thwarted by one undaunted chipmunk that ravaged that strawberry patch down to the last berry. To say I was incensed is an understatement, but I was determined it would not happen the following year.

Why put yourself through the effort to grow a few strawberries? To get the most nutrients from your strawberries, it's best to eat them raw, but strawberries absorb high levels of pesticides when grown conventionally. According to the Environmental Working Group's annual report, strawberries are the second highest pesticide-laden and most consistently contaminated fruit or vegetable. So I recommend either splurging for organic or growing your own.

Growing Your Strawberries

Thieving critters aside, strawberries are easy to grow and maintain if you keep five key elements in mind: sun, drainage, space, pinching, and compost. Most importantly, strawberries need full sun (six or more hours daily). Planting them in a sunny spot will increase your chances for bigger and better-tasting strawberries.

They also need moist, well-drained soil. Because standing water and poor drainage leads to rot, you may need to create a mound or use a tower (pyramid) or raised bed for best drainage results, especially if you have clay-heavy soil. Strawberry towers and raised beds are space savers as well, typically consisting of 8-inch-deep tiers, each 12 inches smaller than the one below—imagine a three-layer cake.

Not everyone has the space for a tower, pyramid, or raised bed. Strawberry barrels and jars work in tighter spaces, and the strawberry's versatility allows it to grow in pots, hanging baskets, planter bags, patio and window boxes, and even containers fashioned from old tires, logs, and rain gutters. Strawberry plant runners (stolons) need space to spread out and create more plants in subsequent years. Pinch (deadhead) the blossoms and runners the first year to ensure that a good root system develops. It may seem counterintuitive to prevent the strawberry plant from bearing fruit, but pinching off the first-year flower at the first sign of blossoming will benefit the yield for next season. Similarly, the clipped first-year runners will produce new plants and fruit the following season.

Adjust clay-heavy or sandy soil with compost, loam, composted manure, or peat moss. Moist and aerated compost is best. That does not mean soggy, and proper air circulation means loose enough that you can dig into it with your fingers.

It isn't difficult to provide the basics of light, moisture, and nutrients to your strawberry plants and stack the odds in your favor for perennially positive outcomes. A mature, healthy plant can yield between a pint and a quart of delicious berries. However, you may need to incorporate creative critter control and companion planting if you find your scrumptious bounty is threatened like mine was.

Creative Critter Control

Suggestions about sun, drainage, space, pinching, and compost mean little if wildlife eat, steal, or destroy your ripening plants. Rabbits, deer, woodchucks, squirrels, mice, birds, snails, and slugs can target strawberries. An adorable, unstoppable lone chipmunk may steal your strawberries whole or leave them partially eaten. The planted roots, runners, soil, and bed may be ripped up and plundered. The strawberry leaves may be chewed and torn. A strawberry bed can get repeatedly ransacked, but you may want to handle the problem by means other than poison or a shotgun.

Bird netting or a mesh cover may be necessary to protect your strawberries from feathered or furry interlopers. Other methods to deter birds in particular include placing rubber snakes and broken glass in the bed (the reflected light can scare them off).

Rabbits, woodchucks, raccoons, squirrels, and rodents can be persistent. Consider using chicken wire fencing with an underground depth of 24 inches for wily rodents and critters prone to digging. Leave the upper netting loose and floppy to discourage climbing. If they still manage to get in, planting mothballs provides those digging maniacs with an untasty form of behavior modification. Hanging crushed garlic nearby will help to deter deer, but be sure to replace it every four to six weeks.

Cover the edge of your strawberry bed with copper foil or tape because snails and slugs are unlikely to cross it. Mixing in some diatomaceous earth (soft powder derived from sedimentary rock) is another option to keep these pests at bay.

Companion Planting

When growing strawberries, be as vigilant about insects and disease as you are about wildlife. Red leaves on your plants or wet and dead roots can indicate a problem with rot, among other things. The only solution is to overhaul the entire bed. Companion planting may help prevent this by assisting with disease prevention and pest control. This involves putting plants together to make use of their different nutrients and properties, with the result that one of the plants deters pests, attracts beneficial insects, and/or provides nutrients or support of the other.

Onions are a companion plant to strawberries because they help with disease resistance by repelling slugs, which feast on strawberries prior to picking. Other companion plants for strawberries are beans, borage, caraway, lettuce, spinach, and thyme. Also consider sage, marigold, nasturtium, and pincushion flowers. Borage is a smart choice because of its multiple functions. It's a culinary herb, strengthens the strawberry plant's resistance to insects and disease, and attracts both pollinators and predatory insects to the garden. Bush beans will repel beetles and fertilize soil. Caraway draws predatory insects, and sage attracts pollinators. Consider using thyme as a worm-deterring border. If you select more than one companion plant, be sure to choose those that complement each other. Do your research and don't assume they will all flourish well together.

Some plants will not benefit your strawberries. Do not plant cabbage, broccoli, brussel sprouts, cauliflower, collard greens, kale, kohlrabi, or rutabaga with them. Avoid planting your strawberries near members of the nightshade family (tomatoes, potatoes, eggplants, and peppers), as they are vulnerable to the nasty Verticillium fungus. Above all, use your common sense. In the end, my strawberry-destroying chipmunk was ultimately replaced with a clover-obsessed, vegetable-chomping woodchuck. While the clover attracts and supports beneficial insects, it also draws this fuzzy, tunneling nuisance to my yard daily. But it's worth it.

More Than Just Tasty

There are significant health benefits associated with strawberries. One cup of unsweetened strawberries is fifty calories and three grams of fiber, making strawberries a filling, low-calorie snack. Strawberries have no saturated fat or cholesterol and are low in sodium. They are also a good source of Vitamin C, folic acid, potassium, and manganese. Vitamin C is an antioxidant, helping to boost immunity and fight infection, counter inflammation, prevent heart disease, and protect against cancer. B-complex vitamins, such as folic acid, help the body with carbohydrate, protein, and fat metabolism. Potassium is involved in the body's cell and body fluid regulation, heart rate control, and blood pressure stability. The mineral manganese is used by the body as a cofactor for enzymes needed in fat and protein metabolism and antioxidant utilization.

Strawberries rank in the top fruits with regard to antioxidant content (others include blueberries, cherries, and raspberries). Why should you care about antioxidants in strawberries? Antioxidants and proanthocyanidins (powerful health-promoting plant compounds) offer protection against degenerative diseases, cancer, heart disease, inflammation, and diabetes. Other compounds in strawberries have also been shown to improve brain function and memory, decrease macular degeneration, and prompt increased short-term memory, faster learning, and increased motor skills. Eight medium-sized strawberries equals one serving. Strawberries are highly perishable so be sure to enjoy

2015 © elenathewise Image from BigStockPhoto.com

them quickly, even if you grow your own. Strawberries provide a tremendous health pay-off relative to the investment of effort.

Be advised it's not all wine and shortcake with strawberries. In some individuals, the consumption of strawberries may provoke a life-threatening anaphylactic reaction. Others may experience Oral Allergy Syndrome (OAS) involving hives, eczema, headache, runny nose, wheezing, gastrointestinal distress, hyperactivity, insomnia, and swelling and redness of the mouth, lips, and tongue. OAS (aka Pollen-Food Allergy) is a result of cross-reactivity between tree or pollen remnants in certain fruits and vegetables. If you exhibit physical reactions after ingesting strawberries, consult with a healthcare professional.

So that first spring, the chipmunk won the battle, the war, and the berries. The following year, I was able to prevent it, and other wildlife, from stealing my strawberries by incorporating critter control and companion planting. But doing so attracted a stocky woodchuck who heartily pillages my yard and garden daily to reach his beloved clover. Seemed like an acceptable trade-off at the time. Luckily, Chip (or Dale) was no Einstein. Time will tell.

References

Bellamy, Andrea. *Sugar Snaps and Strawberries*. Portland, OR: Timber Press, 2010.

Blacke, Mireille. "Strawberry Fields Forever." *OKRA Magazine*. May 31, 2013. www.okramagazine.org/2013/05/31/to-your-health-strawberry-fields-forever/.

Environmental Working Group. "All 48 Fruits and Vegetables with Pesticide Residue Data." *EWG's 2014 Shopper's Guide to Pesticides in Produce*. www.ewg.org/foodnews/list.php.

Phipps, Nikki. "Growing Strawberry Runners: What to Do With Strawberry Runners." *Gardening Know How*. www.gardeningknowhow.com/edible/fruits/strawberry/growing-strawberry-runners.htm.

Riotte, Louise. *Carrots Love Tomatoes: Secrets of Companion Planting for Successful Gardening*. Pownal, VT: Storey Publishing, 1998.

Walliser, Jessica. *Attracting Beneficial Bugs to Your Garden: A Natural Approach to Pest Control*. Portland, OR: Timber Press, 2014.

About the Author
Mireille Blacke is a Registered Dietitian, Certified Dietitian-Nutritionist, and Addiction Specialist residing in Connecticut. She is also a practicing Witch and natural redhead, obsessed with New Orleans and Southern culture. Despite possessing a firm grasp on reality, Mireille prizes her Anne Rice novels and Buffy the Vampire Slayer *and* Dexter *DVDs. She adores her three rescue Bengal cats, which have overrun her Victorian home, allow her little nocturnal sleep, and dominate her life. Find her on Twitter @RockGumboRD or her blog at rockgumbo.blogspot.com.*

Spring Bulbs:
Why You Need Them!

By Peg Aloi

There is no time more magical in the garden than spring, especially where winter is cold and snowy. Spring flowers come
when our souls need it most. Color after months of drabness,
life after months of dormancy, growth after months of stillness.
Spring-flowering bulbs can be a dramatic and vibrant welcome,
and with a bit of effort in the autumn you can ensure weeks of
colorful, fragrant garden blooms that will return for years.

Many spring-flowering bulbs are perennial, returning every
year and increasing in size and number. Their tendency to
increase and spread where they are planted makes them an excel-

lent investment, too. Over time they may require dividing, so simply dig them up in late summer or fall, divide the clumps, and plant elsewhere or share with friends.

Spring bulbs are excellent choices for shady yards because many bloom before trees fill in with leaves. This means they will get plenty of sun in early spring before leaves create a shade canopy. Brightening up shady spots with color is very easy to achieve with spring bulbs.

There are many bulbs to choose from, but the most commonly planted ones are daffodils, crocus, tulips, hyacinths, scilla, and iris. Lilies and allium are planted in the fall as well, but they bloom in mid-to-late summer. You can go to your local garden shop and buy bulbs, or order them online or by mail. Once you order online, you may receive catalogs in the mail and these colorful, detailed listings can be very exciting to peruse as you plan for fall planting! I always get excited receiving my bulb catalogs in the mail; it's like a burst of spring sunshine at a time when I know winter is on its way.

Planning Your Garden

Bulbs will bloom at different times, which are given in your catalog or website listings. You'll want to have flowers blooming from March through June before summer perennials begin blooming. Some very early spring bloomers can be nice, including scilla, crocuses, dwarf irises, snowdrops, and Fosteriana/Emperor tulips. Some daffodils are very early and some are very late, so you can have daffodils from March through May. Tulips likewise bloom from early April through late May depending on the variety, so be sure to plant a selection of varying bloom times to keep your garden full of color.

Plant groups of bulbs strategically to keep your beds blooming as well. Keep in mind that you need to let the foliage of your bulbs stay intact for a while after the blooms are done because it helps feed the bulbs for the next year. Check at your local greenhouse to see how long this should be done in your area. Some gardeners will tie together these clumps of foliage to keep them out of the way until they can be trimmed. Others will plant perennials strategically to cover the foliage of fading bulbs (like planting daylilies next to daffodils so the emerging foliage of the former will cover the fading foliage of the latter).

Preparing the soil for bulb planting means making sure the soil is well drained (does not stay too damp, which can rot bulbs) and has adequate nutrients. If you have heavy clay soil, you will want to add some soil amendments to improve the texture and make planting easier. Dig in with a shovel or pitchfork to loosen the soil and break up big clumps; then mix in amendments. Manure is not recommended at planting time, but mixing in other soil nutrients to help improve drainage and texture is a good idea, like peat moss, wood ash, coffee grounds or other compost, or potting soil with vermiculite. You can mark the spot where you planted bulbs with wooden sticks, and permanent marker works well for labeling.

Crocuses

Dainty but colorful, these early bloomers let us know spring is just around the corner. They will bloom even through snow, and survive early spring weather like little troopers. They come in two basic varieties–small flowering and large flowering. Small (species) tulips come in delicate colors, while the large flowering crocuses tend to be brighter. Some catalogs carry interesting heirloom varieties like, "Cloth of Gold," dating from the 1500s, and rodent-resistant ones like, "Tommies." These are planted 3–4 inches deep and spread widely over time, carpeting your yard in early spring colors.

Daffodils/Jonquils

These cheery flowers are true heralds of spring! They come in many varying sizes, colors, and shapes. There are minis, multi-flowering daffodils with several flowers on one stem, fragrant daffodils like White Lion or Fragrant Rose, white daffodils like the Mount Hood or the delicate Thalia, and even pink daffodils like Salome, Pink Charm, or my favorite, Decoy, that has a strikingly deep pink cup. Some have crisp outer petals, and some are shaggy like the Rip Van Winkles. Some have large trumpets like King Alfreds, or re-curved petals like the Jetfire with lovely orange cups and yellow petals. There are hundreds of varieties of daffodils! Some of my favorites include Avalon, Misty Glen, Fortissimo, Delnashaugh, and Tahiti. I plant them in clumps of a single variety, overlapping the bloom times, while other gardeners like to mix them together.

Daffodils form thick clumps over time and should be divided every five or six years. It's best to plant them by the end of September, and bulbs should be planted about 6–8 inches deep in well-drained soil. If you're planting them for the first time, create a small clump of four or five bulbs that will spread with time. Remember these clumps will more or less double in size each year. Animals do not bother daffodils, making them a good choice for woodland and rural properties. If you plant them in shady areas near larger hostas, the emerging leaves will camouflage the fading daffodil leaves. This same strategy works for planting them near clumps of daylilies in sunnier spots as well.

Hyacinths

With their intense fragrance and bright colors, these bulbs can really liven up the spring garden. They're easy to plant, although squirrels and rodents sometimes dig them up. The most popular variety is the large Dutch hyacinths. This plant likes well-drained soil, and they are usually planted 4–5 inches deep. They do spread a bit over time, but nowhere near as quickly as daffodils. I like to plant them in clumps of four or five for a bright shock of color. Sometimes catalogs or shops offer collections in blue or pink, or in mixed colors. I like to plant them near early blooming tulips for interesting color combinations. Hyacinths come in a range of pastel and deep colors including Delft Blue (medium blue), Woodstock (deep magenta), Fondant (pale pink), and Firelights (warm orange). One stem of the flower in a vase will perfume a whole room! Let the foliage die back naturally and then trim it.

You can also plant grape hyacinths, which are smaller and not quite as fragrant, with a later bloom time. These come in shades of blue, white, pink, and even some two-toned varieties. I like Valerie Finnis, which is a lovely pale blue. Plant these in clumps near the front of your beds and borders; they're small but full of color. Spanish hyacinths and English bluebells are additional varieties great for naturalizing in woodland settings. They also bloom slightly later than the larger Dutch hyacinths. Grape hyacinths look wonderful planted near bright yellow daffodils, making a gorgeous color contrast of warm and cool colors.

Snowdrops

These are probably the earliest blooming spring bulbs in many areas. Their delicate white blooms are sometimes hard to see

when they pop up through the snow, but their vibrant green leaves let us know that they are in fact there, and spring, in fact, is on its way!

Tulips

No flower has a more exciting history than the tulip. In the seventeenth century in Holland some bulbs sold for more than $20,000 each! The endless varieties are a result of many years of breeding and experimentation. Some tulips are perennial and return year after year, while some only bloom for a year or two before fading. Most perennial tulips offer six or seven years of blooms, including the Emperor, Impression, Darwin Hybrids, and species tulips (the latter tend to be smaller but very hardy). Emperors are a good choice because they bloom early and are fairly reliable as perennials. Impression tulips bloom mid-season and boast large, colorful blooms. My favorite is the bi-tone Apricot Impression, which is a soft orange touched with bright pink and has enormous blooms. Triumph tulips are also nice with many colors and lusty blooms, but it can be somewhat less likely to perennialize.

Tulips can be planted as long as the ground is soft enough to dig in. You can add bulb food with tulips when you plant them, and some gardeners think this helps the colors bloom brighter. Perennial bulbs can be moved to different spots as well, but wait until the foliage dies back before uprooting them.

Price can also be a factor in choosing this flower. Some varieties cost more due to rarity or demand, but if you shop around you can find good prices. Triumph tulips are offered in catalogs in many large collections, so the freedom to pick different colors suits many gardeners. Some of my favorite tulip varieties include: Daydream, which turns from yellow to orange; Angelique, a delicate pink with double layers of petals; Queen of Night, a dramatic late bloomer that looks black from a distance; Ballerina, a late-blooming, orange lily-shaped tulip; Cum Laude, a deep purple;

and Yellow Mountain, a peony-flowering tulip in pale yellow. Plant as many as you can so you can cut some for a display.

More Spring Bulbs

These are a few more bulbs for spring blooms. Plant them before mid-October for the best results. Scilla come in blue or white and are small but useful spring bulbs for creating a mass of color. They naturalize beautifully in your lawn, and the foliage fades before it's time to mow the grass. Toss a handful and plant them 3–4 inches deep where they land for a natural look. These look great when you plant grape hyacinths or bluebells for additional spring color in the garden. Dwarf irises bloom early and offer delicate sources of color for the spring garden. Some of the nicest varieties are Cantab in deep sky blue and Katherine Hodgkin in medium cobalt blue. They also come in shades of yellow and purple. They're easy to plant, fairly rodent-resistant, and naturalize easily in most soils.

About the Author

Peg Aloi is a freelance writer and media studies scholar. She has written on subjects ranging from color symbolism in film to aromatherapy to women's health. Her blog The Witching Hour (at Patheos) *explores popular media related to witchcraft, paganism, and the occult.*

Biodynamic Farming

By Michelle Perrin

Often referred to as premium organic, biodynamics is one of the world's first sustainable agriculture movements. For nearly a century it has had a huge following in Europe but has only recently gained popularity in the United States. While it has similarities to organic farming, it is fundamentally different. Biodynamics sees the entire universe, as well as each individual farm, as a holistic organism requiring the use of homeopathic treatments to absorb and distribute earth and cosmic energy. It also believes that it is most auspicious to plant and treat the soil during certain cosmic events.

Biodynamics was the brainchild of German philosopher, architect, artist, and educator Rudolf Steiner. He spent his life advocating the unity of the ethereal and material worlds in a philosophy he named Spiritual Science. Steiner believed that a synthesis of the cosmic and material planes existed, and that pre–Industrial Revolution knowledge could be easily combined with technical advancement. In 1924, he asserted how this approach could also be applied to agriculture.

Some of the fundamentals of biodynamic farming and its preparations can seem a bit far out, but they are very tied to the era in which Steiner lived. He lived in a century that was a bridge between a superstitious relationship to nature and the modern era built on science and technology that was ushered in during the Age of Reason and the Industrial Revolution. Traditions were replaced with chemical industrialized farming. At the same time, the Romantic Movement sprang up to counteract the new world order and its emphasis on logic and reason. Spiritualism, where mediums tried to contact the other world through séances, also gained momentum, especially during the US Civil War and World War I.

The clash between the scientific and spiritual approaches to life was particularly pronounced in the 1800s, and Steiner was not the only one who tried to fuse the material world with the metaphysical one. Entire organizations devoted to this task sprung up filled with prominent scientists, philosophers, and artists. The climate of the time had a deep impact on Steiner, as well as on biodynamic farming, and is key to understanding its philosophy, practices, and techniques.

Spiritualist Revival

The Civil War left an estimated 750,000 soldiers dead, but it's estimated that nearly half of all slain soldiers were not identified, and their families never had the closure of knowing what happened. It is not remarkable that established religion did not offer the solace needed, so a new kind of spirituality arose as families tried to communicate with loved ones. Mediums and séances were common and spread to Europe, gaining particular traction during World War I.

Simultaneously, the Industrial Revolution caused massive societal changes, shifting the world's economy from an agrarian one unchanged for centuries to a mechanized one. Populations shifted from rural to urban living, drastically changing communities and how people interacted. The increased emphasis on machines and science also shifted ways of thinking from folk knowledge—now known as superstition—to rational, academic thought. This brought a need for new spirituality as mankind lost its daily interaction within nature's rhythms. Many scientists and artists were seeking to create a synthesis between the new mechanistic thought and the old organic, cosmic beliefs. Many new societies sprang up either as proponents of spiritualist beliefs or to test their validity. One of the most famous is the Theosophical Society, founded in 1875 by Helena Blavatsky and Henry Olcott.

Helena Blavatsky was the daughter of a noble Russian family who married her off at the age of seventeen to the Vice-Governor of the Yerevan province in Armenia. When naïve Blavatsky realized that she was expected to consummate her marriage with a man three times her age, she ran away in horror. Divorce was illegal at the time so she took to the road. Her search for enlightenment led her to Constantinople, Egypt, Greece, Java, India, and supposedly the then-Forbidden City of Tibet where Blavatsky claimed to have spent four years in the Lamasery monastery learning the mysteries of the ancient Book of the Secret Wisdom of the World.

Her travels eventually took her to the United States, where she met newspaperman and Harvard grad Colonel Henry Steel Olcott at a séance. He was so impressed with Blavatsky's feats as a medium that he wrote a book about it, *The People from the Other World*. Olcott and Blavatsky went on to live in New York City and formed The Theosophical Society to impart the wisdom Blavatsky learned on her travels. Their basic tenet was that the spiritual and physical realms are complementary aspects of our earthly existence, and the goal was to study science, philosophy, and religion to create a synthesis of these traditions that would explain the laws of nature and the life force of man. Olcott said the group's aim was to free "the public mind of theological super-stition and a tame subservience to the arrogance of science." The group believed that all living beings had a spiritual energy field. It was against this backdrop that Rudolf Steiner was made General Secretary of the German branch of the Theosophical Society. He led this until he formed his own movement called Anthroposo-phy (Greek for *man* and *wisdom*), and later invented Biodynamic Farming.

Steiner's Beginnings

While the Age of Reason and Industrial Revolution created a scientific, fact-oriented society, it still took a hundred years or so for the cosmic-consciousness of the spirit world to fully be clas-sified in the realm of debunked superstition. It was in this era that Steiner lived and thrived. Rudolf Steiner was born in 1861 in what is now Croatia. His parents met when they were working for a count who forbade them to marry, so they ran off together. Steiner's father got a job as a stationmaster and took assignments close to Vienna so Rudolf could receive the best education and go to university in the capital.

As a young child, Steiner had clairvoyant capabilities but quickly learned not to share his abilities with others, until he met a kindred spirit as a college student. Felix Koguzki, a man who collected medicinal herbs in the forests surrounding Vienna and sold them in the city, taught Steiner the wisdom of the local farmers that persisted in spite of the scientific approach that was ushered in during the Age of Reason. While at university, Steiner studied biology, chemistry, physics, botany, and anatomy. It was during this period that he discovered Johann Wolfgan von Goethe's scientific writings, which had a profound affect on Steiner. As a student he was given the prestigious job of Natural Science Editor for a collection of Goethe's works. He then went on to work at the Goethe Archives in Germany as an editor. Goethe believed that current scientific teachings did not take into account the spirit, and therefore science could only teach about things that are dead.

Steiner's interest in spirituality was not to communicate with the dead or hold séances, but to create Spiritual Science, which would open the consciousness of mankind to the energies that affected and underpinned all life processes. He went on to write twenty-eight books and six thousand lectures; work as a philosopher, educator, architect, and advocate for people with special needs; and invent movements such as Anthroposophy, Eurhythmy, and Biodynamics. He also founded the influential worldwide network of Waldorf Schools based on his educational principles.

The Advent of Biodynamics

The roots of the agrochemical business reach back to the nineteenth century and German chemist Justus von Liebig, who is known as the father of chemical agricultural due to his invention of nitrogen-based fertilizer. Liebig was the first scientist to propose that plants receive nourishment from the inorganic compounds of nitrogen, phosphorus, and potassium carbonate— what chemical agriculture refers to as NPK. Liebig propounded that there were no distinctions between living and dead—organic and inorganic—chemical processes. Later in his life, however, he came to renounce his earlier theories.

Regardless of Liebig's reconsiderations, farmers soon became dependent on these fertilizers, and a new and extremely profitable industry based on chemical agriculture was born. In 1905, German chemist Fritz Haber discovered a way to create chemical fertilizer from air-born nitrogen—an infinitely free and cheap source. During World War I this process was used for the creation of explosives, and at the end of the conflict surplus nitrogen was dumped on crops, weakening them to insects in the process.

In 1922 or 1923 a group of German farmers approached Steiner. They had witnessed a noticeable decline in the quality of their seeds and plants and an increase in disease. They were worried about the declining nutritional content of their crops and wanted to regain the vitality they had known in earlier times. In response, in 1924 Steiner delivered a series of lectures that laid the framework for the biodynamic agricultural movement. In these lectures, he maintained that, "Nutrition as it is today does not supply the strength necessary for manifesting the spirit in physical life. Food plants no longer contain the forces people need for this." Inorganic chemical agricultural was depriving plants of the vital "ether" the spirit force that contained the living element that empowered life. For Steiner, plants and their nutritional content were merely the spirit that came from living soil and cosmos that then nourishes man and allows its body to manifest and become vital.

Biodynamics is in direct contrast to chemical farming because it relies on living processes. While Liebig fiercely believed that humus—the organic component of soil formed by the decomposition of leaves and other plant material by soil microorganisms—had no affect on crops, Steiner asserted that it played a fundamental role and must be built up and maintained for high-quality crops. He also believed that the energies of the cosmos bestowed a vitality that helped plants thrive. Biodynamics is a method of farming that is sustainable, organic, and holistic. It takes into account the balance and harmony of the material and

2015 © weerapat image from BigStockPhoto.com

spiritual realms in the creation of nourishment throughout the cycle of life. Steiner's lectures emphasized the dangers of chemical fertilizers and the importance of high-quality humus and compost. He also held that there are spiritual and cosmic influences that have profound affects on soil and plant growth. He felt it was important to view the soil as the foundation for plant and human health, and therefore work to restore its balance and fertility and make it a living ecosystem. Soil was not merely a dead substance, but one that was infused with the spiritual realm and influenced by the will of the farmer and energies of the cosmos.

Biodynamics quickly garnered a strong following, and in 1928 the Demeter International certification program was founded for farmers utilizing biodynamic principles. Demeter is one of the world's top three organic certification programs today, and the largest for biodynamics. This method became widely known and used throughout Europe, but it did not initially catch on in the United States because it was seen as an occult method. However, in recent years it has gained popularity, especially with wine makers.

Biodynamics versus Traditional Organic Farming

While biodynamics is a form of organic farming, and the first form of organic in the agrochemical era, it differs in many ways. The primary difference is that biodynamics sees each farm as a holistic unit—manure from animals and fallen leaves create compost and fertilizer for nourishing soil, and plants in turn nourish livestock and humans. Many traditional organic farms do not include livestock. As opposed to traditional organic farming, biodynamics has a spiritual and cosmological basis that sees the energy of the universe and the physical world working as one dynamic, and the creation of energy-rich food depends on planting and tilling based on these planetary rhythms.

Monocrop production is common in traditional organic farming, whereas biodynamics requires 10 percent of farm area set aside for biodiversity. Also, where single crops within a farm can be classified organic, in biodynamics the entire farm must be certified. Organic farming allows the use of imported feed, pesticides, and fertilizers, while biodynamic farms create these elements within the farm itself, and at least half of all livestock feed must be created on the farm.

Soil health is of utmost importance to the biodynamic farmer. It requires the use of special homeopathic preparations that work with the energy of the cosmos to enrich the soil and the plants to increase production. Biodynamics works on the fundamentals of observation, participation, and connection to the land to form a self-regulating system that heals the soil and creates healthier, more nourishing plants. On a biodynamic farm, all cosmic and physical forces (such as compost, manure, and planet emanations) are used to create a continuous cycle of nutritive energy within a closed nutrient system.

One of the defining characteristics of biodynamic farming is the use of nine special preparations using elements from the farm that are then diluted and applied in doses to the soil or plants.

Some of the preparations are to be stirred, preferably by hand, for one hour, changing directions every twenty seconds in order to create a whirlpool-like vortex that infuses energy of the farmer and the universe into the preparation. It is believed that these preparations increase yield, flavor, and nutritional quality by stimulating root growth and photosynthesis, as well as revitalizing the soil, humus, and microorganisms.

To learn more about Rudolf Steiner, read the full Agricultural Course at http://wn.rsarchive.org/Lectures/GA327/English /BDA1958/Ag1958_index.html.

References

Candelario, Elizabeth. "Marketplace Notes...Feeding Our Souls." Demeter USA. www.demeter-usa.org/learn-more.

Olcott, H.S. "Inaugural Address." The Theosophical Society in America. Delivered November 17, 1875. www.theosophical .org/component/content/article?id=1867.

PBS. "American Experience: Death and the Civil War." www.pbs .org/wgbh/americanexperience/films/death/player.

Pfeiffer, Ehrenfried MD. "The Agricultural Course: Preface." The Rudolf Steiner Archive. June 26, 2007. wn.rsarchive.org /Lectures/GA327/English/BDA1958/Ag1958_preface.html.

Tompkins, Peter and Christopher Bird. *Secrets of the Soil.* New York: Harper & Row, 1989.

About the Author
Michelle Perrin writes the Love-Money-Health Horoscopes for Dell Horoscope Magazine. *She is also a regular contributor to astrology .com, and her writings have appeared in* The Mountain Astrologer *and multiple volumes of* Llewellyn's Moon Sign Book. *www.astrologydetective.com, michelle@astrologydetective.com.*

The Moon in Midlife

By: Amy Herring

A midlife crisis is a household phrase in Western culture conjuring up images of middle-aged men in red sports cars trying to recapture their youth. This stereotype has become either sadly ridiculous when being lived out in front of our eyes, or just downright inaccurate when it comes to the personal reality of the experience. Is there more to it? What lies at the heart of the midlife crisis, and does it truly exist? If so, when's that cute pool boy going to deliver my new red car?

The period of life known as midlife can span as many as twenty-five years from 35–60, but the peak age of the culmination of the midlife crisis centers around ages 40–45. While the symptoms can be experienced at many times in life, for a number of reasons these symptoms often gang up on a person during a period of months or years in their midlife, signaling the beginning of a transition. In addition to some physical symptoms such as changes in sleep, eating, or sexual habits, the top three symptoms most commonly experienced are:

A profound sense of emptiness, boredom, or discontent. People on the precipice of a midlife shift often find that a sense of emptiness has crept up on them over time, slowly siphoning away the sense of meaning, joy, and purpose their life once contained until the deficit has reached a point that it commands attention. Relationships, activities, hobbies, and/or spiritual or professional goals may suddenly feel hollow and meaningless, for reasons unknown. These feelings may be accompanied by or shortly followed by a restlessness that's difficult to shake, as a vague but insistent search for something indefinable simultaneously begins. Even previously ambitious and active people may find that their motivation drops precariously low as their present and future direction becomes confused and unclear. Life, or a big part of it, may seem futile or pointless. This often occurs in the early stages of the midlife transition, and prompts an attempt to figure out what has gone wrong. This sometimes happens with frequent daydreaming and reevaluation of past decisions and where they've led.

A general sense of decline. This may manifest as an urgent feeling like of time running out, sometimes bringing an almost manic increase of ambition rather than a decrease, as if we've got to hurry up and get on with living. Alternatively, this feeling may be more sluggish, as though something is slowly ending. Physical changes associated with aging and the realization of them may accompany these feelings or seem to trigger them.

Intensity and/or fluctuation in moods. Moodiness may abound, ranging from unexpected anger out of nowhere to frequent irritability to a persistent or recurring feelings of sadness. These mood swings may make it preferable to escape the confusion of the present through drugs, alcohol, sleep, or any other activity that can consume our attention and divert it from the not-yet-understood underlying issue.

Crisis is not necessarily the focus of midlife, but internal change certainly is. This can prompt crisis if the change is confusing, unwelcome, or unexpected. A crisis is often a sudden development or change that throws us into a tailspin, whose consequences may be long-reaching even though the event may be brief. *Midlife transition* may be a better phrase to describe this period, for while a sense of crisis can certainly accompany the midlife transition, it is not always brought on by an event and is rarely brief. Some type of loss such as losing a job, divorce, or the death of a parent can certainly bring on a crisis, and it can happen at any age. But even when there is no outward event, an inward sense of something changing may arise, surprising us with its intensity even though our outward life goes on merrily.

If a crisis event does manifest, it may be the event that begins the roller coaster of the midlife transition. However, the reverse may be true as well. A crisis event doesn't always prompt the change, but it may be a symptom of an inner change that has started or a change we were ready for, if not yet consciously. We may find, for example, that the person we've become is no longer a fit for the job, living situation, or life we've fashioned for ourselves, even if it used to fit like a glove. Yet, not all midlife transitions result in a crisis, and even fewer result in the traditional red sports car. They are still quietly profound nonetheless.

Midlife's Purpose

Psychologist Carl Jung experienced a profound midlife transition of his own. His exploration and documentation of his own process resulted in his Red Book, a project from which the rest of his life's work and theories emerged.

In alignment with this experience, Jung theorized that the midlife transition is about a sort of changing of the guard, where the Ego (the center of conscious, the part of us that we call "I") must hand over the reins to the Self (the wholeness of who we are, including our divinity and our unconscious, not just the "I"). The first half of life is spent in ascension, strengthening, and building the Ego (the "I"), for we must have a strong identity for self-discovery and self-expression to hold our own and find our way out in the world. But at midlife, that ascension peaks, like the Sun rising and reaching its highest point, after which a more whole self must emerge that is not driven solely by the Ego needs, but by a more complex and holistic approach to life and under-standing of oneself.

Jung postulated that in order to facilitate this shift, a break-down of the persona and a release of material from the uncon-scious must occur. This breakdown can produce a breakthrough, and the process of undoing and releasing frees the shadow (beliefs or characteristics about ourselves that we do not consciously acknowledge). This raw material of self-discovery provides the grit that we'll need in order to change what is necessary to live more fully.

Midlife in Three Stages

Jung saw this process unfolding roughly in three stages: Separa-tion, Liminality, and Reintegration.

Separation

Separation begins the process and is often the crisis part of the transition. Something feels like it's slipping away, whether it's the loss of something real and tangible, or the slow and mysterious loss of vibrancy and meaning that we may have once had.

What are we losing? It may take the form of losing a person, a job, or a belief, but it is not out of necessity that we lose that thing; it is our attachment to or overidentification with some-thing that we are losing. This is often why the loss is so profound. Because it feels like we are losing a part of our very identity.

A person may cope with the loss in a number of ways according to their personality, ranging from continuing to go through the motions and waiting for this phase to pass, to abruptly changing their behavior or circumstances in an attempt to recapture meaning elsewhere. Because this phase is purely about separation and perhaps gaining objectivity and clarity, any flailing attempts to understand or correct the issue seem to fall short. Something is dying, and even if we don't know what it is, attempts to stop or reverse that death are often what author Murray Stein has called "propping up the corpse." Even if we don't fully understand why, we must surrender to the reality of what is happening before we can do anything about it. We must "bury the corpse" and acknowledge a need to move on in some way, even if we're not yet sure how or why.

Liminality

As we surrender to the separation stage, acknowledging that we have to leave something behind, even if it's just a certain idea of ourselves, liminality begins. A liminal state is a state of in-between, as if standing on the threshold of the doorway between two rooms. We are not what we were, and we have not become what we will be.

The first stage of midlife transition is often accompanied by responses ranging from panic to anger to fear, but stillness accompanies this stage. Life doesn't stop and it certainly doesn't need to, but in this stage there is a feeling of suspension as we wait for clues to surface telling us what to do next. This stage is an exploratory one with many questions without answers. Trial and error can allow oneself to be open and leave the shore of the old, but not be in such a hurry to simply land on the next island one sees. It's common during this stage to feel impatient for the people, things, and places that the old self was entwined with. Even if you don't know where you are going, you know you cannot return.

This seeking and exploring is the key to moving through this second stage of the midlife transition. Old longings, pains, or unfinished business from youth may come up in a new way, asking to be addressed. New interests and hobbies, no matter how vague or fleeting, can provide the playground for exploration. Dreams, impressions, feelings, symbols that strike you, interests that suddenly move you, are all fodder for crafting a more whole self, even if the tools only serve in the moment.

Reintegration

In this final stage, we may find that we've not only changed the part of our life and self that was in need of upheaval, but have also shifted the attitude that we approach life and living with itself. In her book *The Astrology of Midlife and Aging*, astrologer Erin Sullivan suggests that the success of this phase lies in the process of "leaving behind the things that are not possible" and living life "as an experience and not a striving."

With this stage comes a sense of freedom, with past goals and old ego attachments either stripped entirely, or streamlined and redefined. A new or reclaimed sense of purpose can arise from the dust, along with clarity about the things that really matter and a consolidation of our energies toward pursuing those things. With an expanded consciousness and a humbled ego, we are at once smaller yet vaster than we once were.

We may never return to the contained focus of the egoic "I," for we have outgrown that uniform. We are bigger than our bodies and minds, our ambitions and plans, and that vastness of soul is reflected in the way we experience life from here. Not in perfection, but in wholeness.

Suffering and Surviving with the Moon

With a process as intense as the midlife transition, it is symbolized by not just one but several astrological symbols, such as Uranus coming to the point opposite one's natal Uranus, urging authenticity and breaking free through change, and Neptune forming a square to its natal position, encouraging us to confront our tried-and-true beliefs. But ever present is the Moon.

Our Moon is, of course, always active in our lives, considering that the Moon corresponds with our emotional body and we're always feeling something. Its presence in midlife becomes center stage because as reason and routine seem to abandon us during the midlife transition, it is only by the heart that we're able to navigate the terrain, feeling our way through.

Our natal Moon is with us every step of the way, providing clues to the complex process of the midlife transition. In the Separation phase, when we feel most threatened and fearful, our Moon sign reveals how we manage those fears and how we might seek comfort. In Liminality, we follow our emotional instincts as we navigate new terrain blindly. In Reintegration, we take what is most essential into the future and secure in our heart's priorities. Below is a brief survivor's guide to midlife with your Moon sign.

Aries Moon

With a warrior's heart, you don't tend to shy away from a battle, but when the enemy is unseen or undefined, your limited patience can run thin quickly. Modern life can get so regulated, safe, and sanitary that the warrior heart within has no outlet for direct and uncomplicated expression. Return to your primal instincts; look to the ways you've become too careful, too practical, or too acquiescent. You may need to live a little closer to the edge in some way, carving out some space in your own life that's just yours.

Taurus Moon

You tend to be nourished, not numbed, by routine so it may come as an even bigger shock to you when the tried-and-trues no longer seem to hit the spot. Change is the name of the game in midlife so embrace it with your usual calm and patience for its slow process. A return to simplicity may be the end point, but based on what truly matters to you now, not just what's easy or what has already come before on the path of least resistance.

Gemini Moon

You may be friendlier with change than some, but a puzzle with no answers will drive you crazy with boredom and impatience eventually! Leave room for the questions themselves and know that the answers are coming. Reclaiming your heart may mean returning to that natural childlike state of curiosity. Not innocence, but openness. Reacquaint yourself with what enlivens you: learning and discovery on a small or grand scale.

Cancer Moon

You put your heart into everything you do and everyone you love, so midlife separation may test your bonds and confuse your alignments. You feel so deeply and give so much that you can be vulnerable to constant overwhelming. Drop those balls you're always juggling and give yourself what you need, even if it's solitude and time, to figure out what is truly most important to the newly emerging you.

Leo Moon

Jealously guard the time in your life that you need to reserve for play and creativity. It's not arts and crafts that you are seeking, but renewal through inspiration itself, which may inspire any number of creative acts. Exploring new hobbies during the liminality phase may reveal short- or long-term outlets for new and more profound self-expression.

Virgo Moon

During midlife, the well-ordered life you've crafted may feel like it's unraveling at the seams. Your instinct may be to work harder to get it back under control, but this will only prolong the process. Focus on short-term goals to continue to provide yourself with a sense of progress even if your long-term direction is hazy to keep your spirits up and recapture new motivation.

Libra Moon

You're no stranger to uncertainty, but this is ridiculous! Decisions you've made may return for reassessment (even if you can't change them), and future paths may seem too diverse. If you can, reserve judgment as you explore your options, but eventually you may find that the midlife transition leaves your choices simpler and your confidence to make them stronger.

Scorpio Moon

You don't surrender control easily, but if you can meet the unmaking and surrender at midlife voluntarily and with ferocity, you will emerge stronger. You know that you come alive when you are pushed to your edges. Let the midlife transition strip you down to the bare essentials and then live the truths you find without fear. Total transformation is not out of the question!

Sagittarius Moon

Your heart has a lightness and buoyancy that can resist blows and setbacks, but the slow plod of time and obligations can be the proverbial frog in the boiling pot for you. It creeps in and weighs you down when you're not looking. Freedom and adventure are the Sagittarius Moon's secret weapon; when midlife gets you down, get on the move, and you'll shake the answers loose!

Capricorn Moon

Watch out. You're a little too good at putting your needs aside when it comes to sticking with the program you've committed to, so you may be most vulnerable to plodding ahead when you should be hitting a rest stop or even rerouting. This midlife layover may challenge you to honestly reassess your priorities and desires, which may mean putting aside goals that you haven't achieved yet because they no longer reflect your priorities. This is not failure; your inner life is being restructured and that must be reflected in your new goals.

Aquarius Moon

Individuality and self-authentic behaviors are at the heart of your journey as an Aquarius Moon, and the midlife transition asks no more than that. Take the opportunity to self-assess, as it's possible that changes in your heart and mind over time call for a realignment. Become friendly with your changing moods and your inner life; now is the time to embrace the subjective experience and not try to remain objective and untouched.

Pisces Moon

You can be prone to depression during this transition, as it's difficult to keep focused on the positive when the realities of midlife press into your consciousness. Find joy where you can to carry you through the intensity, and if you feel you need to escape, be strategic about it. Rather than hiding from life, give yourself a gentle and loving outlet through which to explore your feelings. Reacquaint yourself with your own brand of magic and if you feel you've lost it, take heart; this transition may help you find it again.

About the Author

Amy Herring is a graduate of Steven Forrest's Evolutionary Astrology program and has been a professional astrologer for 19 years. Her first book, Astrology of the Moon, *is available now and she's working on a second. Visit HeavenlyTruth.com for readings, classes, and educational videos.*

Weekly Tips Provided by:

Peg Aloi *is a writer living in upstate New York. She has studied astrology for many years, reads tarot, and makes herbal incenses, perfumes and skin care products, as well as running her own small gardening and baking businesses when she is not teaching media studies to college students.*

Mireille Blacke *is a Registered Dietitian, Certified Dietitian-Nutritionist, and Addiction Specialist residing in Connecticut. She is also a natural redhead, obsessed with the city of New Orleans and Southern culture. Mireille adores her three Bengal cats (all rescues), which overrun her Victorian home, allow her little nocturnal sleep, and dominate her life. Mireille worked in rock radio for over two decades before shifting her career focus to Psychology, Nutrition, and Addiction Counseling. She is presently penning "Life and Times of the RadioWitch" and working as a Bariatric Dietitian at Bristol Hospital in Bristol, CT. Follow Mireille on Twitter @RockGumboRD and read her irreverent RockGumbo blog posts at rockgumbo.blogspot.com.*

Known internationally as an astrologer, consultant, and writer, Alice DeVille *recently relocated to the Tampa Bay area where she continues with her work as an executive coach integrating spiritual insight while meeting the needs of clients in the corporate, government, and small business worlds. Alice specializes in diverse relationships situations that call for solid problem-solving advice to get to the core of issues and give clients options for meeting critical needs. Her clients seek solutions in business practices, career and lifestyle management, real estate, relationships, and training. She has developed and presented more than 160 workshops and seminars related to her fields of expertise.* The Star IQ, Astral Hearts, Llewellyn, Meta Arts, Inner Self, ShareItLiveIt, Twitter *and numerous web sites and publications feature her articles. Quotes from her work on relationships appear in books, publications, training materials, calendars, planners, audio tapes, and Oprah's website.*

Alice is available for writing books and articles for publishers, newspapers or magazines, and conducting workshops, radio or TV interviews. Contact Alice at DeVilleAA@aol.com.

Penny Kelly *is a writer, teacher, author, publisher, researcher, consultant, and Naturopathic physician. She is the owner and director of Lily Hill Farm in southwest Michigan where she teaches courses in Developing Intuition and the Gift of Consciousness, Getting Well Again Naturally, and Organic Gardening. Penny maintains a worldwide counseling and coaching practice, travels widely to speak and teach, and raises organic vegetables, chicken, and beef. She holds a degree in Humanistic Studies and a degree in Naturopathic Medicine. She is the mother of four children has co-written or edited twenty-three books with others and has written seven books of her own:* The Evolving Human; The Elves of Lily Hill Farm; Robes—A Book of Coming Changes; Getting Well Again, Naturally—From The Soil To The Stomach; Consciousness and Energy, Vol. 1, Multi-dimensionality and A Theory of Consciousness; Consciousness and Energy, Vol. 2, New Worlds of Energy; *and* Consciousness and Energy, Vol. 3—History and Consciousness. *Penny lives and writes in Lawton, Michigan.*